D1286943

Group
Counseling

Dr. Wayne W. Dyer
and Dr. John Vriend

Everything
You Need to Know
to Lead Any Group
in Any Setting

for
Personal
Mastery

SOVEREIGN BOOKS
NEW YORK

For William Vollick:
*Educator, humorist, friend,
and a natural group leader.*

Copyright © 1980 by Dr. Wayne W. Dyer
and Dr. John Vriend
All rights reserved
including the right of reproduction
in whole or in part in any form
Published by Sovereign Books
A Simon & Schuster Division of
Gulf & Western Corporation
Simon & Schuster Building
1230 Avenue of the Americas
New York, New York 10020

Designed by Irving Perkins
Manufactured in the United States of America
10 9 8 7 6 5 4 3 2 1

Library of Congress Cataloging in Publication Data

Dyer, Wayne W
Group Counseling for personal mastery.

Includes index.
1. Group counseling.   I.   Vriend, John, joint author.   II.   Title.
BF637.C6D93   371.4′6   79–19788

ISBN 0-671-96043-1

Contents

B4y

D+T 4/3/80 $10.16

Group Counseling
for Personal Mastery

*The worth of the state, in the long run,
is the worth of the individuals composing it.*
JOHN STUART MILL

Introduction

THE BOOK you now hold in hand will provide you with a firm "how to" in functioning as a group counselor. From a careful analysis of the necessary preliminaries, to techniques for "selling" the concept to decision makers, and on through the actual leading of a counseling group, this book covers the whole spectrum. It was not designed as a theoretical exposition (though it is solidly grounded in theory), nor does it carefully review the literature, cite the relevant research reports, and give you a pastiche of library offerings or a summation of what others have done. Rather, what we have done is to take a stand on what we believe to be the single most effective strategem for reaching and helping all people: group counseling. We have chosen not to substantiate all of our work and claims with experimental or other kinds of research studies, nor do we look to texts in the field or other professional sources for documentation. We believe in group counseling because we have done it and are doing it. Whatever else we may be, we are group counseling practitioners. And we have been and are trainers of group counselors. We are certain of the effectiveness of the process when it is practiced by competent people.

We address this book to the professional on-the-job counselor, but we exclude no one. Anyone with an interest and some determination is welcomed. If you seek to gain expertise in any and all phases of the counseling process in a group, this book is for you. We speak to you directly and our goal is to help you in every aspect, in any way we can.

1

There exists no book such as this, a complete no-nonsense guide to group counseling, with all contingencies explicitly dealt with. Herein you have it all: the beginning, the middle, and the end. We go from the fears and resistance of the first stage, through the planning, actualizing, and completing of the counseling process. If you are interested in leading counseling groups, this book is for you.

We have long felt that practitioners have been overlooked by researchers and writers in the field of group work. The bulletins from the "authorities" have been lean, repetitive, full of rehashed material. We have worked to amend this and have written an account which details effective practice.

Although we could have selected any setting (private or institutional), we have chosen the *school* as the specific setting in which counseling groups or a group-counseling program might be inaugurated. There are several important reasons for this choice. First, we could think of no more difficult setting, no social or institutional context that presents as many barriers and problems, or has as many watchers and critics—it is even fair to say "meddlers"— whenever anything innovative or nontraditional is introduced. Of the other social agencies—whether they be family-service clinics, prisons, hospitals, residential centers for the elderly, halfway houses for recovering drug addicts, community outreach programs, rehabilitation settings, private consciousness-raisers, private psychological clinics, the offices of individual practitioners, business or industrial settings, even the varieties of military service installations—none has the same goldfish-bowl character, the complexities of housing and scheduling, the confusions which clog decision-making channels, the difficulties of dealing with the whole spectrum of human heterogeneity (all the people's children go to school), the variability of growth and development curves in the young, the impact of the culture on the people who spend so much of their lifetimes in these buildings. We felt that if we could specifically show how it can be done in a school, then we would have demonstrated that it could be done anywhere.

We see the schools of the North American continent as drastically needing some stabilized form of deliberate psychological education that will work. Counselors, teachers, psychologists, social workers, administrators, and other professional personnel in the schools have not developed viable across-the-board educational structures that succeed in meeting the psychological self-development needs of youngsters, and an effective schoolwide group counseling program affords a means of realistically filling that void. Scores of critics lambaste the schools. Few, if any, offer an alternative program such as we do in this book, one which does not require any great amount of additional funding. In addition to school counselors, the teachers, administrators, and students themselves can take the contents of this book and apply them in any educational setting for the purpose of "emotional" or "psychological" education.

The vastness of the educational system in North America is overwhelming. North Americans believe in education and training, and from prekindergarten through postgraduate university, courses have subscribed to and supported the system. While schools as a setting for counseling groups present many problems, they also afford the time, space, learning atmosphere, and especially the clientele. Membership in a counseling group as an adjunct to a skill- or subject-centered educational program seems to us not only logical and desirable, but crucial to the mental health and self-mastery of every student. And for those youths who fall afoul of the system, where the high cost of providing quality education for all has resulted in mean and enervating environments, a well-grounded counseling program can be the saving grace that makes the significant difference in their lives. It is a feasible alternative which works not merely for those who adapt to the school environment, but for many troubled youth as well. Yet it has not been given its due.

How do we know it works? Because we have helped to make it work in one of the most difficult centers—Detroit, Michigan. Under the most trying circumstances, in some of the most psychologically impoverished school environments, in neighborhoods where the socioeconomic pathology, as measured by any criterion, is as gross as anywhere on the continent, counselors, teachers, administrators, central office personnel, and community folks are working together to support and deliver group counseling for students at all educational levels. We have been closely involved in helping to train group leaders in Detroit and have watched the program mushroom. In other, more advantaged educational settings, we earlier worked to perfect models for group counselor leadership training and group counseling programs.

There are a host of lesser reasons for electing the schools as our setting. As professional counselors, we began in the schools and have served long apprenticeships there, learning what to do, how to help, how to be effective and make a difference. In looking at and discussing the schools, we write not as social critics but as two pragmatists who have given many years to the struggle; as two who know the terrain and can speak of it with the veteran's familiarity. We speak empirically. And we have not lost our zeal to help bring about positive and needed changes. Our experiential backgrounds are long-suited; in public and private institutions, in ghetto schools and affluent suburban schools, in adult education programs, in community colleges, in university undergraduate and graduate programs.

We know from our own experience that group counseling can work in all the settings we claim for it; if we felt that we were overstating our case, in any way, we would so qualify our statements. In each part of this book, from beginning to end, we speak of what is possible to bring about in the real world, not about what *should* be. Everything we say about any part of the process of group counseling has been field-tested many times.

We do not focus primarily on educational settings because these happen to be what we know best. Our group-counseling involvements extend through the alphabet of mental-health-service delivery systems, in every kind of setting, including substance-abuse rehabilitation agencies, marriage and family counseling centers, hospital settings, military service settings, business and industrial applications, correctional counseling programs, in-service training programs, and our private practices. We come to each reader with a track record of tried and tested knowledge of what counseling in groups is all about. When we say that the model presented here, albeit predominantly formulated for the school setting, works in any arena with any group membership, we are not engaging in random speculation. We have demonstrated it to ourselves, over and over, and know how to demonstrate as much to others.

We have not written a manual for each possible setting where counseling can be delivered in groups, because we believe our readers are able to make the necessary interpolations and extrapolations for themselves. In our long experience in training group leaders, we have learned that those who have the readiness, desire, energy, and commitment will work at making it happen without having to be shown the way over each pebble in the path. Counseling, when one fully engages in it, is as energy-draining as any other human activity we know of, and the difficulties are compounded when one has ten or more simultaneous client members in a group.

But excitement and a sense of well-spent mental, emotional, and physical energy accompanies this. A feeling of authentic, meaningful engagement, a sense of self-growth, of self-mastery, of making a vital difference in the lives of others accompany the struggle one undergoes as a counselor of people in groups, and such cannot be purchased at any price, it must be lived through. We know that readers who go from our ideas herein to the hard work of implementation in their own settings with their own charges will find exhilaration, will see their positive impact on others.

What Is Personal Mastery Counseling?

We have given this book the title: *Group Counseling for Personal Mastery.* Just what do we mean by "personal mastery"? It is our view that humans are learners; all of their knowledge is acquired and virtually all of their behavior is learned. Mastery we see as the highest performance level. One is a learner until one has mastered a skill or a set of facts. Then one owns it and can go forth to master another skill or set of facts. Certainly one cannot learn all skills or facts that all humans everywhere have mastered, and any given individual must make choices as to what collections of skills or knowledge are most desirable, as we all have only a finite amount of time and energy to consume in learning. Given this understanding personal mastery becomes a relative concept: the more behaviors one has mastered and the more knowledge one is the master of, the more personally masterful one can be said to be.

Behind the concept of personal mastery, an idea whose time has come, is the question Abraham Maslow asked.[1] In essence, he said, "Why are psychologists so preoccupied with studying the normal and abnormal, in trying to find ways to bring the abnormals up to the norm, whatever that is? Why not look at the other end of the human development continuum and study the human beings who excel in their personal living? Then, if we learn how from these folks, we can help everyone to improve, to grow, to live their lives more effectively, more happily. We can raise the norm." And since these individuals obviously got there

[1] Beginning here and continuing through the next several pages, we have included in a somewhat revised form material that first appeared in *The Journal for Specialists in Group Work*, vol. 3, no. 3, Fall, 1978, pp. 104–112, reprinted with the permission of the American Personnel and Guidance Association.

on their own, without the intervention of therapists and similar helpers, Maslow concocted the term "self-actualized." It was a fantastic placebo and lure, even a threat to the helping professions. *You can actualize yourself.* Haven't others done it? Who needs a therapist or a psychiatrist, preoccupied as they are with sickness, inadequacy, deviations from the norm?

Maslow himself, of course, understood that his study of self-actualized individuals could not be made to fit into the rigorous parameters of the scientific method, that vaunted and guarded superbowl system of thought in which any social scientist must work to receive the approval of his peers and betters. Though Maslow apologized profusely for this, he fumbled merrily ahead anyhow. He was in a territory which was not yet trail-blazed, however much it had been previously trod, and he had to establish his own landmarks. His delineation of the characteristics of self-actualized persons tells this story and provides the bedrock on which personal mastery counseling (PMC) is built. He has pointed the way for us, his heirs.

Let us take just one of Maslow's important characteristics of self-actualization as an example: humor. If it is true that self-actualized persons have a sense of humor, that they can laugh at the comedy which others create, and at their own as well, is it not important for us to learn to do as much, desiring as we do to live more effectively? What is this prized "sense of humor"? One is not born with it. One does not get spanked into the world and immediately begin laughing at the folly of the human experience. It is particularized *behavior*, present in this or that time and place, usually in the company of particular others, and like all behavior it is learned. It is mental behavior first, followed by attendant emotional and physical behavior. As behavior, it can be studied and imitated, its essence understood, its principles learned, its processes incorporated by another who also chooses to make it his own. For whatever reason, we *learn* how to respond to the funniness in others and to be funny ourselves. We *learn* how to worry or to be free of worry, to criticize or to be free of any desire to do so, to feel happy, sad, even depressed. The basic truth about being human is that we are born with no knowledge and with very little ability; we must learn everything.

Why not master those behaviors that benefit us, that help us to be happy, prosperous, and capable, rather than those that harm us, cause our unhappiness, and prevent us from accomplishing our desired ends? This is a rhetorical question to which a simple answer can be given. Either we do not know how to do so, do not want to take the time out to do it, or are not convinced that it is worth doing. The personal mastery counselor, in contrast to the average citizen, is convinced that it is worth doing, has taken the time out to do it, and knows how. This is to say, the counselor has learned ahead of his client how to perform or behave in any dimension of personal mastery on which the counseling focuses.

The concept of a personally masterful, self-actualized, or fully functioning person is, of course, an idealization, a vision of perfection not attainable in a hundred lifetimes, given *all* that a human being can learn. But that vision, like so many others, provides us with directions for growth, for determined self-enhancement in place of willy-nilly opportunistic development. The effective counselor understands this and constantly works on himself, not only empirically understanding and being capable in more and more areas for the sake of his clients, but first and foremost for himself. He practices what he preaches. He is not a quack or a fumbler in the dark. Whether taught by others or self-taught, he has learned how, and he can articulate and give his learnings away. The special skills an effective group counselor has are specifiable, teachable, and valuable to anyone. The counselor is the expert in effective, masterful human living, at least in those areas he proposes to help, and he is expert in the special teaching skills which comprise the counseling process.

Personal mastery counseling in groups first of all presupposes that the counselor knows what individual counseling is all about and is able to do it. The special circumstances of counseling in a group do not obviate the expertise required of the counselor when only one client is present. It is assumed that a group is not an entity with a life of its own. Indeed, the group as such does not exist, only the individual members exist, and each of these is there to receive counseling. Human beings cannot be added together for any purpose without each surrendering his individuality. The personal mastery group counselor is not interested in the totality, only in helping each individual member. He counsels and he orchestrates the counseling that comes from the members. Each of these helpful witnesses is there to learn, to get self-enhancement from the experience.

How does personal mastery counseling differ from other forms of group work? First, the counselor is the avowed expert in the group, the trained deliverer of counseling services who takes responsibility for what goes on in the group. It is unlike group psychotherapy in that no group member is presumed to be sick, abnormal, or inadequate. Each group member is considered to be normal, which is to say that he or she is a person who can benefit from the experience. This is anyone.

The concept of normalcy requires special explication here. The personal mastery counselor ignores the concept, particularly the statistical one responsible for the "normal curve," as having little or no serviceable meaning for him. These are human beings; all of them have human behaviors, some of which are grossly self-defeating, but most of which work efficiently for the individual who owns them. To call anyone abnormal is to compare a unique being with another unique being, to take a part and call it a whole, to label a person for the sake of dismissing him.

The category of group work called "encounter" (a term which seems to have won out over "sensitivity," "human relations training," "growth," or "T" groups, though these appellations have not completely disappeared from the scene and others in the same genre exist or crop up intermittently) differs from personal mastery group counseling in several ways. While both seek to provide a safe human laboratory where members can try on new self-enhancing behaviors, while both are convened to assist individuals in self-development, in an encounter group the emphasis is on a fairly well-outlined group process, not on a counseling process for which the leader takes responsibility. The encounter group leader tends to disavow expertise and likes to call himself the "group facilitator." He facilitates the group process, and it is the process, rather than the facilitator, that accounts for the changes the members experience. His role is that of a more experienced member, a player-coach, so to speak. Encounter group leaders tend not to do individual counseling. Group counselors, on the other hand, take responsibility for what happens to any individual member of a group they head and will extend their services to participants on an individual basis outside the group, if such is called for. It is a condition they establish before a group is even begun, and they consider it unethical not to render themselves available in this way.

There are other special categories of group work such as T.A. (transactional analysis) groups, gestalt groups, values clarification groups, but most of these are highly defined in terms of structure, theory, and particularized purposes, and they are not likely to be confused with counseling groups. Suffice it to say that the personal mastery group counselor knows what he is about, and because he knows he does not denigrate or eschew other group-work experiences. Rather, he is the inveterate student of all of these, seeking to come upon useful learnings which he can adapt to his own practice. What is currently known about how people can best be helped to change in groups is but a scratch on the surface of what will one day be known. What he knows for certain is that the group is an especially potent place in which to do counseling. For most clients, positive behavioral change occurs quicker here.

First and foremost, personal mastery counseling in no way pretends to be a unique way of counseling, distinct from all others. Rather, it is an amalgam of many variables taken from wherever they appear. Thus, at any given moment the orientation of the PM counselor may appear to be Rogerian, rational-emotive, behavioral, gestalt, psychoanalytic. In actuality, how he or she might be categorized is of no possible interest to the counselor, who is, above all, a pragmatist, an empiricist, a utilitarian: if it works, and it harms no one, use it; if it doesn't work, study it, modify it, help it to work.

Whether or not a given PMC action or practice works or doesn't work can only be tested in the client's caldron of experience. The client is the determiner of what works for him, and while PMC insists that clients learn how to know when their behavior has changed productively, that is as far as it can go. PMC sees no need to submit evidence for others' approval that it indeed has worked in this or that instance. Its purpose is to help clients, not to win laurels for itself. This does not mean it defies scientific examination. On the contrary, that is welcomed. The behavioral-science researchers play their games and few of these make any difference to practitioners. Practitioners, hungry for what works, are more apt to set about doing something different in their practice, depending on how convinced they are that a given structure or action will work. Convincing and persuasive writers, talkers, demonstrators, and modelers are the ones who are influential in altering practice, and this is held by PMC to be closer to the reality of people's needs. The researchers and research report writers may influence each other and win points and funding in academia for their efforts, but they make a relatively discountable difference in the trenches of the war on psychological dysfunctioning.

What is lamentable about this state of affairs is not that research learnings are discounted, but that the individual human consciousness and its ability to discern truth is. Somehow modern man has learned to think less of his own mind and its products.

He has become largely other-directed, an approval seeker rather than a truth seeker. He venerates scientific endorsement, while discounting to some degree his own supreme scientific powers. PMC seeks to correct this, to give the proofs for truth back to the people, as it were.

PMC is based on self-evident truths, indeed, it could not exist without them. They are mostly plain and homely truths. However disconnected, unorganized, or diffused they may be, however obscured or distorted by special interest groups, they are staples of Western culture. There are many such truths and the following constitute only an important handful.

Each person is the undisputed authority on his or her life and its parts, however that life may be sliced up for inspection and analysis, and this personal authority can be tapped. Each person lives only in the here and now, never anywhere else, regardless of how the mind can take flight to past or future living. Each person owns his or her own behavior. Each person must first think a thought in order to feel anything or do anything, a *feeling* being what is experienced in the body in reaction to a thought, be it an increased heartbeat, a glandular secretion, an ulcer, or whatever. Each person chooses his thoughts, can change them, and thus can change his feelings. No person, therefore, can make any other person feel bad without the latter's cooperation. A counseling action that works cannot be copyrighted or patented; truth in living is no one's private property; it belongs to the public domain. Thus PMC in its manifestations has stolen or borrowed nothing, nor is it guarded about how it thinks or functions in any way.

PMC knows that the client does all the work. Without client work there can be no client behavioral change, no directional growth. PMC knows that people do not choose to change when they are content, relaxed, and satisfied; people decide to go to work to change when they are dissatisfied, when they are lean and hungry, or when they are helped to see that something good they want is available and attainable. PMC knows that human beings strive to acquire what is best for themselves, however much they are hampered by their bogus past learnings not to see, however much they are conditioned to believe that their learning-yearnings are beyond them.

The concept of freedom is important to PMC. It flows from the concept of choice. A man is as free as the number of alternatives he presents to himself before choosing any course of action; the more alternatives considered in a given instance, the freer a human being may be said to be at that time. Freedom in numerous dimensions of living is looked upon by many souls as a terror from which to be saved, and so they hug their chains. Staying in a house or a job or a marriage they hate is vaunted by many as worth a thousandfold more than the horrors they imagine upon leaving. PMC understands how man can want to cling to what he knows and understands, to remaining static or inert even though the road down to death is thus made steeper and swifter. But PMC is dedicated to helping man alter his condition.

Prized values in PMC are these:

It is better to be alive than dead, and aliveness in any given moment is judged by the extent to which a client is engaged in using all his capacities, both mental and physical, in living. It is better to determine the meaning of one's life and any given behavior than to abdicate from doing so. It is better to love (to accept love and give it to others) and to work (to engage in productive activity) than to do neither of these. It is better to live consciously in the here and now than consciously in future or past time. It is better to be proactive than reactive. It is better to care for one's physical body than to abuse or neglect it.

Historically, PMC came into being because we needed a handle on which to hang all we had learned and were practicing. "What do we call your brand of counseling?" we were asked over and over, a question to which we would always answer, "Call it pragmatism, call it whatever you like, if you need to give it a name." In a conversation over this matter one day, Wayne suggested "personal mastery," and John said, "That's it!" because it fit. It named what we were doing. So we entitled the tape series we had just produced *Counseling for Personal Mastery*. We had gotten together to work at counseling because we had climbed a similar ladder and arrived at a similar place. We had been trained in somewhat the same ways, having been exposed to the client-centered therapy principles of Carl Rogers, gestalt approaches, humanistic ideas, Freudian, Adlerian, Rankian, Jungian, and the neo-Freudian concepts of Horney, Sullivan, and Erickson, and especially the rational-emotive techniques of Albert Ellis. From every approach we absorbed that which worked. Each of us, on his own, had gone after all the informal training there was to get (outside of the degree programs we had attended), including demonstrations, workshops, lectures, and sessions that showed us what some prominent and capable others were doing. We had read the books, thought and worked hard, had understood and used

what was useful and discarded or abandoned what wasn't. Together we co-led groups for thousands of hours, monitored each
other, invented new ways to function, and endlessly evaluated
what we were doing.

As stated earlier, the work and findings of Abraham Maslow
were a significant beginning for us. We added to his list and
learned how to eliminate negative emotions in ourselves, to abol-
ish worry, guilt, anger, loneliness, boredom, and more, and then
how to counsel others into doing so. We were impressed by the
concepts of discovery and mastery in learning which Benjamin
Bloom and others delineated and explicated. Karl Menninger provided us with a five-part stepladder of categories which we used to
describe particular behavior: panic, inertia, striving, coping, and
mastery. To locate any particular behavior at any particular step
gives both client and counselor a benchmark with which to work.
We were impressed by, and adapted to our own work, the internal-
ity/externality concepts of Julian Rotter. Our influences, or better
—our sources, have been many.

We, in turn, have trained and influenced many others. But it is
the validity and practicality of personal mastery counseling which
make it potent. "If it works, use it, if it squares with the truth of
human experience, use it," is still the only empirical injunction
for any practitioner worth his salt.

As for training, the apprenticeship or protégé approach is the
best. It amounts to learning by experience from a journeyman personal mastery counselor, and this is best done as a co-leader of
groups. In the group it will all happen, sooner or later, if one
spends enough hours counseling there. The reading and thinking
are necessary, but knowledge untested is only theory, and hypo-
thetical. A skill cannot be memorized. We want to shout, "Group
counseling works! Try it! Here are all our secrets. A blueprint for
action. Go to it!"

You will find in this book much of what you need to know to
get started, to advance your level of performance if you have already tried your hand at leading groups, to enlarge your repertoire
if you already are a veteran.

One of the persons who handled the manuscript before it became the book you now hold in your hands was a typist who had
no connection at all with counseling or groups. Her unsolicited
remarks were, "Wow! I feel I can lead a group now, after digesting
all this!" We didn't have her in mind when we put it all down, but
we were pleased with the statement and felt confirmed.

Our book, *Counseling Techniques That Work*, has been a best-seller in the field two times, first with the American Personnel and Guidance Association Press, and again when it was reissued in hardcover by Funk & Wagnalls. In their promotion literature for that book the APGA said, in part, "Drs. Dyer and Vriend offer a refreshing approach to a subject that has too often suffered from ponderous, overstuffed prose written merely to gain academic acclaim. Each student or practitioner who reads this book will welcome the direct, straightforward style which has become an emblem of these two fine authors."

We repeat that style herein.

1

So You Want to Start a Counseling Group: Why You Don't Feel Ready

YOU'VE HEARD about it. You've read about it. You've even taken a course or two which attempted to teach you about it. You know that it works, and that it is endorsed universally by leaders in the profession. There are literally hundreds of books about it, some of which you've read. Yet you still don't make it a major part of your professional activity.

School teachers and counselors all across the country know about the virtues of group counseling and pay lip service to the advantages of group counseling for students at all levels. Like you, they are not taking it upon themselves to sit down with their students and actively lead counseling groups. Why do you, and the overwhelming majority of your colleagues, avoid the actual leading of counseling groups when you know that group counseling works? Very simply put, you avoid group counseling because you do not feel competent to lead groups, and because of a flock of fears you have about group counseling as a school guidance function. So you spend a lot of your time in "wheel spinning" activity. You try to reach all of your students through individual counseling, even though such a task is both absurd and impossible. You spend a large part of your working day acting like a clerk, reviewing endless lists of students who need counseling: absentees, students who are failing subjects, disruptive students referred by other teachers, potential dropouts, suspected drug users, underachievers, students with emotional problems and vocational and educational indecision, and on and on through an interminable chronicle. And all the while telling yourself that you would like to be able to reach more of your students. You know that every single student could benefit from counseling, and yet you shun the potentially most useful, implementable, and effective technique for delivering counseling services to the majority of your student body: *group counseling*—a strategy that you've considered, but essentially are reluctant to offer on a schoolwide basis.

YOUR FORMAL AND INFORMAL TRAINING

Let's look at the basic reasons why you are resistant to becoming a practicing group counselor in your school. Your formal training. If you proceeded through the typical Master's program toward guidance counselor certification in the United States and Canada, you have had next to no practical training in group counseling. Perhaps you were in a course called Introduction to Group Guidance, or Group Process, or some such appellation; or you took a broad survey course which included lectures and small group discussions about group dynamics, large versus small group interaction patterns, content versus process in small groups, group guidance as a school counselor role, student government, special groups in our culture, and some talk about group counseling as an effective strategy for school counselors, in which much emphasis was placed on discussions about the advantages and the disadvantages of school group counseling. If this was the extent of your formal training, it is small wonder that you feel ill-prepared to get into the foray and function as a group counselor, with all of the attendant risks and responsibilities.

Perhaps your formal training went one step beyond the "typical" group counseling exposure in the graduate schools of North America. Perhaps you enrolled in an advanced group course in which you were a member, maybe even leader, of a counseling group and submitted tapes for evaluation by a trained professional on the counselor education staff at the university. Given this tentative hypothesis, you have still had minimal training in group counseling. As a member of a group you had the opportunity to observe group process, but this is in no way to be considered an effective training strategy. As a member you were there to get something out of the group. To grow in some ways, not to learn leadership skills.

If you have served as a trainee in group counseling by working alone and submitting tapes, you received a lot of *ex post facto* advice about how you should have functioned back there when the group was going on. It is not at all a hazardous pronouncement to assert that the practicing school counselors of North America have had virtually no formal training in group counseling leadership, and particularly lacking have been on-site, supervisory co-leading experiences offering critical feedback about group skills as they either emerge or fail to develop within the context of an actual "live" counseling group.

Your training in group counseling has been almost exclusively limited to reading textbooks about the research results of counseling groups, assertions about various theoretical approaches to group counseling, and a smattering of some techniques which seem to be useful in groups. Actual experience in leading and co-leading counseling groups is next to impossible to come by in counselor training institutions at the Master's level. As you assess your formal training in counseling you begin to realize that the emphasis has been placed in areas other than those that would have helped you to gain skills and knowledge about effectively leading counseling groups.

But your training in counseling goes beyond the actual course work requirements of your counselor education department. Perhaps the most valuable training you receive is the firing-line experience of functioning day to day as a school counselor. You probably learned more about individual counseling, academic programing, teacher consulting, curriculum planning, attendance list checking, working with parents, lavatory supervising, and the thousands of other tasks you perform on a daily basis, as a result of trial-and-error work on the job. Very simply put, you learned by doing. You developed your individual counseling skills, as you did all your guidance counselor activities, by counseling every day. Your personal reinforcement schedule helped you to become trained in a host of activities within the school, and the things that you do well are those that you have systematically practiced and worked at diligently. Conversely, those things that you are not skilled at are those you have not reinforced on the job.

Enter group counseling. Your personal reinforcement schedule has not permitted you to grow in this area and so, because you have not done it and have not extended your university training as you did in so many other guidance areas, you have extinguished the very limited knowledge that you gained while a student counselor.

It is not our purpose to bemoan the fate of group counseling in the counselor education training facilities across the continent. We believe in group counseling (when properly conducted) as the single most effective counseling strategy available to school counselors and all people in the helping professions. We have devoted a large chunk of our professional energies to upgrading and expanding group counseling training at the university level. The subject of this book is you and group counseling in the schools or any other appropriate setting. Recognizing that you feel ill-prepared to function as a group counselor is an important first step. But you need not use your lack of training as a justification for avoiding group counseling.

YOUR LIFE EXPERIENCES

There are additional reasons why you do not feel ready to lead counseling groups, and becoming aware of them will help you eradicate your inertia in getting out there and beginning your first group. Your life experiences have not prepared you for the role of effective group leader. As a member of hundreds of groups you are expected to act in very prescribed ways. When you sit on a committee you have unwritten group rules to follow, including tasks that all members must accept and become subservient to. In social groups you know how to function, and you do so based upon your family training and the reinforcement you've received throughout your life. Similarly, in "strained" groups such as crowded elevators you have learned enculturated behavior. In large groups you have learned not to speak out, while in small groups of two or three you have learned that silence brings upon you an uncomfortable pressure to participate. At social gatherings you have learned that long silences are cumbersome, and that in movie houses prolonged noises are equally distressing. You have had a lot of group training in your life, and essentially you have learned how to function in literally thousands of different groups of all sizes and compositions. None of this life "group experience" has prepared you to become a group counselor, wherein you are the unquestioned behavioral expert on effective living. You must learn to function uniquely as a group counselor, much differently than any of your group life experiences have up to now dictated.

As a group counselor you know that *you* must be alert to a multitude of things happening at any one time, yet your life experiences in groups have never demanded such diligence. You will be expected to be able to *interpret* group member behavior, and certainly you've never had to do that before in any of your life groups. Also, you will be expected to observe communication patterns, something you've always been able to ignore in your group life. You will need to *listen* to everyone and separate the cream from the crap. Up until now you could just ignore the crap or argue with the crapper—although, in general, your life experiences have taught you that arguing with someone in the group is taboo, certainly a poor preparation for leading a counseling group.

You will need to *encourage*, when never before was this needed. You will need to endure painful silences, when always before you could just tell a joke. You will need to help someone over an emotional hurdle, when always before you could just change the subject when it got sticky. You will need to make decisions on what gets focused upon and what gets discarded within the group; not so before, this burden was never on your shoulders. You will need to *summarize* group activity, and when was this ever required of you in your group life? And you will be responsible for *effecting closure* and *initiating counseling content* areas, when always before this was just a naturally developing element in your groups. Group members will be relying on you to know how to solve problems, and to help them to become more effective with the many concerns in their lives. Always before you had only yourself to worry about in your groups. By now the point should be crystal clear: your life experiences in groups, which have been vast and impressive, have in no way prepared you to become a group counselor, and so your reluctance to initiate this new group role for yourself is reinforced.

Your Built-In Fears

Your formal training and on-the-job experiences, as well as your life experiences in groups, which are so dissimilar from the role of group counselor, have provided you a cop-out from initiating group counseling. You also resist becoming a practicing group leader because of some intrinsic fears that you have about groups. While all of these apprehensions may not apply directly to you, most of them are a built-in part of the defense system of those counselors who espouse individual counseling over group counseling, even though they are aware that exclusive, one-to-one counseling is the quickest road to obscurity for the practicing school and institutional counselor.

PARENTAL OBJECTIONS

Perhaps your most troublesome fear about group counseling in your school is that omnipresent demon who looms very large on your potentially innovative horizon. That is, the threat of parental objections and possible reprisals. You do not want to become involved in any activity that might be construed as potentially explosive, and you have many reservations about counseling groups because they fit so neatly into that danger zone. You are well aware that parents fear groups. That some parent-inspired organizations have initiated lawsuits against school districts because of some highly questionable activities that took place in sensitivity groups that alleged to be "helpful" in purpose. Moreover, you know that parents are suspicious of their children participating in any "tell it like it is" group in which students are encouraged to relate juicy tales from their family storybooks. Your awareness of parental objections in this area has taught you that one-to-one counseling minimizes the risk of parent insurgency in the school, and that a group multiplies the risk by a ratio greater than the given number of group members. What if students start talking about another student's alcoholic mother? Suppose Maryanne starts talking about her mother's interminable parade of boyfriends? You know that students who talk about their home life in an individual session are not likely to take the news to their friends. But in a group? You have visions of parents storming the counseling office in search of your professional jugular vein.

Your fear of parental gainsay is not your only misgiving about becoming a practicing group counselor. Groups themselves are a frightful concept to you and to most of your counselor colleagues. Strange things have happened in groups. Group members have been encouraged to touch each other, to become more intimate, to show their affection by removing all enculturated inhibitions, and they have even gone so far as to encourage feel-up games and removal of clothes. The things you've read about the conduct of group members in a "familiar" environment are certainly not something you would even begin to condone for your students. The proliferation of a multitude of encounter-type experiences, and the attendant risks involved in any group which has intimacy as a goal, are clearly not for you in the schools, and so you back off in your thinking and action when it comes to labeling yourself any kind of group devotee.

While you know that many parents might object to group counseling for their school-age children, you are also aware that the administrative machinery is even more keenly attuned to any school activity that might be seen as potentially vexing to parents in the community. Administrators are in many ways slaves to parental pressure, and least of all can they afford to alienate the mothers and fathers of their school district. The very existence of administrators depends upon their pleasing rather than distressing parent groups. And so you, as a school counselor, know too well the potential ill-wind that blows in the area of administrative sanction of a possibly controversial activity. The rule that you have come to abide by is, Don't make waves in an area that might cause trouble for my administration, particularly since it is at the mercy of the parents.

Is it Therapy?

More fears. You also fear becoming involved in anything that might be construed as therapy. You think that counseling groups can get heavy and be emotionally draining, and that group pressure can build to encourage members to tread into unfamiliar "therapy only" territory. You do not want school officials to think you are involved in group therapy, and since you are not sure of the distinctions yourself, you'd rather not enter the area at all. Just the term "therapy" conjures up notions of your lack of training and experience, of deep psychological problems, of psychotic episodes, or journeys into psychological waters that for you are uncharted. Rather than even get into a setting which might suggest group therapy, it is easier simply to avoid the small group as a device for delivering your counseling services. You also have heard of the groups labeled sensitivity, encounter, human-potential, TA, and numerous other descriptions. Somehow you know that such group experiences do not belong in the school, and since you are not sure of how they are distinguished from group counseling, it is another source of restraint. Why institute something that might be labeled inappropriate by other community officials?

You also fear the possibility of psychological damage that might result within the group. You do not want any casualties, and you've heard that a group can, in fact, leave a member helpless by encouraging him to tear down his defenses leaving him with nothing for the purpose of rebuilding. You've heard that people have gone berserk after participating in a group, and that the pressure to "let it all hang out" is strong. You know that small groups stress feelings and emotions, and that you aren't quite sure what to do when someone gets very emotional.

CAN YOU HANDLE THE GROUP DYNAMICS?

You don't want to take any risks that might hurt your students who are innocently signing up for group counseling sessions. Additionally, you want to protect your own position and avoid inaugurating a program that might become explosive because you are not trained for, or capable of, handling group-inspired emotional material.

Conversely, you fear counseling groups because you are not sure how to keep them going, how to avoid having simple discussions and gripe sessions, or just plain boring "out of it" group meetings in which two or three members try valiantly to keep it going, despite the fact that it really is going nowhere. The fear of failure in this regard is very great in you, perhaps even more significant than the fear of having problems come up that you aren't equipped to handle. In simple terms, it is the fear of bombing, of having nothing to say yourself and creating an uncomfortable environment in which everyone just sits around and nothing gets accomplished. Or of being the only one doing the talking and running out of things to say when no one in the group volunteers to help you by getting things started. You know you can never bomb if you don't get into a group and lead, and so your avoidance of the group is reinforced within yourself.

You also have resolute doubts about your ability to handle effectively circumstances that are likely to crop up within the life of the group. You don't know if you could deal with anger, or depression, or crying, or blatant emotional displays within the group.

You know that this behavior could occur, and you have had no experience in coping with it, or in using it for the benefit of the acting-out (or acting-in) group member. Similarly you are unsure of what to do in the event that a group member asks to leave the group or group members gang up on one individual, in the event of long, painful silences, or attacking behavior, or confessionary outbursts, or boredom induced by a member who rambles on and on at the expense of everyone else. Because you have self-doubts about your ability to deal with any number of potentially trouble-some activities, you find it difficult to envision yourself function-ing as a group counselor on a regular basis. The most efficient way for you to deal with these group leader deficiencies is to avoid taking on the task, then you never have to answer the question, "Could I handle it?"

Another question that you would be forced to grapple with if you decided to become a group counselor is, "Who gets into my group and who should be eliminated?" or "How do I go about screening for group membership?" Since you have no guidelines whatever, you have dealt with the fear of a faulty group composi-tion by having *no* group composition. The fear of a bad mixture, or a totally homogeneous (or totally heterogeneous) group is a gen-uine reservation. Also, how do you conduct intake interviews, how do you advertise, how do you communicate precisely what the components of group counseling are to the students, so that you leave no room for misinterpretation, and on and on through an everlasting list of questions which get answered by you very simply. That is, if you don't seek out the answers, you don't even have to ask yourself the questions, and inertia wins another pro-fessional battle within you. These are very real fears, and they have all served to reinforce your non-group counseling behavior within the school setting.

Essentially, you shun group counseling because it is *easier* to avoid it. Group counseling, although exceedingly useful as a tech-nique for providing most of your students with a counseling expe-rience, is hard work. It involves the kind of firing-line activity in which willingness to take risks is the price of admission for be-coming a practicing group counselor. You, like many others, are not enthusiastic about risk-taking. You succumb to the stomach-wrenching queasy feeling about having to counsel large numbers of students at one time. It is easier to make the following kinds of self-explanations for your avoidance of becoming a functioning group counselor.

I don't have the time.

Parents would object.

Students won't really want to talk about personal problems in groups.

The administration wouldn't want anything so controversial in the school.

The mechanical problems involved in setting it up are too great.

The teachers wouldn't let the students out of class.

I have so much paperwork to do, that leading groups is impossible.

I can't get all of my work done now, let alone the work of leading groups.

I'm really not trained for it, and God knows what could happen in a group.

You may genuinely believe these excuses, but in essence, it is easier to avoid group counseling than to fight your passivity and inaugurate a group counseling program for your students. For each of the above reasons, there are equally persuasive arguments for the opposite point of view, as is pointed out in chapter 2.

Whenever you begin to examine critically the things that you don't do but would like to do, you should recognize that it is *easier* for you to avoid doing it. Perhaps you don't paint pictures or undertake mechanical chores, or maybe you avoid athletics or entering a Ph.D. program. Whatever it is that you avoid, a systematic examination of your avoidance behavior turns up such causative elements as fear of failure, a shunning of risks, fear of the unknown, or slavish adherence to what you have always been. So, too, in your avoidance of becoming a group counselor. It is just plain easier to be a counselor who talks about group counseling rather than one who does it. As a counselor you are always asking your students to take personal risks and to come to grips with their own reluctance to change. And yet you exhibit the same kind of avoidance by staying away from the "riskiest" of all counselor activities, that is, GROUP COUNSELING.

The remainder of this book is designed to help you take a step-by-step approach which will allay your fears and help you avoid the trembling feeling you have about dropping a bomb. The extent to which you succumb to the fears elaborated in this opening chapter will be a direct measure of the disservice you do to the students you are paid to serve. Overcoming your resistance and taking the first step is the way to become the most effective deliverer of services to your students. Group counseling works!!! But only if you, the practicing counselor, make it a vital part of your program.

2

You Need to Be Certain That Group Counseling Is Worth Doing

IF YOU were forced to decide on the single most glaring deficiency in contemporary education you would very likely assail the schools for doing almost nothing about the gross state of mental health in our culture today. Between overlooking the emotional concerns of our students, and failing to provide curricular experiences that would genuinely contribute to making the child a fully functioning person, the schools appear to be indifferent to the "personal worlds" of the students they are pledged to serve.

You know that the ability to "make it"—without immobilizing emotional reactions—in every operational area of one's life is perhaps the most significant index of a "together" individual, and yet our schools almost totally ignore activities which aid the developing person toward achieving these functional skills. You've heard the new educators' plea for affective education, in lieu of a program that focuses exclusively on the cognitive realm. And you, as a practicing school counselor, have somewhat absolved yourself of responsibility for redirecting the curriculum, since you are not in the business of curriculum planning or design.

What is your school busy, busy, busy stressing? Knowledge, academic mastery, and problem-solving. Where are the course offerings on how to eliminate guilt? How to avoid worry, how to develop confidence in yourself? Where does the child learn how to avoid self-defeating approval-seeking behavior, how to be psychologically independent, how to get along effectively with neurotics, and how to function every day in an unfair and nonegalitarian society? The crucially important areas are ignored by school officials, all at the expense of learning how to master the academic curriculum.

The result of this cognition-based approach to education is that we mass-produce neurotics at an alarming rate. People who truly believe in themselves and have positive self-images are profoundly few in number. Individuals who seek out therapy in order to function in their everyday lives are multiplying at an alarming rate. The student who graduates from a typical American high school has learned some intellectual facts, has mastered the necessary tools either to get by in a chosen vocation or to pursue higher education, but he or she is often incapable of functioning independently. Certainly the schools can take little or no credit for helping graduates develop healthful, positive feelings about themselves as worthwhile human beings. In fact, by stressing many externally imposed standards, the schools work at tearing down and removing many of the internally developing structures of self-confidence in young people. Rely on the teacher to know the right answer or the correct interpretation. Check it out with the teacher. How many pages should it be? When is it due? Ask your counselor what courses you should take. What did you get on the exam? Teacher evaluation rather than self-evaluation. These are the touchstones of American education.

If you look at the philosophy of your school, which was probably written under the pressure of an accrediting-agency visitation, you will likely find a statement that goes something like this. "Anywhere High School believes in the full development of each individual child. We strive to assist each child in becoming a self-actualized person and to meet all of his or her needs in both the cognitive and affective domains." You know, as a school counselor, that this is so much claptrap. You have seen, far too many times, how a student who begins to show evidence of self-actualization by self-assertion or resisting enculturation (absolute indices of self-actualization) is systematically "put in his place" by well-intentioned but psychologically unaware school officials. There is almost no room in your school for a truly self-actualized student. That student is forced to conform, both in thinking and behavior, to a set of standardized norms that have been unilaterally imposed on him. And you, as a school counselor, are actually an agent of that external force; daily you seek to develop "self-actualized" young people by engaging in behavior that is diametrically contrary to the attainment of personal mastery, or self-actualization.

The Case for Group Counseling

The case for group counseling is implicit in the preceding paragraphs. It is a curricular intervention which has the affective domain of the student in mind. It is a structure which aids young people in learning how to make decisions, how to take charge of their own emotional worlds, and how to reorder their externally skewed thinking systems to put the focus on themselves as human beings. It is an arena in which the individual student is more important than the group itself, and where learning how to become as effective as possible is the goal, as opposed to memorizing some externally imposed curriculum. It is the students' place. The individuals within the group are the data, and the gaining of self-confidence and the ability to think and behave in self-enhancing ways comprises the homework. It is truly a move toward focusing on, rather than paying lip service to, affective education.

If you could provide an atmosphere in which students were totally free to be themselves and work on their own behaviors in safety, wherein the most important thing to be dealt with was the unique and individual concerns of the group members and how they could change any and all self-debilitating thinking and behavior, you would have taken a step in the direction of bridging the gap in affective education. Group counseling is the only structure that affords the students in your school just such an environment. Where for once it is the student, rather than the teacher or someone else, who is of value, who is the most significant piece of data. Where the one thing the student is an absolute expert on—himself —can be examined, understood, and improved in a spirit of common helping.

In making up your own mind about group counseling (and you must be considering it if you are reading this book), you will need to make your very own case for the value and effectiveness of this procedure. To help yourself make the decision to try it out at least, you need to consider what positive kinds of outcomes are indeed possible for you and for the students you are paid to serve. We summarize below some specific reasons for adopting group counseling as an effective counseling strategy, one in which the *student* receives the payoff.

• It is a move in the direction of affective education for each and every student in your school. That is, the emotonal world of every individual student is given careful consideration, not ignored as it is in virtually all schools.

• It is an arena in which the student has an opportunity to work on himself in absolute safety. Risk-taking is certainly a part of group counseling (as it is in all counseling), but the fear of reprisal or violation of confidence is minimized, and each group member is seen as important; while his or her fears and concerns in every area of life are given important consideration by people who have only one goal, that is, TO HELP.

• It is an opportunity to assist students to become "in-charge" people in all areas of their lives. From getting along with parents and friends, to more productive use of their time, to getting and receiving love, to establishing strategies for achieving psychological independence, the focus is on becoming more in charge in their worlds. The one treasure individuals can possess is to be masters of their selves, rather than slaves to an indifferent environment. Showing young people that this is possible for them without having to master a set of curricular learning principles, is indeed sound justification for establishing counseling groups.

• A counseling group is a place wherein the building of self-confidence is a necessary adjunct to the process itself. The stress is always on the person, and how she can become more personally effective (within her own set of goals) in her own life. But the hidden agenda of every group counseling intervention is to teach group members to believe in themselves, to rely on their own strengths and worthiness, rather than on others. Self-esteem and self-confidence are the by-products of effectively led counseling groups, and nowhere else in the school curriculum is the opportunity so dramatically and forthrightly presented than in a group counseling setting. Whereas the classroom has as a spin-off objective the development of self-confidence (by learning to master curricular problem areas), the counseling group attacks directly the problem of poor self-esteem, and sets goals for all individuals to maximize their feelings of personal worth in all phases and activities of their lives.

• Perhaps the single most significant index of a young person's movement toward personal mastery is the degree to which he is able to establish himself as a psychologically independent human being. A counseling group exists for the very purpose of assisting each group member to become autonomous and independent from the *need* for external approval and support. Achieving psychological independence is not a course offering to be found in any of the schools in North America. Yet virtually all developmental psychologists stress the importance of having children become autonomous and independent in their thinking as a prerequisite to effective living.

• Becoming a completely free and effective human being means being able to selectively resist the enculturation process when it behooves the individual to do so. You are well aware how schools enculturate young people, and how they serve as instruments of conformity and "adjustment" to the culture. In almost all life settings, young people are being channeled into ways of thinking that are externally imposed and other-directed. Thinking for oneself is clearly discouraged, and becoming a conforming member of society is most often belabored. Somewhere students must have the opportunity to express their own values, to make up their own minds about what they will be, and yes, even decide what facets of their own culture they are going to resist. Individual thinking is a crucial component of self-actualization, and having an arena to explore one's individualized notions about life is just as crucial. A counseling group is such a place. A setting in which conformity has no necessary payoff, and where the free expression of one's values and contrary stances is encouraged. A fully functioning person sees no threat in resistance to enculturation, and in fact recognizes that it is important to be a questioner rather than blindly accepting all rules and external standards. A counseling group is a place where learning to resist and ask why is not only tolerated, but it is encouraged as effective behavior.

• A counseling group is a place where students can learn to achieve in all areas of their lives, rather than exclusively in "academic" endeavors. Every single facet of the person is considered to be important, and no one element is given any more prominence than any other. So learning to be outgoing is just as weighty a skill as learning to solve equations. And gaining "friend-making" behavior is as primary as essay writing. Similarly, learning to understand one's feelings and how to control negative emotions is subject matter for the counseling group. Learning how to avoid feeling hurt, or how to avoid anger or prolonged depressions is considered a necessary lifelong skill. All of the substantial aptitudes that are absent from the school curriculum are given utmost concern in the counseling group. These include learning to avoid senseless worry and guilt, to function effectively in the present as opposed to living in the past or the future, to welcome the mysterious and the unknown rather than rigidly clinging to the familiar, to develop skill at making people laugh and having an unhostile sense of humor, to accept oneself without complaint, to avoid shame about the self, to avoid "blaming" as a strategy for living, to be nonevasive and honest, to love oneself and receive love in the world, and most significantly, to take control of one's own world and function optimally and happily.

• A counseling group affords young people the opportunity to identify all areas of their own lives in which they feel less than effective, and to set goals for themselves to become more productive and happy in their own lives. Having an arena to identify self-defeating areas is vital, since not identifying and working on these areas often means ignoring them and *hoping* they will go away. Being able to state one's deficiencies without feeling silly or embarrassed is a solid reason for having counseling groups. Identifying and declaring personal goals is the business of group counseling, and nowhere else in a student's life is this opportunity presented. If a student declares his weaknesses or vulnerabilities in the classroom, he invites criticism and social ostracism, and yet you know full well that being able to admit and declare an infirm area is the first step in ultimately bringing about change.

• Many young people have adopted inertia as a strategy for living. That is, they live with the internalized notion that if they wait long enough, the problem will go away, or they will somehow magically become better. Obviously this is not so, and a counseling group is a setting in which young persons can begin to see that they have indeed adopted this self-defeating strategy in their own lives. Students who are having difficulties with a given subject area often fit into this category—"If only I wait long enough, the problem will disappear." Meanwhile their inaction is magnifying the problem. Fearlessly labeling inert personal behavior is a function of group counseling. Recognizing that most of one's "problems" are really a misapplication of personal energy and priorities is a significant learning objective. Rather than preach or cajole or otherwise "imposed from the system" efforts at getting students to change, the counseling group is the one place where the student can search out the real reasons why he behaves in self-squandering ways. What he gets out of avoiding and rebelling is examined in a nonthreatening environment, and no one (least of all the group counselor) assumes the role of trying to decide ethnocentrically what another person should become. Rather, the individual is encouraged to examine what it is that he gets out of his behavior and if it is, indeed, self-forfeiting, then to select new and more self-expanding goals and rally himself to the credit rather than the debit side of the personal-effectiveness ledger.

• The last in this potentially endless list which builds the case for group counseling in the schools, is the most momentous and pressing of all. The counseling group is the student's place, unlike everywhere else in the school where it is either the teacher's or the authority figure's place. The most important piece of data in this place is the student herself. The most important goal is in the student herself, not in her learning something that someone else feels she must know. A place where the school and its agents (you) actually practice what they espouse in their written philosophies, that the self-growth and "actualization" of the individual child is of paramount concern. Here this is translated into meaningful action. The students' personhood and their own personal worlds are examined and improved in a threat-free minisociety. Here the student is free to be herself without reprisal. And crucially, here the student can come to an understanding of what she is, and simultaneously learn to develop passionate self-love, while setting goals to become as personally self-expanding as she is desirous of being. The school does not offer this mentally hygienic environment anywhere else in its milieu, and if you do not provide it for your students, it is almost a sure thing that they will never experience it in their school lives or, even more devastatingly, in their entire lives. (The same logic applies to all institutional settings. If you don't offer the group counseling, your clients will simply lose out.)

You can see from the ten points made above, that group counseling affords you a unique opportunity to make a difference in the lives of your students. In deciding if group counseling is indeed worth doing, you must also ask yourself the question, "What is it that happens to students who participate in counseling groups?" You will find that your students, after experiencing group counseling, will demonstrate some new behaviors, and some innovative and exciting ways of thinking which were previously not even considered.

It is very likely that students who participate in your group counseling offerings will begin to look at themselves differently. They will see themselves as having potential to become almost anything they choose. They will begin to challenge some notions that others have laid on them during their young lifetimes. These new notions include not needing others' approval, being emotionally free of guilt about not behaving as others dictate, feeling free to confront or challenge what were previously expected behaviors, and on and on through an array of new and more positive thought patterns. Very likely your students will begin to examine and change their thinking and behavior as related to school concerns. Group counseling often serves as an impetus to "get something done" that has been put off for a long time, such as assignments, college applications, or seeking out tutoring. Moreover, students often begin to demonstrate a different attitude toward school itself. As they develop self-confidence and esteem, they begin to see school as an opportunity rather than an imposed structure. As they start to think about themselves as important individuals, and want to avoid self-defeating behaviors, they recognize that *they* should *use* the school and the system for their own benefit, rather than having the school abuse them, as it so effectively does in a multitude of ways. Students who emerge from a skillfully led group counseling experience often take on a different attitude about school life. They have been challenged to get out of life all that they can, and to recognize self-debilitating behavior for what it is.

This is not to suggest that a student can be molded and shaped into a conforming robot by sitting through group counseling sessions. Rather, the student begins to think for himself, often for the first time, and to carefully scrutinize all of his behavior by attempting to answer the question, "What am *I* getting out of it? If I am hurting myself in any way, then I need to reexamine and decide if, in fact, I want to continue the behavior." This kind of independent thinking is what group counseling is all about. When participating in extended group counseling programs, a student begins to think first and foremost about himself, and how he can get all of the available goodies for himself. If he behaves in ways that *he* admits are dysfunctional in any way, then he is encouraged to set goals for himself to avoid such behavior. There is no imposition of a set of rules for living. Only a chance to get genuine feedback from a skilled leader and from peers who are also learning to be nonevasive and direct in their communications.

Obese students can start working effectively at shedding their excess baggage and developing a positive self-image. Truant students (if you can get them to commit themselves to coming) can begin to challenge their behavior and see if it is getting them where they really want to be, or if there are more effective avenues for reaching their goals. Underachievers can begin to understand that their often recalcitrant attitudes toward schoolwork are choices that they have made, rather than the inevitable result of being in a boring or irrelevant school atmosphere. Students begin to respect each other as having feelings. They become caring people. Even the toughest of school rebels often becomes a caring, helpful person, given the climate of an effectively led counseling group wherein understanding rather than contumely is the watchword. Students who have had little or no chance at being important often shine in a counseling group and begin to develop genuine feelings of self-importance as they see, by doing, that they can be of help to another person. Often students see for the very first time that their fellow classmates have many of the same kinds of fears, apprehensions, and "problems" that they themselves have experienced. Observing and participating in a counseling session within the group can have a marked effect on each of the group members. Learning that "I am not alone in my fears" is often the elixir that begins to take hold of a young person and change his life around.

Students love group counseling. Attendance is almost never a problem in effectively led counseling groups. As the word spreads in the school, students will clamor to get in. You will learn that your students look forward to their group counseling time, that they see it as productive and exciting. You will find that they are learning things about themselves for the very first time, something that almost never occurs in their daily classroom activities. The answer to "What happens to those who get group counseling in the schools?" is not difficult to deal with, but is exceedingly complex to delineate, in that the possibilities are endless. A cogent summary to such a question is that *students learn to believe in themselves; to understand why they think and behave in the limitless ways in which they do; to develop alternatives to the thinking and behavior which they identify as self-depriving; to actively set goals to change, test out, evaluate, and either incorporate or reject their new behaviors; and to set priorities for themselves that will optimize their own personal living in every single area of their existence.*

Group Counseling and Counselor Accountability

Beyond the numerous payoffs that group counseling offers for the student body, you need to apprise yourself of the benefits that it offers you, as a functioning school guidance counselor. The term "accountability" has been given considerable press in the literature of your profession in recent years. School counselors have been accused of being highly paid clerks, and local boards of education have used their budget-cutting scissors to neatly excise many guidance positions, with little or no protest from students, parents, or school officials. In plain language, the school counselors of North America are not DELIVERING. You have said many times that you would like to spend more of your time counseling, rather than pushing papers, filling out forms, writing recommendations, and being a pawn for administrative fiat. You have also asserted that you would like to be able to reach more of your students, and offer your counseling expertise to the large numbers of students who so desperately need it. Group counseling is the tonic you have been looking for.

As you examine the "delivery of services" dilemma, coupled with the "not reaching your students" syndrome, you must see that the most economic use of your time, in terms of what you are paid to do, is to begin to offer your counseling services in groups, so that larger numbers of students can benefit from your services, and to demonstrate to the entire school community (including yourself) that you are a vital component of the total school picture. It boils down to very simple arithmetic. If you spend your entire school day doing paper work and squeezing in as many individual counseling sessions as possible, you are lucky to have more than four or five appointments in a given day. If you were to spend just one half of the time that you devote to individual sessions to counseling in groups, you could reach ten times as many students, and they would be participants and active observers in effective counseling.

Speaking from a purely practical budgeting-of-time point of view, you cannot continue indefinitely to serve a tiny proportion of the students in your caseload, while ignoring large numbers of students who are in need of counseling. The inefficiency of counselors in budgeting time to provide for the greatest number of "in-need" students is the single most pronounced reason for the assertions of nonaccountability in the school counseling profession. Group counseling, on a schoolwide basis, is perhaps the one approach to your job that will make you more accountable and, in fact, make all of the students in the school emphatically aware of the significant contributions that guidance counselors make to the student body.

In schools where the majority of students have an opportunity to participate actively in counseling groups there is very little talk about the nonviability of the counseling office as an integral part of the school program. You will find that if you can successfully inaugurate a schoolwide group counseling program, the spin-off benefit will be a new attitude, permeating the entire school, about the significant contribution that the counseling office is making. Administrators, teachers, parents, and of course the students, will hear via the grapevine that an innovative, exciting, and worthwhile service is available to all of the students. It will come home to them that the counselors are "out there" helping rather than sitting in their cloistered offices, available only to a select few—usually the troublemakers and the class failures. A schoolwide portrait of effectiveness is the payoff for becoming an active group counselor. And there is a renewed sense of self-satisfaction in knowing that you are delivering counseling services on a schoolwide, rather than a limited and severely restricted, basis.

In Response to Your Objections and Fears Elaborated in Chapter 1

My training has been insufficient to begin leading counseling groups.

While this is perhaps your most legitimate concern, it is not a reason to stay away from group counseling entirely. You are avoiding the most potent instrument for delivering your counseling services. Essentially, if you have been trained in individual counseling methods, you have the groundwork necessary for becoming an effective group counselor. You know how to counsel, and you know how counseling differs from discussion and conversation. You have some training in diagnosing self-defeating behavior, and you have done some supervised counseling with clients who are not functioning at their optimal capacity in many areas of their lives.

Certainly you can seek out some additional specialized training in group counseling methodologies. You can hire a consultant who is expert in group counseling procedures to give you some updating on specialized skills necessary for effective group counseling leadership. You can make an effort to see that your entire staff gets some training in group counseling by hiring competent trainers to spend some time in your school to meet your specific needs in the area of group counseling. But all of the training in the universe is not going to give you the confidence to get out there and begin leading groups on a regular basis.

You will become good at group counseling by forming your groups and applying your individual counseling skills in the groups. You will gain competence in group counseling by taping your sessions, listening and relistening with experts and colleagues, and putting into practice what you are gaining from the experience. If you remember how you learned to counsel at all, you are likely to admit that it wasn't through your training but rather through your on-the-job experience. You would certainly be wise to have consultants to help you at the beginning, but saying that you have not received the proper training and using this as your reason for avoiding group counseling is essentially a cop-out. You can receive the training right now, by doing, and by receiving expert supervision. The only way to become an expert at anything is to *do*. The old maxim of the pragmatists is applicable. "I *hear* and I forget. I *see* and I remember. I *do* and I understand."

My life experiences have not prepared me for group counseling leadership.

While this self-statement is certainly accurate, it is in no way a defensible reason for avoiding group counseling. Because you were never expected to exercise leadership in the groups of your life, you feel discontented about assuming this role now. You are fearful about venturing into uncharted waters. However, you should keep in mind that any new skill you have acquired largely required the same kind of venturing. If you know how to paint, or play tennis, or swim, or even swat flies, there was a time in your life when you couldn't do these things; you had no past experience in these specialized activities. Being effective in your world involves not living in the past; it means overcoming your internal self-descriptors which are based on what you have learned in your past. If you are interested in becoming something that you haven't always been, then you must take new steps in unfamiliar areas.

Conversely, you can stay the same by simply relying on all of the things you have done up until now, and using them as your self-description, thereby using your past as a guide, nay, a restrictor, on what you will be now. Using the logic of your past as a reason to avoid something new, if applied universally in your life, prohibits you from ever visiting new and exciting places, from attaining any new interests, and on and on. Many people use their past as a way of avoiding something new or possibly mysterious. It's not unusual for a person to have the same kind of friends, see the same type of movies, buy the same newspapers and the same kinds of books, and read only those journal articles that discuss an "interest" of their own.

Venturing into the unknown is a characteristic of fully functioning people. Not being a slave to one's past experiences involves fighting the internal attraction of the familiar and trying something new even though you have not been well prepared experientially to be immediately successful.

So it is with group counseling. If you let your past experiences guide or restrict you, you are likely to avoid it. But if you see it as a challenge, as something to be mastered, then you will not let yourself be tied to your past. The alternative is to be forever precisely what you have always been.

I am likely to incur parental and administrative objections if I inaugurate group counseling.

Of the things you fear, this is the least likely to occur, provided you take the necessary precautionary steps. Chapter 3 will elaborate, in detail, the preliminary steps to take prior to inaugurating your group counseling program.

In many of the schools which have made group counseling a vital element in their school guidance offerings, the parents have been among the most enthusiastic supporters of the program. If parents are well informed about the goals of group counseling, and if they can be in on the explanation of exactly what it is that constitutes group counseling as it will be practiced in your school, then the fear of parental reprisal is unfounded. Certainly, if parents feel that students are going to be sitting around in unstructured group settings and encouraged to let it all hang out, then you can expect to receive a great deal of parental flak.

Informing the parents does not mean letting them in on what is going on in the group itself. Instead, it means covering all your bases, anticipating what might be taken as objectionable, and being careful not to provoke obstructionism. Parents genuinely want help for their children, they want to feel that your school is taking steps to help their child at every turn. If you, as the school counselor, are sold on group counseling as a way of reaching more students and as an arena for coming to grips with age-pertinent concerns, then the parents will be supportive. Certainly you are not going to insist on taking a student into a counseling group over serious parental resistance. Parents will assuredly support any program which your school adopts and which you as a functioning school counselor have endorsed as educationally and psychologically sound.

Your fear of arousing parental anger over group counseling in your school or agency is essentially unfounded. Try to communicate that group counseling is a positive, healthful experience, and one which does not include focusing on others (including parents) as a part of the process. Parents want for their children what will help them in any way and you, as a counselor, can help them to see the worth of group counseling.

Your fears of administrative nonsanction are similarly unfounded. Your administrative staff will enthusiastically endorse any procedure that will remove some of the thorns from their busy day. Certainly, counseling itself has been endorsed by the administration, and counseling in groups is just your way of offering already sanctioned services to more students. Often administrators are at their rope's end with a small disruptive segment of the school population. Truants, troublemakers, drug-related problems, and so on. They know full well that nothing is being done for these professional system-disrupters and your offer of group counseling, as a way of reaching them, will generally be welcomed rather than rejected. "Anything, I'll try anything," your principal laments, "we're certainly not reaching them now."

School principals genuinely want to help, while simultaneously running a smooth, trouble-free organization. Group counseling can meet both of these goals if presented in the manner discussed in chapter 3. Your anxiety about both parental and administrative displeasure is largely a projection of your own uncertainty about the value and effectiveness of group counseling.

When you believe, really believe, in the process and in your ability to deliver the service, then your fears about antipathy from other interest groups will subside. You, not they, will become the governing force behind the delivery of your professional services. Moreover, you will be surprised to learn, that others are just as interested as you are in providing growth-producing activities for the students. Like you, their fears are based on the unknown. Your job is to take the mystery, and thereby the apprehension, out of the unknown by presenting yourself as a knowledgeable, competent professional who is earnestly interested in maximizing his effectiveness as a school counselor.

I've heard that groups are places where weird things can happen.

Once again, you have heard much about what can happen in a group. What you need to store in the deepest caverns of your brain is, "What happens in a group is what the group leader allows to happen." Period. In groups where people play feel-up games, where out-of-control emotional episodes crop up, or where any of an array of inappropriate activities are allowed or encouraged to occur, the leader has assumed a role which is inconsistent with ethical and professional standards for group counselors.

As the group leader, you are the orchestrator of the activity. You establish what will take place, and clearly verbalize the forbidden areas. Disallowing touching and group pressure, ensuring the right of group members to be silent (or nonrevealing), being cautious in emotionally sensitive areas, all this can be determined unequivocally by the group leader. You as counselor can make your own professional assessment, decide what you will say in the first session (see chapter 7 for recommended opening statements), and see to it that the rules are followed. There is no need to have "weird" things crop up in your group counseling activities.

Were you to investigate those groups in which you've heard of strange "goings on," you would undoubtedly find a leader who was either ill-prepared, or who had not thought through and stated the ground rules for group counseling. And, tellingly, you would discover a leader who had endorsed, rather than discouraged, unethical group procedures. If you know what kinds of behaviors and occurrences you do not want in your counseling group and act consonantly with your stated beliefs, then any fear of bizarre or unsuitable activities is essentially a lack of confidence in yourself and in your ability and willingness to carry out your professional commitment. It won't happen if you won't let it happen!

I do not want to be accused of doing group therapy in my school.

The word "therapy" has come to be associated with mental illness in the psychological circles of our culture, and for this very reason, your activities as a school counselor should never be confused with the practice of therapy. You will not be accused of doing therapy if you avoid this tag altogether. Group therapy and group counseling, although alike in many respects, when applied to the school setting are miles apart in definition and operation.

As a group counselor you should avoid the labels of sickness, pathology, or mental illness. You might note that group counseling is for everyone, and that its purpose is to help anyone, certainly everyone who desires to grow and become more personally effective. You should note that while everyone can use help, certainly it does not imply that to receive help one must be sick. Essentially, you can avoid the label of therapy by making it crystal clear that you are providing counseling services and that *anyone* in the school can avail himself or herself of this opportunity. You should also steer clear of using the therapy label yourself, since it sounds "sicky" and will provoke avoidance signals in the school.

You are a counselor. You are paid to deliver counseling services. In conducting your counseling groups, should someone surface who obviously needs the services of a therapist, then you are well aware of the referral channels available in the community. While it is rare indeed for any group member to show severely disturbed behavior, nevertheless emotionally laden concerns will certainly emerge in a counseling group. Very often, the inexperienced group counselor will associate the expression of feeling, or the communication of strong emotions, with "heavy stuff" that only therapists are trained to deal with. This is patently not so. You are certainly equipped to clarify and encourage affective expression by students in a group. Moreover, a student should not be thought of as disturbed simply because he or she displays a strong inclination toward "emotional" expression.

The "psychotic episode" in a counseling group is a rare phenomenon. Should it occur, and strong evidence of hallucinatory and detached behavior be present, then it would be treated as a referral, very much as it would if it occurred in a one-to-one counseling session in your office.

There is no basis for your fear that the counseling group itself will bring about psychologically damaging results or actions that would require a specially trained therapist. You must keep in mind that you, as the counselor, are the most significant determinant of group activity. You can ameliorate any group pressure with a potent intervention. Similarly, you can help an individual to relax, or make an appointment with you later, if you feel that he or she cannot handle an emotional interaction. You, not they and not some metaphysical factor of group composition, are the definer of limits. As long as you know this, you can play the key role in directing group activity. Accept that students are not brittle, frail creatures who will crack at the mention of a feeling or of an unhappy episode in their lives; you do not need to act as a therapist toward them or engage in any activity with a potential for psychologically damaging a young person in a counseling group.

If you don't call it therapy and don't act like "Sally Psychologist" with funny jargon about sick kids, then you will not be stuck with the "group therapy" label. If you have a reputation for practicing amateur therapy in your school, a very thorough investigation will probably show that you, and not any "they," are responsible for your reputation.

I want to avoid dropping a bomb, and since I've never led a group, it's a real possibility.

Here is one piece of self-logic that you can vigorously attack. There are two significant points in this "fear" of yours.

First, so what if you do "bomb"? What is the worst thing that would happen to you as a result of bombing in your first efforts? Will the students hate you or lose respect for you because you attempted to provide a helping structure for them? Of course not. You can really benefit from bombing in your early group counseling efforts, by using the same counseling logic you would employ with any student who uses fear of failure as an escape or avoidance ploy. You can do nothing but grow from a bomb-dropping episode. You will know and understand what not to do in the future and thus you will have gained some exceedingly valuable data for your future group counseling activity.

Failure is good. It is the greatest teacher, and the only way to learn what doesn't work. How did you learn all of the things you know about yourself? By taking the risk of failure. How did you learn to counsel effectively? You tried, you blew it, then you changed your method. But maybe you feared failure so much that after you experienced it in any specific endeavor, you dropped that endeavor—forever. Which means that in all of your areas of ineptitude you are doomed to ineffectiveness. Similarly, all of your limitations are really restrictions of the most debilitating sort, because you use failure as a reason to avoid that activity in the future, rather than as a piece of treasured data to apply to self-improvement.

You need to tell yourself that your fear of bombing is something that you could use in becoming a proficient group counselor, rather than using it as an evasive strategy. Tell yourself that the most useful thing that you could do on your road to effectiveness in group counseling is to have an occasional miscarriage and thereby learn not only what to do, but what *not* to do. Failure, or bombing, is good. By keeping this in mind, and by remembering that failure can never diminish your self-worth, you will be able to eliminate "the bomb" as a reason for avoiding anything in your life—specifically, becoming a practicing group counselor.

Second, there is very little likelihood that you will bomb in your initial efforts at group counseling, not if you prepare yourself, know what it is you are going to do, master effective group counseling leadership behavior, and explain what it is you are doing to the group. Your fear of failing as a group counselor is based on your awareness that you do not know how to behave in that role. However, when you enter your group with a game plan, alternate structures and strategies, and a knowledge of the process of group counseling, then you have taken steps which are predictive of being effective. Later chapters of this book provide you with highly detailed techniques and strategies for being effective from the opening moments of group counseling.

Should you enter your group with a fuzzy notion of what you are going to do, with no thoughts about specific strategies, and armed solely with a basketful of hopes and wishes, and a game plan of just being yourself and doing what comes naturally, then of course your fear of failure is actually an expectation of failure, a self-destined prophecy, if you will.

To summarize: you are unlikely to fail if you know what it is you are going to do, and if you do fail, it can only be to your advantage as a professional group counselor. Either way, the fear itself is useless mental activity.

I don't know if I could handle some circumstances that might crop up in the group.

This final reservation of yours stems from your wariness about the unknown. You tend to stay with the familiar and eschew those life situations wherein extemporaneous behavior might surface, and certainly a counseling group is a place wherein spontaneous behavior is not only likely, but predictable. This fear relates significantly to the bombing concern. That is, you know you can't fail if you stay only with the familiar, so you dodge the mysterious and take no risks, thereby leading a safe, albeit mundane and stunted life. If you studiously avoid them, you will never learn to handle perilous or uncertain conditions. You will always see yourself as wobbly in an unsettled group circumstance, unless you wade in and try it out. Consider the actor or professional ball player who fears how he will perform in the big leagues; he languishes in the minors for a lifetime, out of fear of being unable to handle the pressure. YOU LEARN BY DOING!

You will learn how to deal effectively with emotionalism, resistance, acting-out, crying, anger, and thousands of other possibilities, by arming yourself with as much knowledge as you can acquire, and then making the foray and testing yourself where it really counts. *In the counseling group.*

You can handle most counseling situations that occur in the privacy of your office. You learned how to do so by taking it upon yourself to counsel effectively. The same logic applies to group counseling. You learn how to work effectively in group circumstances by leading and calling upon your own skills and senses. Certainly you can equip yourself to deal with predictable group counseling behaviors, (reading this book is one of the ways to do so); thus you maximize the resources you will have to call on when the situation crops up.

You know it's possible to hit an airborne baseball with a thin wooden sliver, not because you read it or saw it, but because you've done it. Similarly, you'll know you can deal effectively with precarious group counseling circumstances, not because we've told you, but because you've experienced it. Action is the only genuine source of self-knowledge.

Chapter 5 details some understandings of and strategies for handling anticipated group-member behaviors. A careful reading and rereading of the contents will surely be helpful to you. In the final analysis, though, what matters is the realization that you have the capacity to function effectively in group counseling circumstances on the basis of your *own*, rather than anyone else's behavior.

Having closely examined your own resistance to group counseling, and having made your own personal assessment that it is worth doing, you will need to be absolutely certain about what group counseling is, and what the fundamental assumptions are that underlie effectively led counseling groups. These assumptions have to do with the purpose of group counseling, which is to help students take charge of their thinking while simultaneously achieving more effective and self-enhancing mental and physical behavior.

Group Counseling Defined

A brief but operational definition of group counseling is a contradiction in terms. Group counseling is complex; a multitude of considerations are necessary to identify the process. As you lead a group of students through a counseling experience, you should keep in mind that it is very easy and tempting to do activities other than counseling in your group. Any activity in your group that does not follow the model given below is probably a deviation from *counseling*.

Group counseling is a helping procedure which begins with the group members exploring their personal worlds for the purpose of identifying *thinking* and *behavior* which are in any way self-defeating.[1] Group members state to the group the behaviors that are counterproductive, and the group counselor helps each member set individual goals for himself. The counselor helps the individual members to verbalize the significant people and places in their lives in which the self-defeating behaviors are most evident and troublesome, and then helps them toward self-understanding by examining: a) the psychological maintenance system for the beha-

[1] This definition and the assumptions that follow are a restatement of those which first appeared in *Counseling Techniques That Work*, by Wayne W. Dyer and John Vriend (Washington, D.C.: American Personnel and Guidance Association Press, 1975), pp. 131–141. Reprinted with the permission of the American Personnel and Guidance Association.

vior (what the client gets, both positively and negatively, from the behavior), and b) why that self-crippling behavior persists.

The counselor or a group member, acting as a helper, then moves the individual to explore possible alternatives to his self-defeating behavior. The process then involves the setting of goals which are specific and attainable for the individual member or additional members who share a like concern.

After goal-setting, the individual tests his new behavior right in the group through either simulated or genuine helping structures. Psychological homework assignments are then mutually initiated and agreed upon, and the group member tries out his new behavior in his own world.

In ensuing sessions the group member gives a report on his new thinking, new feelings as a result of his new thinking, and on his new behaviors. The individual then either incorporates his new thinking and behavior, or he rejects them or gets recycled back for further exploration, self-understanding, and goal-setting. The total emphasis is on helping individual members set and work toward goals for themselves that involve new self-enhancing behaviors.

Twenty Basic Assumptions Underlying Effective Group Counseling as Defined Above

1. *Each individual member is more important than the collective.* A counseling group is an amalgamation of people—individual people. There is nothing magic about the group, nor is there anything to the notion that the group, as an entity, has significance. Group counseling should be thought of as *counseling,* that is, helping individuals to understand themselves and thereby function more effectively in their own worlds. There is no goal of helping the *group* to function more effectively in its own world, because the group has no external world to function in. The group is a myth. People are real. Therefore the use of words such as we, us, and the group, is discouraged. Instead members speak of you, I, me, him, her, Mary, George, and so on. Students come to the counseling group with their own set of concerns and difficulties. You must remember that as a group they do not exist; rather, they exist as individuals who are attempting to learn and grow. You should make every effort to singularize your behavior as a group counselor, and to keep uppermost in your mind that you are deal-

ing with individual people, not with a collective. When you say "the group," or "us," or "we," you are not talking to anyone, and most often no message gets conveyed, simply because each person assumes that you are talking not to him or her, but rather to those who make up this entity called a group. So the signal that you send gets received by individuals only if they want to identify with it; but if they choose to ignore it, you have made it simple to do so by your collective references.

2. *The leader is not a "member" of the group.* It is assumed also that the group leader does not have member status within the group. The one all-embracing characteristic which separates the leader from everyone else, is that he or she *never* uses the group to serve his or her own needs. When you are leading a group you are being a counselor, and hence you are being paid to deliver counseling services to the group members. You only make self-references when they are designed to help someone (or several people) in the group.

There are two very basic reasons for you not to use the group for your own self-growth and development, or to work on concerns of your own. First, when you "get into" yourself and begin sharing with the group for the purpose of being helped, you lose sight and sound of what is occurring around you. The process of being counseled is a deeply intense experience, and the client tends to screen out everyone around him, or to put it more graphically, to get lost in himself. If you, as a leader, begin to move into this "getting lost in self" behavior, you will not be aware of what is going on in the group. Obviously, if you lose contact with the group, you are not able to serve in a leadership capacity; you will be unable to interpret, summarize, clarify, protect, and most importantly, read the signals within the group.

Second, your role is to counsel and not to receive counseling. When you shift the focus to yourself to receive help, you are not working as a counselor, but rather as a client. This is an unprofessional and unethical stance to assume within a group that you are assigned to lead. A very clear statement about your leadership role and responsibility should be verbalized in the first session. (See chapter 7 for a sample introductory leader statement to the group.)

3. *Group counseling is for everyone.* Anyone on this planet who can admit to being able to improve in some way in his life, can benefit from group counseling. Whereas the price of admission to a therapy group is the admission of some pathology, the

entrance dues for membership in a counseling group are only an admission that "I can grow" in any area of my life. Group counseling is for everyone. Normals, maladjusted, geniuses, and those who are not living a totally self-actualized life. You will need to make this very clear to your group members and thereby allay any anxiety they may have about being sick or "screwed-up" because they are participating in group counseling. Group therapy operates from the premise that the group and the therapist are there to restore the individuals to healthy living. The touchstone of group counseling is that growing, becoming more effective and productive in your life is possible for everyone; there is no interest in making the group into an Easter egg hunt in search of juicy, neurotic prizes to be cracked open by inquisitive, albeit well-intentioned, peers. As stated in the Introduction to *Counseling Effectively in Groups* (by John Vriend and Wayne Dyer), "A counseling group is a supercharged learning environment where new behaviors can be acquired and practiced, where members can learn to master themselves and develop competencies and skills which are useful in numerous areas of their lives, where even creative and self-actualized geniuses can get more mileage out of their natural endowments. For each member, the overall personal goal becomes the greatest totality of personal effectiveness: How can I take charge in more parts of my world?" There is nothing in there about the eradication of sickness.

4. *Group counseling is nongimmicky and nonfeely.* The business of group counseling is counseling. Whereas encounter groups encourage intimacy and utilize a raft of touching exercises to break down intimacy barriers, a counseling group uses talking and techniques that communicate effectively without physical contact. The environment of a counseling group is straight, not contrived in a minifamily atmosphere. The techniques that are used are counseling strategies rather than gimmicks to provide temporary escape into a fantasy world.

A school counseling group is an inappropriate arena for engaging in intimacy games and touching exercises designed to build trust, cohesiveness, and love among group members. Group counseling has a set of guidelines, it has strategies that are exceedingly useful, and it has a scientific base built upon measurable and observable components of the helping process. To make it into a miniature love affair between members, or any such forum where members are encouraged to explore, feel, and tear down defenses is to engage in something other than group counseling. The service of group counseling is delivered in a verbal rather than a sensory mode. Nonverbal behavior is certainly noted and examined; however, touching or groping exercises are in no way a component of the constituted process of group counseling.

While "feely" exercises lend themselves readily to the group process, and in fact may have significant value in the growth process in groups, they should be seen as a part of the "encounter group scene" which should be reserved for volunteering adults who know the waters they are wading into. In schools and agencies, "feely" gimmickry in groups leads to outraged parents, litigation, and trouble with a capital T; but most importantly for you as a practicing group counselor, it is unethical behavior and not a part of the group counseling process.

5. *A counseling group has individual rather than group goals.* Basketball teams have group goals. Committees have group goals. Juries have group goals. Counseling groups have individual goals. Each individual in the group is unique and consequently has unique expectations for himself or herself within the group. The group is only a means toward helping individuals become more effective human beings; it has no significant end for itself. People should be encouraged to think for themselves rather than thinking like everyone else. Consequently, any emphasis on treating the group as a private entity with goals to achieve reinforces the self-immobilizing notion that the collective is more important than the I. Each individual is encouraged to think for herself, and to set goals for herself, and to use the resources of the total group to reach her goals. To subordinate oneself to the "other" is to engage in self-defeating behavior. To emphasize group goals is to teach the group members that others are more important, thereby solidifying a poor rather than a strong self-image. The group is a myth! The individual, using the group process and the social opportunities for valuable interaction and feedback, is the function of group counseling.

6. *Individual counseling in the group is not only permitted, but necessary.* Just as individual goals are stressed in group counseling, so too is individual counseling within the group. While feedback and interaction are important, the notion that somehow the "group counsels" is ludicrous. You are the counselor, and until you teach the group members what counseling is by modeling it, you are the only one who knows how to counsel within the group. Moreover, it is absurd to assume that if you counsel one person in the group setting, no one else will benefit from your

helping efforts. By observing you counsel with another group member, and by absorbing the helping messages that you are sending, others within the group can see and implement your counseling activities. You must also remember that there are only individuals in this world, and that counseling deals with those individuals. A group does not counsel nor does it receive counseling. Individual people do! And any and all helping efforts that occur in your group are directed at unique, original, unparalleled, special, unmatched individuals. Help is always directed at a person, rather than a collection. For you to feel that everyone must be participating verbally, or that you must constantly involve everyone, is to engage in high-level folly. Group counseling focuses on people in groups, and until you, with the help of other group members, have moved through the group counseling process with an individual and brought about closure with goal-setting and the trying out of behavior, you have not counseled. Moreover, when you are counseling an individual within the group and encouraging others to "help" that person, you are paradoxically, doing the most collective good. The others benefit most from help that is directed individually, rather than collectively.

7. *Group interaction and group feedback are not goals in themselves.* This is positively related to the assumption above. You should not measure your success as a group counselor on the basis of how much the group was involved. This is the criterion of the novice. Interaction, just for the sake of talking and involvement, is conversational chit-chat rather than counseling. Far better to have only two people interacting, and one person receiving help directly (and countless others vicariously), than to have eight people talking and none growing. While interaction will come as the group gets moving, it is certainly no virtue in itself to have everyone contributing. Ironically, in the groups that have the most interaction and participation, the least help is often being offered. Such a session takes on the character of an interrogation rather than a helping exercise, with attention being taken from the individual who requests help at the time in favor of a lot of self-seeking personal references by everyone in the group. Or the "totally involved verbal group" becomes an advice-giving forum in which the protagonist is barraged with personal advice from every direction. While interaction certainly is valuable, it is not a goal all by itself. You are seeking to deliver help, not to create a lot of group interaction. Contrary to a whole literature of "group interaction" as a desired trait of counseling groups, the general way that groups

work is through individual counseling, with individual members having an opportunity to use the group resources to receive help for themselves, with the leader counseling more in the beginning sessions, and group members picking up the helping techniques via the modeled effective counseling behavior. Looking for some magical "group doing the counseling" or "group receiving the counseling" will lead you down endless psychological dead ends in your group; the end product is conversational chawing rather than help for individuals within your group.

8. *There is no pressure applied to group members.* Individuals within the group have the right to choose whether they will or will not participate. The group leader protects the right of a group member to make a choice without having the group members coerce, cajole, or otherwise apply group psychological pressure to divulge or to seek help. While pressure will undoubtedly mount on group members to take part in the process, there is no direct duress applied to achieve total group participation. Each individual has the right to talk or not to talk. Similarly, each member has the right to resist changing, even though others within the group, including you as the leader, might have contrary views. If an individual does not feel ready, or does not view self-defeating behaviors as something he is willing to change, then this is more than tolerable, it is understandable and acceptable. Change is a personal matter, and very often just confronting someone with their behavior and not asking them to change it now is enough to get them started on the road toward self-improvement. The counselor protects the right of each member to make these choices for himself, and to have the focus shifted elsewhere if this is the individual's inclination.

9. *A counseling group is not a confessional.* The encouragement of a spirit of confession within your counseling group will inhibit effectiveness. Every individual has something in his past he is ashamed of and prefers to maintain as personal rather than public data. If a member chooses to pour forth juicy stories from the past to gain the attention (and sympathy) of the group, you as the leader must ask yourself some vital questions. How will this person benefit from releasing closet skeletons? Is this person seeking sympathy? If so, won't group support reinforce this kind of thinking?

The psychology of the confessional is debilitating to the progress of the confessor as well as to those listening to the confession. When you, as the group leader, lend your support to this kind of activity, you reinforce the self-immobilizing need of the confessor to maintain focus on past behavior. If you want to be effective within the group, you can ask the group member who is prone to emotional storytelling, "How can we be of help to you now?" A confession is only a reminiscence about the past for the purpose of being forgiven, or for getting sympathy and support. A counseling group is a here-and-now activity constituted for the purpose of helping people become more effective in their lives. If the telling of a past emotional experience will help an individual to become more effective now, then it should by all means be explored. If, however, the group member wants to tell sympathy-producing stories for the purpose of getting attention, then you will need to intervene to bring the focus onto present-moment concerns. You will also want to keep in mind that "letting it all hang out" as a strategy for counseling within the group is not always productive. Very often, the fact of "putting it away forever" because nothing can be done about it (except to feel guilty or helpless) is a sign of mental health, and you as a group leader may be encouraging neurotic thinking by instigating recollection and confessionary behavior.

10. *A counseling group is not a gripe session nor does it focus on "others."* There will be a strong temptation on the part of the group members to turn the group into an arena for complaint about a host of Others, most particularly the bad teacher, the principal, the unfair rules, or even the "out-group" kids. You, as a group leader, will need to be on guard for such activity, and effectively squelch it before it becomes a way of life within the group. If your group becomes a gripe session, you will be reinforcing the very kind of behavior that is self-forfeiting in the individuals within the group. To blame or to otherwise focus on someone outside of yourself is to give them, rather than yourself, responsibility for what you are and what you will become. (Chapter 5 deals more in depth with this typically recurring group member behavior.)

You are always alert for group member behavior that attempts to shift responsibility to someone or something outside of self and particularly outside of the group. How will churning around complaints help the individuals within the group to become more effective in dealing with people who do not fit neatly into their expectations? Gripe sessions, while having some cathartic value, tend to unite the group in an "against" mentality, rather than helping them challenge each other into alternate ways of thinking and behaving which could become more self-serving. Grumbling is not growth-producing behavior. Similarly, focusing on anyone who is not in the group teaches abdication of self-responsibility, and certainly will not serve to change "them." Many so-called counseling groups turn into forums for griping about the system in which the students find themselves unavoidably immersed. And most often students leave these groups (1) without any new insights or strategies for dealing more effectively with their impersonally imposed system; (2) with their "blaming as a strategy for living" philosophy reinforced; and (3) with the "system" remaining exactly as it was when they entered the group. In other words, they leave without having gained anything from an experience that might have helped them become more productive human beings.

11. *Confidentiality is a watchword of group counseling.* What goes on in the group is for group members, and no one else. Students need to know and BELIEVE that this is one place where a report to the authorities is not forthcoming if someone gets out of line. Just as individual counseling is viewed as a privileged relationship, so too is the counseling that takes place in the group. This is something that should be dealt with in the very beginning of the group. You, as the leader can assert that what goes on in this group will not be talked about by you, unless you first receive the permission of the group members. (If you cannot live with this ground rule, then you should make it clear to everyone what the boundaries of confidentiality are in this group.)

This is not to suggest that group members should be discouraged from talking about group-related data outside of the group, but rather, that bringing *others* in on the data-sharing would be a breach of ethics. You can make it clear how you will treat data. And you needn't make a big thing out of your statement; the group members will decide if you are to be trusted on the basis of what you do, not what you say. It will suffice to make a simple statement about confidentiality and who has access to the group data, and to poll the group members to see if they can live with this ground rule. Once it is established, you will not find violations to be a problem. Rather, the group members appreciate it as a safeguard of their own right to privacy and most often will observe it religiously. Any group member who feels that he or she cannot live with your confidentiality requirements should not participate in the sessions, and should be encouraged to seek out individual rather than group counseling. You must act as a model protector of confidentiality at all times, and tenaciously fight any temptations you may have to share group data with others, without the permission of the group members. Your modeling will help others to see how important and easy it is to act ethically.

12. *Group members speak for themselves in a counseling group.* Each member of the group is encouraged to talk for himself. Individual and independent thinking are regarded as healthy goals, and when one member begins to speak for another it is pointed to by the leader and explained as behavior that is counterproductive for everyone concerned. Because a group is a social arena, there will naturally be varying degrees of introversion, verbal skill, and personality expression among the members. When a more verbal member speaks for another and you as leader don't point to it, then you are encouraging rather than helping to extinguish psychologically dependent behavior. If a member is unable to speak for herself, then she can begin to work at becoming a more effective communicator as well as a more independent person. At no time in the counseling group should speaking for others become a way of group life as it so often is in many of the groups that people find themselves involved with. (These include family groups, committees, peer groups, clubs, teams, and classes, wherein speaking for each other, or having leaders who speak for everyone, is a necessary condition of group survival.)

13. *Counseling groups do not emphasize feelings over thoughts.* It is quite possible for group members to confront each other on a variety of levels without becoming emotional or "gutsy." While feelings are not to be devalued as appropriate content for a counseling group, neither are they to be considered as having mystical properties or any desirability over nonemotional content areas. There is no goal of "getting down to feelings" within the group. Many group counselors also assume that there is a clear measurable distinction between a feeling and a thought, and that somehow the latter is unpalatable, while the former is fruit to be coveted within the group. Not so! Feelings are quite impossible without thoughts; they are essentially physical reactions to cognitive processes. To attempt to separate them is to induce confusion. And to insist that group members express their feelings as if they are separate entities to be called upon at will, is pure and simple psychological folly.

Keeping in mind that the purpose of the group is to help all persons work at becoming more effective in the self-chosen areas of their lives, you must then examine the role of feelings within the group. Helping a group member to understand her feelings, to feel unthreatened by her emotions, and most importantly, to learn how to control her debilitating emotions and use them more productively is certainly a laudable goal and significant group counseling activity. However, if you have the expression of emotions merely in order to show how "gutsy" you are with no specific objective toward self-improvement, you merely foster psychological gamesmanship rather than self-understanding for the purpose of individual-betterment in the counseling group.

14. *Group cohesiveness is not an end in group counseling.* The rather peculiar aim of the counseling group is that it strives to dissolve itself. Cohesiveness as a unit results from *time* spent *being together;* it can happen to people stranded on an elevator for twelve hours, or to a group waiting for a bus for several hours. It is not a goal of the group counseling process to have a cohesive, together, bound-up group. All goals are for the individuals, and the group itself is only a tool in helping members grow. At the end of the allotted time for the counseling, the group will die, while all of the individuals will go out and attempt to function in their own private worlds.

The significant thing here is that cohesiveness will develop whether you actively foment it or not. Spending group time to advance cohesiveness is a waste of time, when you consider the goals of group counseling. The cohesiveness factor is an offshoot of the counseling experience, but whether it occurs or not (and it almost always will), it is unrelated to the tasks you have as a group counselor. *The business of group counseling is counseling individuals in groups.* The business of group counseling is not to foster friendships, solve intellectual problems, change the school, or create cohesive units with in-group support. Don't spend your valuable group counseling time in exalting an activity that can just as easily be accomplished in a sewing class, at a party, or on any occasion in which "time" and "being together" are inescapable components of the socialization process.

15. *Session-to-session follow-up is an integral part of group counseling.* A counseling group is not ten or fifteen distinct experiences, but rather one experience which has continuity and follow-up throughout. A member who has had time in the spotlight to get some help in the group is not forgotten for the remainder of the life of the group when the spotlight shifts to others. Each session should have some degree of carry-over from previous sessions; follow-up on every goal and homework assignment is

crucial. Follow-up teaches the group members that you, as a leader, care about their goal accomplishment.

Reporting back to the group should become a regular part of the group counseling agenda. Even a member who has gone to work on a self-defeating behavior after the first session should be encouraged to give a brief report at the beginning of every session, so that continuous intermittent reinforcement for the new behavior is provided. A report back to the group should have very specific components, and these are examined thoroughly in chapter 8.

Follow-up reports are vital to effective group counseling. Without them, you are not actually engaging in continuous group counseling, but rather in singular, isolated sessions, that in their unrelatedness vitiate the benefit of long-term help. Since your goal is to help each individual maximize self-selected areas of his life, then each individual must be held accountable for going to work on his behavior. Session-to-session reports reinforce the importance you attach to the group member's continuing work on stated areas of ineffectiveness.

16. *Some counseling should take place in every group session.* While some of the activity that takes place in a counseling group may not be defined as counseling, there should be no session in which *individuals* are not receiving some counseling. The emphasis here is on the individual receiving counseling. Certainly, many legitimate activities take place within the group that would not be identified as counseling per se. They include process analysis, summarizing, reviewing, examining the content of previous sessions, and so on. No one session should be filled exclusively with these ancillary activities, and particularly not the early sessions.

It is important for the group members to see first-hand what constitutes a group counseling experience, to see an individual, or several individuals, receiving help in the form set forth in this chapter as operationally correct. A session, or an entire group experience, could be consumed by summarizing, or goal-setting, or reviewing, or process-analyzing, all to the exclusion of helping the individuals within the group. At the end of every group session, you should be able to say who specifically received help today as a result of your counseling and that of other identifiable group members. This is not to minimize the importance of group process activities, but to put the stress where it belongs in a counseling group, on *individuals receiving and providing counseling services.* It is possible to analyze, summarize, plan, revitalize, scrutinize, and examine group movements to death. While these are bona fide group counseling activities, when practiced with exclusivity they become excuses for avoiding counseling within the group.

17. *Counseling groups contain no chit-chat or conversation.* The business of group counseling is counseling. While discussions, conversations, and chit-chatty behavior are certainly fine and acceptable social practices, they have no place in a group constituted for the purpose of helping individuals through the counseling process. Talking about the upcoming party, football game, or who is dating whom is tempting for group members, simply because it is easier than participating in counseling. If you condone such activity, you are robbing your group members of the opportunity to receive help from the group counseling experience. It should also be a clue to you that you are avoiding counseling and encouraging noncounseling activity in the group.

Just as using the group to complain or gripe is nongroup counseling activity, using it for the purpose of socializing is also unethical and nonproductive. When you see conversational interchanges cropping up, you can point to them as avoidance behaviors, or ask what the participants are getting out of this behavior, or you can simply ignore it and not reinforce it by joining in. But it is far, far better to have some uncomfortable silences in the group, than to fill in with small talk which, if unchecked, can become the primary activity of the counseling group. Once you demonstrate that this is a place where business gets transacted in the form of delivering helping services, then the inclination toward conversational "fillers" will not only subside, but group members won't even consider it as an activity, since it receives no reinforcement from you, the leader.

18. *There is no connection between comfort and effectiveness in group counseling.* Your goal is not to make group members comfortable, and statements which indicate that everyone is comfortable and cozy are often indicators of immobility rather than progress in the group counseling process. When people are comfortable they are least likely to change and most likely to stay as they are, simply because that behavior gets rewarded with comfort. Accompanying any change toward new thinking and behavior is a degree of provocation and, yes, even some self-irritation. To the extent that you encourage group members to be comfortable and snug, you are stimulating "standstillism." This is not to suggest that outright anxiety is a goal for the group leader, but certainly some degree of anxiousness about self does far more to promote change than do self-satisfaction and comfort.

Change involves coming to grips with the "whys" of our behavior. Usually the answers to the whys will get our adrenaline flowing, and that is when changes in our behavior are most likely to occur. If a group member is experiencing some discomfort, that is no reason to shift the focus to "safer" territory. The degree of discomfiture is of course important; a total emotional collapse will serve no good and is of course to be avoided. A preoccupation with solace and a commodious atmosphere is, however, the least likely climate for effectively helping people to understand and ultimately change their behavior. Anxiety that accompanies ultimate going-to-work on the behavior is desirable. Anxiety for the sake of anxiety or exacerbation is as self-hindering as comfort for the sake of comfort in a counseling context.

19. *Negative emotions are not bad, and should not be avoided in group counseling*. While the expression of negative feelings has no inherent value unto itself, certainly to avoid expressing them does not promote growth. A placating group which shuns any expressions of anger, fear, hostility, sadness, anxiety, or hate is one which teaches the group members that having negative emotions is bad, something to be ashamed of, and certainly to be avoided in a counseling group. People are not good at handling negative emotions largely because they fail to deal with them, and because they operate from the philosophy that getting back to emotional homeostasis is a goal for everyone.

If negative emotions are debilitating or psychologically immobilizing in any way (and they almost always are) then working at not having them would be a laudable goal. However, pretending that they do not exist, or that you should be ashamed of them, teaches people to run away from the things that they don't like or understand. If some members in the group are angry, hostile, or depressed, allowing them to work on it, to come to grips with it, and maybe to work at having different, more self-enhancing reactions in the future is valuable group counseling activity.

While it is not recommended that individuals be encouraged to feel negative emotions within the group, it also is not recommended that when they do arise, they be tabled in favor of more succoring thoughts and feelings. The one fear that you probably have as a group counselor is that the expression of anger or some such emotion will tear the group apart. The opposite is almost always true. When group members struggle with some of their frustrations both in their own lives and in the group itself, the resolution of the battle often serves as a unifying rather than a rupturing element. When you see negative emotions surface, rather than think, "Oh my God, what can I do to get out of this?" think about the potential value in working it through, and begin to label behavior for what it is. Running away from anything only teaches running-away skills. Most students have learned throughout their lives that having anger is bad, and that no one is able to handle it. A counseling group should not be one more occasion where the shame of having negative emotions is reinforced by disdain for their presence.

20. *Your effectiveness as a group counselor is measured by what goes on outside rather than inside of the group.* If the members of your group are behaving in textbookishly perfect fashion within the group—interacting, helping, agreeing, and being cooperative counselees—yet their lives are unchanged and they continue their self-defeating behavior patterns, then you as a group counselor are ineffective, and your group counseling activity might better have been spent filling out forms in your office. Changing behavior in a growth-producing direction is what group counseling is all about.

Armed with this information, you are not interested in having your group members agree with you or accept a counseling stance that you might support. Nor are you interested in winning arguments and being convincing. Looking for exactly the right response is not your business, nor is having heavy doses of communication within the group or covering lots of emotional topics. Essentially, your success as a group counselor is measured in those weekly reports that the group members give. Are they taking charge in more parts of their world? Are they happier, more fully functioning, more productive than when they entered the group? These are the questions that the thinking group counselor asks himself. Not, "Did I convince him?" or "Were we interacting?" but "Are we making a difference?" This is the important question to be asking. And the difference is measured out there, in that person's individual life, where he must learn to function effectively forever.

The group is certainly real; members do not bring an *ersatz* self to the group. But the important reality is the individual's private world, which is external to the counseling group. By looking to see how much impact you and the entire group are having on individuals in their own lives, you can begin to assess how effective you are being as a group counselor and a helping person. The group activity is meaningless if it is not having an impact on the individual's world. You can increase your overall efficiency as a group leader by asking, "What kinds of things can I do differently in the group that will make a difference in the lives of these people?" Not by asking, "What kinds of things can I do to get the group off of the ground so that it is more lively and interesting?"

This then is an extended operational definition of group counseling as it is practiced with the purpose of making a difference. In answering the question, "Is group counseling worth doing?" which is posed in the title of this chapter, you will need to examine, very carefully, all of your own personal fears and reservations about becoming a group counseling practitioner, as well as the components of group counseling and the twenty basic assumptions that go hand in hand with a thorough understanding of group counseling in the school and all settings.

The case for group counseling is demonstrably clear. It is a needed activity which focuses on the most important components of everyday living, that is, being in charge of one's own world in every operational aspect. While many group experiences are available to young people—group therapy, the multitude of group activities under the encounter umbrella, rap groups, and peer discussion groups—group counseling is the one kind of activity that offers a student a skilled counselor in combination with well-intentioned peers working together in a safe but challenging environment for the purpose of becoming more self-aware and self-productive persons.

If the students whom you serve are to receive the counseling services you are prepared to offer, then you must come to grips with your reticence about becoming a group counseling practitioner. Chapter 3 offers a discussion of the necessary preliminaries in inaugurating a full-scale group counseling program, or even just a trial balloon of one counseling group. If you are beginning to give it more serious consideration, read on!

3

You Are Thorough About Preliminaries

BEFORE PLUNGING into your group counseling activity on a schoolwide basis, you will want to make a comprehensive assessment of the school's readiness for accepting group counseling. You will identify those persons who might be apprehensive about your group counseling activities, those who are the potential supporters, and most importantly, what *strategies* you will implement for assuaging skeptics and fully utilizing the available support system within your school and community.

These are the most significant questions that you will be asking in making your pre-group counseling assessment within your school:

Who cares about this activity?

Who is, or might be, apprehensive, and why?

How can I best allay the fears of those who are skeptical?

Who is supportive of group counseling?

How can I best utilize the existing support structure within the school?

In your thoroughness about preliminaries, you are taking every precaution to ensure the smooth transition from a traditionally one-to-one counseling system to one in which you deliver your counseling services in groups. Obviously you will need the cooperation of many factions within your school in order to make it come off effectively. You are now thinking about reaching your entire student body with counseling services, something that has never been contemplated by the school staff. And so, your preliminary activities take on a crucial tone, in that your "selling" of the process is dependent upon how efficiently your groundwork is carried out.

Every school has a set of interest groups that are concerned about any innovative program that becomes a part of the school curriculum. Group counseling is no exception. Certainly you must consider your entire school administrative structure—superintendents (if applicable), district offices, regional supervisors, your school principal, and assistants to the principal. You must consider also the teachers within the school. In addition, the parents of the students certainly are interested in any program that is going to involve their children on a schoolwide basis. Also, your colleagues in the counseling office and other school psychological personnel are vital to the success of a group counseling program. Certainly the community in which your school is located will have some interest in this approach to school counseling. Most importantly, your student body, those who will receive group counseling, comprise a significant interest group to be dealt with in your planning for a workable program.

Your work is cut out for you. You must devise a plan that will be most predictive of success, and yet satisfy those in-school and extra-school interest groups mentioned above. What follows is a suggested model for your pre-group counseling activity, a model that can have a multitude of variations. The one all-embracing characteristic of this model is that it is a well-thought-out plan for making your group counseling program one in which the impediments and potential snags are minimized, and the supportive and abetting factors are maximized, in the school/community setting.

Your Plan of Action:
A suggested model for dealing effectively with the six interest groups who can affect the success of your group counseling program.

1. YOUR COLLEAGUES

Colleagues include any and all school student personnel professionals who might have an interest in providing counseling services to your student body. While it is not absolutely necessary for you to have departmental consensus in order to implement group counseling services in your school, it is most advisable to have your entire school psychological services staff in on your preliminary planning for introducing group counseling into your school.

By having unanimity among staff members, by having them interested and involved in the actual leading of counseling groups, you will appear convincing and professional in your approach; certainly you will have more clout in selling to the powers that be your idea of total school involvement in school group counseling. If you have a permanent staff of school psychologists, or have only visitation arrangements, you would be wise to involve any and all school psychological personnel in your planning activities. It would be advisable if the school psychologist could be in on the group counseling itself, serving the double purpose of improving the psychological services offered to the school, while also strengthening your over-all helping structures available to the student body.

You will need to think through carefully how you are going to implement your program from a logistical point of view (see part 3 of this chapter). Moreover, you will want to decide, departmentally, how you are going to sell your program to the total school community. As staff, you are indeed committed to the notion of group counseling as an effective helping strategy for reaching your students, then you will need to present a unified portrait of this feeling to the students and educational decision makers in your school. Getting staff agreement to endorse group counseling, while not mandatory, is certainly advisable, particularly in the pre-group counseling planning stages.

This should be your very first consideration in the long-range implementation of a group counseling program in your school. Staff should meet regularly to discuss the pros and cons of becoming activists on the group counseling front; assessment of potential barriers to the group counseling can best be accomplished in staff meetings. And plans for co-leading beginning groups, bringing in consultants, arranging counselor time schedules, planning with teachers and on and on, can be accomplished most propitiously in preliminary staff meetings with trained counselors and psychological personnel who know full well the need for providing outreach counseling services on a much wider scale in the schools. Staff planning can also include a philosophical examination of the assumptions presented in chapter 2 and the way the entire guidance staff feels about becoming active group counselors.

This crucial first step in planning your action on the group counseling front can eliminate many potential hazards and impediments to your program. A unified staff, in agreement at least on the importance of expanding your services to more students, is your single greatest weapon against the fears and apprehensions that so often confront any approach that smacks of innovation. Obviously, if you are the only guidance person in your school, then all of this strategizing about working in committee with your staff can take on the tone of a well-thought-out soliloquy, and then you alone can present a "unanimous" guidance position on the need for group counseling services in your school.

All of the above is not to suggest that a departmental dissenter can thwart your efforts at becoming an active group counselor in your school. By having it all out on the table in departmental meetings with your colleagues, you can probably overcome any intradepartmental objections and neutralize obstructionism. It is unlikely that your desire to implement group counseling will meet with vehement resistance from any trained counselor, particularly if you present your case in a manner which clearly demonstrates the potential benefits to the students. If some departmental members choose to divorce themselves from the group counseling efforts, this is perfectly acceptable and even predictable. But having dealt with it on a departmental level first, you have taken that big precautionary step toward "making it happen" in your school, and avoided any clogging of your group counseling machinery further down the pike, when it would be most troublesome.

2. Your Administrative Structure

The entire administrative structure of your school will present little opposition to your implementation of group counseling.

However, you must remember the cardinal rule, that *your principal must be in on the permission-giving aspect of your program.* If you present your plan for becoming an active group counselor to the administrative staff you will need a solid rationale that goes beyond the "case" built in chapter 2. You must approach the administrative staff from a pragmatic point of view, and actively demonstrate how your becoming a group counselor will make the principal's job easier, while simultaneously illustrating the educative value of your activities. In addition, you must keep in mind your principal's fear of parents and community pressure groups, and your strategizing must include how you will avoid any unforeseen problems with these factions.

Essentially, you can approach your principal with a plan that involves trying to reach those students who have been labeled as *unreachable.* The chronic troublemakers, the failing students, the truants, suspected drug abusers, and any of an endless list of students who create administrative headaches. You also must be prepared to tell the administration how you will deal with parents, faculty, and the community. (See the pertinent sections in this chapter.) By conferring with your administration from the point of view of attempting to reach, via the group counseling channel, those students who are most in need of counseling services, you will be touching a particularly receptive chord. Your administrators want to help. They are harried by a multitude of impossible demands, and they feel helpless about those students who are obviously operating independently of the school system's expectations for them. By genuinely presenting a plan that purports not only to reach but to help these anti-schoolers, you are striking at the principal's most sensitive and responsive needs.

Selling group counseling is not a problem. It is a procedure that has received professional endorsement at all levels. You are being paid to deliver counseling services. Delivering those services, in groups, does not present any conflict, particularly when the process of group counseling is recognized as a healthful experience advocated by the entire student personnel services profession. Your selling job to the administration will likely take on the posture of assuring them that none of the interest groups they are responsible for will be offended in any way, and that no personal or professional flak will come their way as a result of your group counseling activity. And since counseling is already an accepted part of your school curriculum, certainly group counseling will not be viewed as a threatening enterprise.

If you enter the administrative offices with a well-thought-out plan for implementing your group counseling program, armed with the self-confidence to make it work in your school, you will meet with little or no resistance. Your plan must include answers to the very practical questions about having students released for participation in the groups, when and where you will be leading the groups, and how you intend to deal with parental inquiries. You will not need to launch into any lengthy explanation about the difference between group counseling and other group activities, nor will you need extended definitional data giving a theoretical perspective on the group counseling process. Essentially, you are looking to avoid trouble spots on the administrative horizon, and to inform the principal that you will be attempting to reach students who get no help from anyone, and students who represent sources of irritation to the administration on a daily basis. A big part of your strategy is in how you intend to sell the idea to the faculty, and for this you are eminently well prepared (see below).

Every administrator is different, and certainly some are much more guidance-oriented than others. You know what the limitations are in attempting to convince a school principal of the inherent value of an effective schoolwide group counseling program. But you must also keep in mind that your principal, like all administrators in every profession, is keenly aware of the need to have a smooth-running organization, and that every instance of trouble focuses primarily on the top banana. In presenting your case, you must stress group counseling as a process that seeks to eradicate trouble spots at all levels of the school organization, rather than being a procedure that will create additional migraine episodes for the chief. As the group counselor, you and not the principal, will be dealing with the problem students (as well as with those who are not seen by the administration as troublesome, but who are in need of counseling). You will not be doing anything differently. You will only be counseling in groups rather than in your traditional and uneconomical one-to-one style.

A statement to your principal about your decision to inaugurate group counseling might go something like this:

> I have been giving a lot of thought lately to the notion of attempting to reach more of the students in the school. We don't seem to be reaching a large segment of the school population,

and I would like to see the counseling office play more of a significant role in "making a difference" here in the school.

We have talked it over in many departmental meetings, and have agreed to try out group counseling on an experimental basis. We have worked out a plan to present to the faculty, and we have sample letters to send to the parents to allay any community or school disapproval.

Initially, we would like to start three groups, composed of several factions of student groups here in the school. We would like to have in these groups some of the students who just aren't making it on any level. They would interact with some of the students who are "successful" but who are certainly not without their own problems.

A counseling group is merely an arena for the students to meet regularly and work on any concerns they have which they can turn into more useful and self-enhancing behavior. It is not therapy, and not a rap or gripe group. Basically, it is just counseling, only in groups.

I feel that we owe it to our students to make every effort to reach out to those who are most in need of counseling services, and to provide a forum where they can go to work on themselves in safety. I've talked to many students in the school and they solidly support the idea and would be willing to participate.

If the program is successful, and many of the students who are administrative headaches become less conspicuous in their recalcitrance, perhaps we can then inaugurate a schoolwide group counseling program, and shift our emphasis from individual to group counseling.

This has been tried in many schools with a great deal of success, and most school counselor educators are retooling their training emphasis to group counseling, and strongly advocating that the road to accountability, in the schools, is via the group rather than the one-to-one counseling approach. I think we can make it easier on everyone, and most important, reach many students who are untouched by the school, given our present approach to helping them.

3. YOUR SCHOOL FACULTY

By far, your most challenging and important task is convincing and gaining the support of your teaching staff. Any group counseling program that is worth anything functions effectively because it receives the endorsement of the entire school teaching faculty. You must have their cooperation. Without it, you can forget about having a schoolwide outreach group counseling program. This is not to suggest that you cannot run counseling groups without teacher consent, but in order to have it as a schoolwide practice, teacher cooperation must be elicited and nurtured assiduously.

Without this valuable cooperation, you must run your program around a complex array of teaching and student schedules, making every effort not to alienate *anyone* for fear of having your program canned before it gets off the ground. At best, without teacher cooperation, you can run maybe one or two groups of students who *happen* to have some collective free time. But with total staff endorsement, you can inaugurate a total school approach to the business of counseling students in groups, without the constant sword of teacher reprisal hanging over the soft spot in your head.

Your plan of action for convincing your faculty of the worth of group counseling involves a straight "pitch" on the need for providing students with an opportunity to receive counseling services on a more available basis. The first thing that you do is ask the principal for an "in-service day." If this is impossible, then you request a half-day for presenting your case to the staff. The least that you settle for is a faculty meeting in which you will assume full responsibility for the agenda. Whichever of the three strategies you are able to secure, you will be at an advantage, in that you are going to present a bang-up, dynamic, and convincing case for implementing schoolwide group counseling. Generally speaking, faculty meetings are dull exercises in which one individual talks down to the entire staff about a variety of school-related items. Faculty members are almost always bored nonparticipants, who have one goal, that is, to have the meeting end as soon as possible. You are going to capitalize on this attitude.

Below are three strategies for presenting your group counseling case for the school faculty. In each case, your goal is to demonstrate to your staff the absolute need for group counseling in the school, based upon students being unable to obtain counseling services within the present organizational structure. More importantly, you are going to elicit their support and cooperation in making this program work. Chapter 2 delineates very carefully, the "case" for group counseling in the schools. You can use these persuasive principles in building your own case. You will most certainly want to allude to the many students who are not being reached, as you did in talking with your administrative staff. You will want to include the need for deliberate psychological education in your school, as well as the necessity for providing a place where students can work on the most important ingredients of a fully functioning person—self-respect and self-confidence. You will build a solid case to present to the staff, but beyond your own BRIEF talk to the staff, you will want to keep in mind the cardinal principle of learning: *I hear; I forget. I see; I remember. I do; I understand.* All three elements of hearing, seeing, and doing must be included in your presentation to the staff, in order to guarantee their support and cooperation in implementing your group counseling program.

In each of the three agenda presentations below, you the school counselor assume full responsibility for conducting the program. It is assumed that a longer presentation (the full in-service day) is more effective than the short one-meeting agenda. But you can *do the job* using any of these formats or variations thereof.

A Single Two-Hour Faculty Meeting. In seeking approval to conduct a meeting with the entire faculty, you must keep in mind that your main goal is to get faculty cooperation for your group counseling efforts in the future. It is crucial that you make a dynamic, convincing presentation on group counseling. You will need to do your homework thoroughly before conducting the meeting. Your opening statement can be very much like the one you made to your principal, with the necessary addition that you must have the cooperation of the entire faculty if the proposal is to succeed. You will want to include your very own "case" for group counseling in your school. The "lecturish" aspect of your presentation should be brief but dynamic and to the point. In building your case, consider the needs of the students first, then how badly the school needs to expand its counseling services, and how very much you want to reach those students who appear to be operating on the fringe of your school program. Then you will address yourself to the significant part that your faculty plays in the success of the counseling program. You will want to urge them to send referrals, to cooperate in allowing students to occasionally miss a class, and to consult with them about the progress of your program.

Demonstrating what takes place in a counseling group is perhaps the single most important element in your two-hour faculty meeting. You must allay any fears that this is a pseudotherapeutic enterprise that represents just one more effort to mollycoddle students who should be dealt with firmly by the school. Here you will want to extract student volunteers to actively participate in a counseling group before the entire faculty of the school. The students you select should be made aware of their vital role in selling a program that is totally student-oriented, and therefore you will want to make selections for the demonstration group very carefully, securing only those students who are sold on the need for innovative counseling practices designed with the students in mind.

After having made your pitch for the need for faculty support for schoolwide group counseling, you will inform the gathered faculty that you are going to demonstrate for forty-five minutes what goes on in a counseling group. Perhaps you are beginning to feel a tad shaky about doing this before the entire school staff. If you are totally unsure about your ability to bring it off effectively, perhaps you can hire a consultant to make the demonstration with you as a co-leader to insure your making a solid impression on the faculty. At any rate, having them see, hear, and participate as active observers will give the staff a mind-set of readiness for cooperating with your school group counseling efforts.

An alternate strategy would be to have eight to ten faculty members volunteer to participate in a counseling group, while you serve as a leader of the group. Here you can demonstrate "how to begin a counseling group" with a strategy that is guaranteed to produce results. (See chapter 7 for the "beginning-a-group strategy" detailed therein.) Once again, a community consultant who is an expert on group counseling would serve to allay any fears you may have about bringing this off effectively. The important thing in demonstrating any process is *to show* the staff that this is indeed a valuable and needed experience for the students.

You end your presentation with a plea for cooperation on all fronts until the logistical bugs have been worked out. Noting that you are attempting to extend your counseling services to every student in the school, and that in order to provide these kinds of needed counseling experiences, you must begin to deliver in groups, rather than in the traditional and limiting one-to-one mode. Moreover, you urge them to send referrals to you on any student who might be interested, and to talk about this new service in their classrooms. Answering any questions that they might have is certainly appropriate, and asking them to write them down and submit them to you so that you can address yourself to them at a future meeting, or in writing, would be an effective strategy, rather than getting bogged down with a host of questions at the presentational meeting itself.

A sample agenda for this meeting would be as follows:

2:00–2:15	Explain the rationale for group counseling on a schoolwide basis.
2:15–2:45	Define group counseling and what goes on in a counseling group. Use the twenty assumptions in chapter 2 as a guide. Emphasize the need for a place where the student can work on his concerns in safety.
2:45–3:00	Discuss the need for total school cooperation in making it work.
3:00–3:45	Demonstration. Either with student volunteers or with faculty members who agree to participate in a one-session demonstration. Emphasize goal-setting in the demonstration.
3:45–4:00	A closing plea to the staff and a wrap-up identifying what took place in the counseling group.

A Half-Day In-Service Training and Orientation to Group Counseling. In conducting a half-day training session in group counseling, it is urged that you bring in a skilled consultant to participate in the activities. Once again your goals are essentially the same, only you have additional time in which to accomplish them. Here you will concentrate on the experiential base in planning your activities, as well as actively demonstrating how you can inaugurate a schoolwide group counseling program with minimal disruption to the orderly functioning of the school. A sample agenda for a half-day training program is included below, keeping in mind the same precautions elaborated in the previous section.

8:30–8:45	Explain the rationale for group counseling on a schoolwide basis.
8:45–9:15	Define group counseling and what goes on within a counseling group. The content of group counseling.

9:15–10:15   One-hour group counseling demonstration with volunteering students. Students work at identifying self-defeating thinking and behavior in themselves, and establish goals for themselves in the group. *Some counseling takes place.*

10:15–10:45   Total group interaction. Here questions are directed at the students, and the basic fears that students will collapse as a result of receiving counseling are demythicized. Students who received focus and help can testify how they feel and felt during the experience.

10:45–11:30   Counselor presents a model for implementing group counseling on a schoolwide basis, including scheduling adjustments, teacher cooperation, use of counselor time, and how the parents are to be informed of the program.

11:30–12:15   What the school can receive from a group counseling approach. The difference it will make to the students, what it will mean to the staff, and the significance of initiating a step toward deliberate psychological education.

12:15–12:30   Wrap-up. Questions submitted or dealt with here in the final minutes. An effort to extract written reactions and support from the staff is presented.

A Full In-Service Day Devoted to Group Counseling Training and Orientation. Using this most productive of formats to convey the group counseling message in your school, you can provide a surefire sales job on implementing group counseling in the school. Here you will spend most of your time actually providing nonthreatening group counseling experiences for your staff. You will need the services of at least one expert consultant in group counseling. Essentially, you will be showing the validity of group counseling as a process in which anyone can benefit, by asking your staff to partake of the group counseling goodies. While many might perceive this as a "threatening" experience, in reality, it is a well-received, highly effective technique for demonstrating the utilitarian value of counseling groups.

The value of this day goes beyond demonstrating and selling

group counseling to your staff. It is an opportunity for faculty members to come together and work on individual concerns that affect their teaching performances within the school. "Looking at ourselves in terms of behaviors that we can work on to improve our ability to function effectively in the classroom," and "improving communication and listening skills" are appropriate activities for individual goal-setting in this group. The benefits of this all-day approach can be two-fold: 1) convincing the staff of the need to support group counseling experiences for the entire student body, and 2) helping individual teachers and staff members to identify areas of self-improvement, and work on them in a safe, albeit working, environment. By seeing it work for themselves, the staff will become far more amenable to endorsing the process for the students they serve.

Those staff members who are reluctant to participate in counseling groups will be gratified to learn that there is absolutely no pressure on them to be revelatory. They can absorb vicariously, and they can admire your ability to function in a group in a way which is nonthreatening. Simultaneously, they will leave the experience seeing what a boon group counseling is for those who choose to take advantage of it. Here your skill (and the skill of your consultant) is crucial. The ability to present an environment that is conducive to growth and risk-taking, without being frightening, is the mark of a skilled group leader. Your ability to be an "accepting confronter" will determine the success of your day-long activities.

A sample of a day-long workshop schedule, for the two-fold purposes discussed above, is as follows:

8:30–8:45	Explain the rationale for group counseling on a schoolwide basis, and for the day's activities.
8:45–9:15	Define group counseling and what goes on in a counseling group. The content of group counseling.
9:15–10:15	Demonstrate a counseling group which works on individual goal-setting. Eight to ten staff members in a fishbowl, with you and a trained consultant expert to lead the group.
10:15–10:30	Group interaction in the counseling group.

10:30–11:30	Form as many counseling groups as possible with approximately ten to a group. Have appointed leaders (co-leaders for each group, which includes other counselors, staff with some counseling background whom you have prepped, and consultants). You serve as a rotating consultant to each group and take notes on what is happening. Emphasis is on counseling in the groups as defined in chapter 2 with goal-setting being of highest priority.
11:30–12:00	Lunch.
1:00–1:45	You present a model for implementing group counseling on a schoolwide basis, including scheduling adjustments, teacher cooperation, use of counselor time, and how the parents are to be informed.
1:45–2:45	Reconvene morning groups. Focus on each member setting a goal for the hour (in writing or privately to themselves). You set a goal for the leader to facilitate helping at least three faculty members through the group counseling process elaborated in chapter 2.
2:45–3:15	Total group reconvenes. You provide roving consultant report to the entire group.
3:15–4:00	You present the benefits to the school of a group counseling program on a schoolwide basis, making analogies with those who received help during the day. Teachers who received help can testify how they feel and felt during the experience. Debunking the notion that help is threatening, or that you have to be a "sickie" in order to benefit from a counseling group.
4:00–4:30	You make a pitch for cooperation on a schoolwide basis, offer them an opportunity to have a place to work on their own concerns, while simultaneously making your own counseling efforts more effective and more accountable.

These are only suggested models for selling your program to the entire staff. They are offered because we know that they work. We have used them on many occasions to acquaint a school or agency staff with the need, value, and importance of group counseling. It is also suggested that you provide recommended readings for the staff which show conclusively the benefits of group counseling. Also that you involve any and all school personnel who evidence an interest in counseling outreach in the school. Your staff has several people who, though untrained, are superb in working with students and who have a natural ability to help and be understanding and effective with students. Using them in the selling of your program is a most propitious stratagem. Any and all resources that will facilitate total school acceptance of group counseling should be utilized. You must have the willingness and energy to gain the school staff support before you can even begin to "think big" about offering your counseling services to the entire student body in counseling groups. If your staff supports you, you are in. Work firmly at gaining and sustaining that support.

4. THE PARENTS IN THE COMMUNITY

While the parents in your school district will not represent any barriers to the implementation of your group counseling, they will certainly be interested in what you are doing. In dealing with the parents, you will want to avoid stirring up any concerns about group counseling being a potentially controversial school activity. You can treat it very much as if it were an expected part of your school responsibilities, and certainly not in a cautionary or alarmist fashion. You are the school counselor. You will be conducting counseling sessions in groups. You would like the parents to be aware of this. It is not necessary for you to call a meeting of all parents, since this particular innovative program does not require that much special attention from them.

The most effective tactic for informing the parents about group counseling is in the form of a letter, or in whatever channel the school uses to communicate with the parents, be it a newsletter, memorandum, or announcement to the homes. A special announcement that the parents would read could be worded in the following manner.

ANNOUNCING
*Group Counseling for the Students at Anywhere
School*

The counseling staff will begin, next week, to offer their counseling services to the student body in groups. Students will participate on a voluntary basis. Group counseling has the advantage of reaching far more students than the counseling staff is presently capable of reaching. In these groups, students can work on a host of age-typical concerns: vocational indecision and doubt, academic concerns, program planning, personal problems, and any and all areas which might be causing troublesome worry or concern in the individual.

Group counseling is universally endorsed as the most effective way for counselors to reach students in the school, given current case-load size and responsibilities. The school staff has supported the counselor's efforts to reach more of the students with counseling offerings, and has agreed to do everything possible to facilitate the smooth transition from exclusive one-to-one counseling at Anywhere School. While individual counseling services will certainly continue to be available for the students, it is felt that far more students will have the opportunity to avail themselves of school counseling.

This kind of announcement will assuage any fears related to group counseling that the parents might have, while simultaneously treating the inauguration of group counseling as a natural school function and an effort on the part of the school counseling office to be more efficient in carrying out its responsibilities.

If your school has a policy of acquiring parental permission in order to have students participate in a counseling session, then a simple letter of consent to the home is in order. A model of this kind of letter is presented below.

Dear Mr. and Mrs. _____,

Beginning next week I will inaugurate the new group counseling project which was announced recently by the school administration. I would like very much for your daughter to participate in this program. I have discussed the objectives of the sessions with her and she has indicated that she is willing to be a member of this group. It is important for you to recognize that these group counseling sessions will in no way be considered as therapy, nor will anyone be required to talk about anything that they deem personal or private.

The counseling sessions will take place during the school day and will be confidential in terms of general student body and faculty. If you have any questions please feel free to consult with me at any time. Please sign below and have your daughter return this letter to me, if you consent to her participation.

Sincerely,

I.M.A. Counselor

_____

Signature of parent

While parental permission is most likely unnecessary, it will be important for you to devise strategies for dealing with parents who call and want to know what is going on in the group. Typical satisfying responses to parental inquiries about group content include: "Students deal with age-typical concerns, and do not reveal private family matters under any conditions. Students are encouraged to talk about how they themselves can take charge of themselves and become more effective. So while they might like to make it a gripe session, the emphasis is on personal goal-setting, and becoming all that they choose to be. Your son/daughter is a member of a group. If I revealed the content of what took place I would be violating a confidence that I set as a ground rule of the group. Specifically the content was to be held confidential in order that trust might be established and an environment that is nonthreatening would prevail. I can assure you, however, that nothing that would be considered slanderous, inappropriate ethically, or exclusively private, would be permitted in the group. Essentially, your son/daughter is participating in group counseling in order to set and achieve goals that will aid him/her in every area of his/her life. I can assure you that all provisions for ethical conduct are taken, and that the same conduct that goes on in an individual session, is observed by me in group sessions." These kinds of responses will assure the parent that this is a purely student-oriented procedure, and that they have nothing to be concerned about.

Parents want help for their students, and 99 percent of them will strongly support your group counseling efforts. Those few skeptics can be dealt with in sure and effective terms. And if you have a parent who absolutely demands that his or her child not participate in groups to which the parents are not privy, then you can make the decision to have that student see you on an individual rather than a group basis. This is a rare occurrence, however.

Parents will enthusiastically support your efforts to provide more counseling services to their children.

5. THE COMMUNITY

You can help yourself gain support in the community by providing publicity that will send the message out to the masses. The community itself should not be viewed as potentially averse to your group counseling program. Rather, you should think of the total community structure as providing support for your program, provided you are able to utilize this vehicle effectively.

You would be wise to inform local newspapers and community helping agencies of your plans to implement schoolwide group counseling. Perhaps you could invite any and all community "helping" officials to an indoctrination and informational meeting in your school. Here you might explain what you are attempting to do in offering group counseling. You need not become overly concerned with community reaction to group counseling. Most likely it will be treated as a part of the overall school guidance program and nothing to become alarmed about.

Publicity can be an exceedingly helpful adjunct to your program. You can receive parental acceptance of your group counseling approach if it receives attention in the newspaper. Similarly, your program will be the recipient of attention in the community, and you can expand it at will if the community is behind your efforts. You need not develop any long-range involved strategies for convincing the community leaders of the validity of your school group counseling program. On the other hand, you can certainly add strength to the program by having it endorsed locally. If community leaders, agency personnel, and ancillary psychological helpers back up your group counseling efforts, you will have minimized any difficulties that come your way from a small percentage of dissidents.

The following excerpts from articles appeared in local newspapers as a result of school officials instituting group counseling programs. The ensuing publicity brought much acclaim to the schools, counselors, and participating students, and reinforced in the parents the notion that group counseling is a valid and significant approach to helping students.

The New York Times, Sunday, September 16, 1973, excerpt from the article by Francis X. Clines:

One of the subjects was loneliness at Archbishop Molloy High School last weekend.

"I understand her loneliness," a senior speaking in a gentle tone of his widowed mother, declared to some colleagues. "I'm not saying I'm turning my back on her. But I'm sixteen and she's fifty and I'm going to have to live my life."

. . . It is the peer-group counseling course in which the school has been tapping the greater life experience of the seniors to help sophomores deal with personal, family and school problems.

Last weekend, the forty students selected from among 375 volunteers in the senior class received their first training in the area of leading a group counseling session. Next week, after additional days of training, they will be assigned in pairs to groups of sophomores who will be invited to attempt a more candid understanding of themselves.

. . . From largely unstructured gatherings and conversations among students, the program grew in size and format to the point where, this year, two outside consultants were hired to teach the seniors the best ways of guiding counseling sessions. The consultants, Dr. Wayne W. Dyer of St. John's University in Queens, and Dr. John Vriend of Wayne State University in Detroit, spent three days over last weekend at the school, on Manton Street near Queens Blvd., assisted by the school's regular guidance staff of six full-time and four part-time members.

Long Island Press, Monday, September 17, 1973, excerpt from the article by Stan Trybulski:

> A unique educational innovation which can trace its roots back to the concept of the one-room schoolhouse, with big kids helping little kids, is going on at Archbishop Molloy High School.
>
> . . . The sophomores are counseled by twenty-eight picked seniors who have gone through a twenty-five-hour peer-group counseling training program.
>
> . . . The program originated as a spare-time operation by the guidance group but this year it was felt a comprehensive program was needed. The school brought in two outside consultants to conduct the training, Dr. Wayne Dyer, professor of counselor education at St. John's University, and Dr. John Vriend, professor of counselor education at Wayne State University in Detroit.

Group counseling is not an arena for confession but an up-grading of everyone's ability to handle their emotions and increase their social skills. However, what is discussed in the group sessions is kept on a confidential basis.

The school community can become an agent of support for your program if you are thorough about preliminaries. Actively going after community endorsement will bring a sense of status to your group counseling efforts that is generally reserved for athletic or dramatic events in the school. Moreover, the credibility of your group counseling program will be established via the community-support route, and help to guarantee you a smooth-running operation in your daily efforts to deliver group counseling services.

6. The Student Population

You will have no difficulty in selling the students on group counseling. Young people throng to groups which provide them with an opportunity to be themselves and to work on their concerns in safety. There are almost no opportunities for young people to receive help in a group setting, and they almost always take to it willingly and enthusiastically.

Before organizing your groups, however, there are several preliminary considerations which you will want to resolve. The following checklist of pre-group student-oriented tasks will aid you in effecting an unwrinkled program, while affirming a strategy that will tease the students' curiosity and kindle interest in group counseling participation.

• Keep a list of potential group members. Whenever you see a student in individual counseling, consider to yourself whether he or she would be able to receive help in a counseling group. If your suspicions are that this student has trouble with the socialization process, lacks confidence in self, is having the same kinds of personal and academic difficulties that many of your students are having, then approach him or her about the possibility of getting into a group to deal with personal concerns. With the exception of some devastatingly private matters, almost all student concerns can be handled more effectively in a group counseling setting. By maintaining a ready list of students who would like to participate, and by adding names to the list daily, you will be able to organize many counseling groups from your own counseling caseload. Similarly, if you encourage your colleagues to do the same, you could almost organize a new group every day or two. This procedure will enable you to maximize your counseling activities ten-fold. Rather than conducting ten individual sessions on the same kinds of personal difficulties, you can lead a group and reach ten students at once.

You have often felt that sense of frustration that comes from spending an hour with a student, feeling gratified at the success of your diagnostic coups and exhausted at having struggled for so many important insights, only to have the next student walk in and present you with an identical concern. The entire process begins all over again, the same resistance, denial, and gradual recognition that the difficulty is lodged in the student rather than the hostile environment he fantasizes as the cause of his ineffectual living. You start over, the process is neverending. Imagine having a list in your drawer and suggesting to potential counselees that you will be forming a group next week, and that you would like very much for them to sign up for it now.

• Visit classrooms and study halls and make your pitch. Here is an ideal opportunity for you to form counseling groups, and it is a sure-fire, guaranteed method of extending your counseling services in the school. Arrange to visit given classrooms or study halls, and have your invitational address all prepared. You will have a multitude of students signing up. You must remember that students should be participating in group counseling on a *voluntary* basis, and that they need to know what it is they are volunteering for. Here is an example of an open invitation for students to sign up for group counseling. It should be presented in an informal, "non-talking-down-at" manner.

> "Beginning next week, I am going to be forming a series of counseling groups, and I would like to extend an invitation for you to participate. It is very likely that you don't know anything about group counseling, and that is why I am here today. To explain the offering, and to answer any questions that you might have.
> "Essentially, group counseling is a place where members can come to work on themselves to become more effective human beings. It is for everyone, rather than for "sickies" or people in trouble. What goes on in the group is an honest presentation of

yourself, and the identification of anything, and I mean anything, that you see as thinking or behavior that is not self-enhancing or helpful to you. It is a confidential setting, but it shouldn't be thought of as a rap group or a gripe session. Rather, it is one place where you can work on yourself, with other students and a trained counselor, in safety, and leave the group after resolving some of the areas of your life that are in any way troublesome or difficult to handle. From school-related problems, to feelings about yourself, to personal and emotional problem areas, you will be able to receive and give help in the counseling group.

"It is an exciting place to be, in that everything that goes on in the group is serious but meaningful and, most important, helpful. The purpose of the group is to provide help, in every way, to individuals who would like to grow. I can personally assure you that it will be a rewarding and exciting experience. There is no other place in the school where the only thing that counts in the group is you and the other group members, and working on self-chosen improvement. I am not asking you to join so that I can change you to what I would like you to be. Rather, you can assess for yourself what thinking and behavior is helpful and destructive to your own goals and happiness, and then either decide to work on them, or to help others to do the same. There is no pressure on you to participate just because you sign up. If you would like to know more about it, or ask any questions, feel free to come to my office for an interview."

This kind of approach will generate many questions, while serving as a catalyst for students to sign up for the counseling goodies. And once they see that the counseling group can be an exhilarating experience, the word will spread like wildfire throughout the school.

• Conduct preliminary, group or individual intake interviews. If possible, you should conduct an intake interview with each student prior to entering the counseling group. If large numbers preclude individual intakes, then a small group-orientation session is a secondary alternative. At any rate, you will want to provide an opportunity for every student to participate in a precounseling group interview with you, the group leader.

The intake interview should have the flavor of an information-giving exercise. It will be important for you to cover each of the twenty assumptions detailed in chapter 2. You must avoid turning the interview into a lecture or one-way communication street. The following points should be crystal clear to each individual before he or she enters the group for the very first session. (And, incidentally, they will be repeated and dealt with in your first session as well. See chapter 7.)

An understanding about what constitutes confidentiality.

As clear a picture as possible of what goes on in a counseling group.

An opportunity for the student to elaborate any concerns that he/she might have.

Why you are recommending him/her to participate in a counseling group, and what you expect he/she can get out of it.

A commitment to the process itself. Asking individuals if they can commit themselves to attending a minimum of three sessions, after which a decision can be made about the effectiveness of the group counseling and continuation in the group. This is crucial, because many times, after one session, students will see that a degree of discomfort is attached to changing their behavior, and running away from this (which has likely been their strategy in the past) seems like the natural thing to do. The commitment in the intake interview will help the individual to stick it out and then make a decision about remaining, on the basis of a fair trial period. The commitment to stay for three sessions has nothing to do with participation. You are not asking the student to promise to actively engage in the counseling group, rather just to stay with it for a given period of time, and then come to their own decision about the usefulness of the group.

A checklist of the twenty assumptions in chapter 2. This will help the student to see that it is a counseling group, rather than just a friendly place to air gripes, or talk about parties, cars, and upcoming dates.

The purpose of the intake interview is to allay anxiety about the group experience, and to be sure that the students who enter the process do so with a clear understanding of what they are signing up for. You will make every effort to be informative about the upcoming process and to communicate that you see it as a businesslike enterprise, which you treat seriously and with great importance.

If this message gets conveyed to the students, you will have taken a giant step toward eliminating the floundering that characterizes most beginning counseling groups. The "I don't know what's going on" behavior, and the fuzziness that accompanies so many beginning sessions, are all eliminated. If you have been thorough about your preliminaries, and conducted intake interviews designed to defog the group counseling horizon, then you will have set a path for clear, effective and utilitarian sailing in your group counseling.

• *A word about group composition.* There is no magic formula that, if followed, will help you in forming a highly cooperative and effective mixture for your counseling group. However, there are some precautions you will want to observe.

Primarily, you should look to avoid a totally homogeneous grouping. When you group together a collection of students who all share the same difficulty, you are magnifying the potential resistance within the group. Ten truants, or children of alcoholic parents, or underachievers, or what have you will not have any internal group opposition to their self-defeating thinking and behaviors. Group members who identify with each other tend to reinforce their self-immobilizing thinking, and consequently there is little opportunity for challenge by group members. You as the leader might very well represent the only opposition to a self-forfeiting behavior pattern in a group member, and therefore you will have little or no support for alternative behaviors by the group members.

Supposing you group together ten chronic truants, and one group member begins to receive counseling from you. As the counseling develops, you begin to confront the individual with his truant behavior and try to identify what he is getting out of this behavior, pointing out that he is genuinely putting himself down with his behavior; the other members of the group, however, will be reinforcing his reasons for skipping school. "It's a drag," "School is out of it . . . ," etc. You have created an environment wherein students will tend to reinforce their unhealthy behavior, rather than helping each other understand the self-deprecating nature of their thinking and behaviors. On the other hand, if there are representatives of a different approach to school attendance, students who can challenge the notion of the inevitability of the boredom and irrelevance of school, then your task as the leader is made easier.

Group composition which has a cross section of students will certainly help you in creating an environment of change, rather than the reinforcement of self-defeating behavior. Students can help each other to see contrary points of view, rather than just assuming that one way of living and reacting is the most natural and expected way for a person to be. While it is not *impossible* to function effectively in a homogeneous group, it is certainly much easier and more effective to have a heterogeneous quality to your group whenever possible. If for no other reason than to minimize internal group resistance, having psychological "lookalikes" is not a useful way to blend your groups. It is recommended that you randomly assign people to your groups, rather than search for labels to organize yourselves around.

Arranging Your Schedule

Now that you have planned and acted out your strategies for dealing effectively with the six major interest groups within your total school community, you are ready to begin thinking about your own schedule and the logistical concerns related to making your group counseling plans into a reality.

Your number-one goal is to work out a method of freeing students for group counseling sessions while causing minimal disruption to the everyday running of the school. Since you were careful to work very closely with your teaching and administrative staff, you are far more likely to elicit their support and cooperation in instituting your program. You will want to offer your counseling sessions on a rotating basis, utilizing a different time slot, and perhaps even a different day of the week, for your weekly meetings. Beginning with first period on Monday in week one, and alternating your schedule as indicated below, you will incur almost no faculty opposition, in that students will miss a given class period only once over the entire semester. This alternating scheduling also frees you to perform your multitudinous tasks; it does not lock you into an inflexible group counseling schedule. If you allow yourself just one-third of your time for group counseling, you will be able to meet with your entire caseload over the two semesters that comprise the school year.

SAMPLE COUNSELOR SCHEDULE
For Group Counseling Using Different Time Schedules

Group counseling one period per day for eight weeks, with five different groups. Fifty students reached with a commitment for only *one* group counseling session daily.

	Mon	Tues	Wed	Thurs	Fri	
Period 1	Group A	Group B	Group C	Group D	Group E	Week #1
Period 2	Group B	Group C	Group D	Group E	Group A	Week #2
Period 3	Group C	Group D	Group E	Group A	Group B	Week #3
Period 4	Group D	Group E	Group A	Group B	Group C	Week #4
Period 5	Group E	Group A	Group B	Group C	Group D	Week #5
Period 6	Group A	Group B	Group C	Group D	Group E	Week #6
Period 7	Group B	Group C	Group D	Group E	Group A	Week #7
Period 8	Group C	Group D	Group E	Group A	Group B	Week #8

Using this kind of an alternating scheduling, you are able to devote only one period per day to group counseling and reach fifty students in your case load every eight weeks. You can post the schedule so that students and faculty are aware of the time slot for group counseling. But the beauty of your plan is that no student will be required to miss a particular class session more than once over the entire eight-week group counseling time span. You have taken great pains to arrange a schedule which will be least offensive to the entire teaching and administrative staff. While your group counseling sessions occasionally may fall during lunch periods, there is certainly nothing to stop you from arranging to have lunches served during the group time, particularly since it will occur only once during the life of each group. Obviously there are an infinite number of possibilities for juggling this one-period-per-day group counseling schedule to fit your own day conveniently.

If you decide that you can devote two periods per day, or about 25 percent of your working day, to group counseling, then you can reach a total of one hundred students every eight weeks, or approximately four hundred students over the two-semester calendar year. The following breakdown offers a model for scheduling which requires you to devote only two periods daily, on a rotating basis, to the practice of group counseling, and simultaneously to reach every student in your caseload. This also takes into account final exam time, as well as the infinite number of interruptions that plague you throughout your school year. You can minimize the disruptions to your schedule by publicizing the schedule in advance, having it printed in the school paper, and posting it for the faculty and student body to see.

Group counseling schedule using two periods per day, rotating ten students per group, and ten ongoing groups.

	Mon	Tues	Wed	Thurs	Fri	
Period 1	Group A	Group B	Group C	Group D	Group E	Week #1
Period 2	Group F	Group G	Group H	Group I	Group J	Week #1
Period 3	Group B	Group C	Group D	Group E	Group A	Week #2
Period 4	Group G	Group H	Group I	Group J	Group F	Week #2
Period 5	Group C	Group D	Group E	Group A	Group B	Week #3
Period 6	Group H	Group I	Group J	Group F	Group G	Week #3
Period 7	Group D	Group E	Group A	Group B	Group C	Week #4
Period 8	Group I	Group J	Group F	Group G	Group H	Week #4

Repeat the sequence, not duplicating any periods.

Arranging your schedule, while an important consideration, is certainly no obstacle to the implementation of an effective, all-reaching group counseling program. It can be done.

Final arrangements for rooms, furniture, and other incidentals. If rooms are a problem in your school, you will want to use all of your ingenuity to come up with a place you can truly call your own. The only requirement you have is that you can fit twelve folding-type chairs in a circle, as close together as possible. Scouring the building for such a room will probably turn up something quite useful. An old janitor's closet, storeroom, or unused closed-in space in the library. Even your office can be used, although it would probably be a pretty tight fit. You will be surprised to see how easy it is to fit ten or twelve chairs into a small space. Closeness facilitiates communication without having to raise one's voice. Comfort is to be programmed out. Soft, cozy chairs and couches are not conducive to effective group counseling interaction. They tend to help people relax and sit back. Also you will want to avoid using a table or desks, which tend to stultify communication and provide barriers to hide behind when the group begins. Simply stated, you want a circle of chairs, pulled as closely together as possible, with an absence of barriers and comfort-inducing furniture. This is your best physical arrangement for conducting your group.

That does it. You have completed your preliminaries. You have been thorough and organized in your pre-group counseling efforts. Before your debut, you will want to get into some anticipatory thinking about your own and the students' behavior in the group. Read on to chapter 4, which details leader behaviors that you will want to anticipate and master before your auspicious debut. Chapter 5 will help you in anticipating group member behaviors, while chapter 6 focuses exclusively on the goal-setting process in group counseling, for leader and members. You still have much to do before your first group counseling session.

4

Before Your Debut:
Leader Behaviors to Know[1]

AS A GROUP leader, you will want to master a set of highly specific group counseling leadership behaviors. You are not setting
out to practice an art form, or to "do what comes naturally" as a
group counselor. You recognize that if you did what came naturally, then you might engage in all sorts of typical group behaviors
that are unrelated to leadership. These would include chit-chatty
conversations, joke-telling, hanging-back, and on and on through a
long list of "natural," albeit nonproductive, group behaviors.

Leading a counseling group is more than a science; it is a humanistic technology. There are inherent skills and leadership behaviors that you must be able to muster and put into practice in
the life of the group. You are embarking on a highly professional
journey when you elect to lead a counseling group, and pretending that you can be effective by "winging" it makes you one more

[1] Major portions of this chapter first appeared in *Counseling Techniques That
Work*, by Wayne W. Dyer and John Vriend (Washington, D.C.: American Personnel and Guidance Association Press, 1975), pp. 142–176. Reprinted with the permission of the American Personnel and Guidance Association.

practitioner who takes the easier road by failing to master the skills of your craft. You have heard of group leaders who make a case for being spontaneous and natural as group counselors. In fact, this is one of your fears discussed in chapters 2 and 3. In your heart you know that just allowing things to happen within the group is a clear-cut abrogation of your professional responsibilities. Moreover, it is a bona fide cop-out from the word go. You are a counselor. And you are paid and trained to deliver counseling services. The same holds true when you enter a counseling group as a counselor. You are going to deliver counseling services rather than do whatever you feel like doing as the "spirit" moves you or as the "group spirit" moves the group collectively.

You understand the basic assumptions elaborated in the extended definition of group counseling in chapter 2. You can see that group counseling has more to it than just sitting together and talking about problems. And you are beginning to see that the process of group counseling moves through rather predictable steps, from exploration and self-understanding, to the development of action alternatives for self-forfeiting behaviors on the part of group members. But you are still fuzzy on exactly what it is that you must do throughout the life of the group in order to maintain your status as an effective group leader. Well, hold on friend, because you are about to take an excursion down the river of explicit group leader behaviors. Each of the twenty stops you will make as you paddle this ne'er-before-navigated pathway will contain examples from counseling groups which will spell out in operational terms how, when, and why to use each of these group counseling leadership behaviors. Once you understand that these are the behavioral components of group counseling leadership (and you get good at them not by reading about them, but by practicing, practicing, practicing them in the group), you will be on your way to mastering them by constantly appraising your competency in each one, and striving to improve your skill in those behaviors in which you are most deficient. Very much like any professional who works at becoming more effective. Assess those components which need stress, and work on them. But first, be aware of what the components are, and even more important, admit that the components exist in the first place. Far too many group practitioners deny that there are specific leadership skills to be mastered, other than a chronicle of nonmeasurable and nonobservable traits such as kindness, warmth, genuineness, good-intentions, empathy, and love. Below is a detailed analysis of the specifics of group counseling leadership, followed by your own personal rating score at the end.

Specific Group Counseling Leadership Behaviors

Skill #1. One of the skills that you will need to possess and use regularly as a group leader is the ability to *identify, label, clarify, and reflect group data.* This is an exceedingly important group leader behavior, and one that many fledgling group leaders falter at badly. You are certainly aware that there will be a vertible flood of data occurring within the life of any counseling group. As a leader, you must do more than just observe it or be aware of it; you will need to assume responsibility early in the life of your group for labeling and clarifying group happenings.

Essentially, you will find three specific kinds of group data cropping up within your group. These kinds of group behaviors, or trends, include (1) feeling or emotional data, (2) behavioral data, and (3) cognitive data. Each of the three kinds of data calls for special skills in identification, labeling, clarification, and reflection on your part as the group leader.

The *when* of identifying, labeling, clarifying, and reflecting the emotional, behavioral, and cognitive data is impossible to lay down; it is a constantly recurring group leader responsibility. You are always on the alert for "fuzzy" areas, concerns that are unclear to the group members, behaviors they don't understand, avoidance of obvious feelings, and so on. Whenever group members ignore, avoid, or systematically deny emotional, behavioral, or cognitive data, you as the group leader must facilitate identifying, labeling, clarifying, and reflecting responses. This is a highly specific and measurable group leader behavior. The more of this kind of group leadership behavior you engage in, the better you will become at it. Moreover, as you model this kind of identification, other group members will see that this is the business of group counseling, and you will have actively demonstrated what it is that constitutes group counselor leadership behavior.

The *why* of this intervention has been explained in the basic assumptions underlying effective group counseling practices. The counseling group is not a place for aimless conversations, discussions, or fun-and-games behavior. In a conversation, you don't label, clarify, reflect, and identify feelings or anything else; you are polite, and you wait for the others to stop talking, and never, but never, do you label something that someone subtly wishes to avoid. In a counseling group there are uncountable circumstances in which the group members will choose to avoid something. In addition, the group members, being untrained, will not even be aware of many group happenings that constitute group data. If they are aware, they have been conditioned by their culture to overlook the unpleasant or the uncomfortable, such as any negative emotions (fear, anger, sadness) or even positive feelings of love and excitement.

Part of your repertoire of behaviors as a group counselor leader is to expose and make clear for the group (not just for yourself) any and all problem-related material, all intellectual or attitudinal group data that are not being picked up and dealt with by the group members. It is an important skill; without it, you will gloss over the most meaningful group counseling content and end up focusing on things that are comforting, and unproductive of change.

Examples of skillful identifying, labeling, clarifying, and reflecting of feelings as a group counselor include leader behaviors such as the following:

When an entire group appears to be reluctant to talk about anything that has emotional overtones, you as the group leader label and clarify with a statement such as—

> "Everyone in the group appears to be afraid to talk about things that are difficult to deal with. For example, when David mentioned the problem he has at home in getting along with his father, everyone fell silent, and Mike, you changed the group focus to something else by talking about your math class. David expressed frustration, fear, and some sadness about his inability to talk with his father. By running away from these feelings, we are teaching David, and everyone else here, that we can't help someone who has a serious difficulty. Now Mike, were you aware that you had difficulty in talking about touchy concerns? And David, perhaps you could tell us something about these feelings that you get whenever you bring up your relationship to your father."

This kind of leader use of identifying, labeling, clarifying, and reflecting feelings within the group brings the focus to the business of group counseling, and helps David—and others in the

group with similar concerns—to explore, set goals, and ultimately
come up with alternative modes of thinking and feeling in relationship to his father or to any other troublesome individual(s).

A typically *ineffective* utilization of this leader behavior involves the group leader chewing out the group, or otherwise not
labeling and clarifying the feelings within the group.

> "David, you must not be afraid of your own feelings. This is a
> place for you to examine your hurtful emotions, and to go to
> work on them. I want everyone in the group to remember that
> we aren't afraid of negative feelings, and that we are not going
> to avoid talking about them here in the group. Now, why were
> you so upset when your father's name came up?"

Skill #2. Labeling, identifying, clarifying, and reflecting *behavioral data* within the group is sometimes difficult even for the
most skillful group counselor. Here is an example of how to effectively utilize this group leadership skill.

> "One of the things that I've noticed within the group is how
> almost everyone seems to want to protect everyone, and deny
> things that appear obvious to an objective observer. For exam-
> ple, Bob was mentioning how he skips school because it's bor-
> ing and Mary suggested that maybe he didn't have the skills to
> avoid boredom in his life, and that the responsibility for not
> being bored was in Bob, rather than the school. When she did
> this, almost everyone came to Bob's rescue. George moved
> closer and got very intense in his defense of Bob. Suzi changed
> her position for the first time today, and complained about the
> lousy teachers. Maryanne laughed sarcastically at Mary's sug-
> gestion to Bob, and Leroy waved his hand in obvious disgust
> and disapproval. Bob, are you aware of all this rushing to your
> defense, and can you work at setting some goals for yourself in
> this whole boredom area?"

Most frequently, behavioral data of the kind clarified above get
ignored by the practicing school group counselor. This is called
"missing it." You will want to become skillful at attending to everything that is going on in the group so that you can be proficient
at implementing this group leadership behavior. Careful observation of everyone and their in-group behavior will permit you to

identify and clarify it, for the benefit of each member who is interested in learning about himself and how he typically behaves. You cannot help a group member to change his or her behavior if you aren't aware of it in the first place.

Skill #3. An example of a propitious use of identifying, labeling, clarifying, and reflecting *cognitive data* is evidenced in the leadership excerpt below.

> "I'd like to point out something to everyone here in the group about something that has been recurring each week. Almost everyone tends to get into 'explaining for others' behavior. It's almost as if being a student here at Anywhere High School entitles one to know everything about everyone else who is also a student. All of you seem to explain things for each other all of the time, rather than helping each other to more effectively explain yourselves. When Darcel talked about being tempted by drugs, Mary, Sylvia, and Spencer attempted to explain Darcel's feelings, rather than helping Darcel to examine his own motives. Mary and Sylvia even said that they could explain it better than Darcel. Were you aware that you have the tendency to do this for each other almost all of the time, and what it means to explain something for someone else rather than attempt to help them to see it for themselves?"

This kind of a group leader application of identifying, labeling, clarifying, and reflecting cognitive data will again help you to keep the group focused on the business of group counseling, that is, counseling individuals in groups. What has been explained to the group is purely cognitive information about their behavior within the group. It comes from acute observation and unhesitating leadership behavior.

A typically *ineffective* application of identifying and clarifying cognitive data involves the leader waxing intellectual himself, and engaging in the same kind of nonproductive behavior as the group members. For example:

> "I'm sure you're not aware of it, so I'm going to have to stop here and explain just what it is that you are all doing in the group. You all tend to explain things for each other. Now this comes from the group moving too quickly through the cohesiveness stage, and bypassing understanding, and getting

trapped in the 'too-much-action-too-soon' syndrome that so typifies many counseling groups. Explaining something for someone else is a violation of the person's right to choose to be. Maslow discussed this very point in his treatise on self-actualization. We must guard against becoming too psychologically dependent on each other, and certainly be aware at all times of our roles within the group of being mutually concerned about group syntality. I trust that you will now avoid such behavior in the future. You may continue, Darcel."

You can see the point. Becoming cognitive and flowery in your leadership behavior will help to turn all of your group members into avowed skeptics of the process, and of your own sanity as well. As you practice identifying, labeling, clarifying, and reflecting cognitive data, be on the lookout to avoid being mysterious yourself, and always watch out for your own inclination to wax intellectual and philosophical about others' intellectual and philosophical behavior.

Skill #4. Another group counselor leadership behavior that you will want to master is *questioning or drawing out and evoking problem-related material within the group.* This is a highly specific behavior that unfortunately often becomes the inexperienced group counselor's one and only mode of behavior within the group itself. While questioning and drawing out is certainly important, and is a leadership behavior that you will want to rate yourself on regularly, it should not be considered your exclusive *modus operandi* as a group counselor.

The ability to question and evoke pertinent data comes from asking *yourself* some very important questions before engaging in questioning behavior as a group leader. Your most important self-question is, "Am I seeking out important and relevant data, or am I just asking questions for the sake of having noise, or to sound important?" At any moment in the life of your group, when you are asking questions of group members, you are doing it from an established rationale, which involves taking a group member through the group counseling steps outlined in chapters 2 and 9. You will not want to rate yourself high on this skill simply because you are able to ask a lot of questions, but rather on the basis of how significant your questions are, and how much important counseling-relevant information you are able to elicit. As a persistent questioner you can take on the tone of an interrogator, and also you will be teaching your group members to conduct interrogations rather than being of help in their queries. Your questions should relate to helping individuals to explore, work at self-understanding, and ultimately develop action alternatives in specific areas of their lives. Any other questions are useless and should be programmed out of your group. Often, your group members will ask a whole series of extraneous questions, simply because they do not know what else to do, and this is because *you* have not modeled effective questioning and drawing-out leadership behaviors. You should also keep in mind that you never, repeat *never*, ask the group itself a question. Groups cannot answer questions, only people can, and any question directed at the collective is really not directed anywhere.

Typically ineffective counseling groups are those in which rapid-fire questioning has gone rampant as a strategy for conducting group sessions. While questioning is absolutely necessary for evoking pertinent data from individuals, it is also the one leadership behavior that gets readily misused. Questions, questions, questions, without reflecting, interpreting, encouraging, and focusing becomes threatening, inappropriate, and most important, ineffective. On the other hand, without the ability to evoke concerns from group members through effective questioning practices, your group will die faster than a fish out of water.

Below are some examples of the effective utilization of questioning and drawing-out:

> Johnny, have you ever considered what *you* get out of your being upset when your girlfriend rejects you?

> Lulu, can you tell us a little bit about how you've gotten along in school before you came to Anywhere High School?

> Sammy, can you give an example of what you mean when you say nobody seems to understand you?

> Danny, have you ever considered that others might feel just like you do about approaching a girl for a date?

> Patty, did you notice that both George and Manny expressed concerns very similar to yours?

Some typically *ineffective* applications of questioning in counseling groups are evidenced in the examples detailed below:

Why are we all afraid of our teachers and parents?

Julius, do you always get embarrassed like this?

Mary Ellen, how many children in your family? Do you like being the youngest? Is your mother fond of you when you behave like this? Your older brother never seemed to be shy like this, how come you are?

Why do you all just sit there when I ask you a question?

Why don't you just stop taking drugs, then you wouldn't have a problem?

Why don't you just tell her off, then you would get her respect?

The list could be endless. Questions which are irrelevant, rapid-fire, directed at the entire group, which convey advice rather than understanding, tend to get you nowhere and create a question-and-answer environment almost identical to the classroom

Skill #5. You will also need to learn the group leadership skill of *confronting.* This is an observable and measurable dimension of being an effective group counselor, and one of the most difficult of all specific skills to incorporate into the beginning group counselor. Once again, your culture has taught you to avoid confrontations on all fronts. To confront is to be rude, unkind, or impolite, and so you are unaccustomed to the business of being a confronter. In addition, it is a perplexing task to learn how to confront as a group leader and simultaneously to maintain an accepting demeanor. To confront is to indicate disapproval and dislike in your culture. And so you avoid confronting, because you are unable to be confronting and accepting at the same time.

In order to be effective in helping individuals change, you must be able to identify the discrepancies in their thinking, feelings, and behavior. This, very simply, is what confronting is all about: the identification of discrepant behavior, without conveying any disapproval or being in any way judgmental. Indeed, it is a talent that few in the helping professions possess. Confronting means that you are not just one more individual who turns his head when you see something that is obviously a discrepancy. You fearlessly label, identify, and point to behavior which is self-defeating or inconsistent. Discrepancies can take many forms. The most common are listed below. In each case, it is your responsibility as a group leader to identify and deal with the discrepancy in an accepting fashion, or to see to it that it gets dealt with in the group by other group members, who have learned (because you have been an effective model of confronting behavior) that the business of group counseling involves no self-delusion when personal growth is at stake. For each kind of discrepant behavior detailed below, one example of both effective and ineffective leader confrontation is offered.

• A discrepancy between what a member is currently saying and what he said earlier.

> **Effective Confrontation:** "Larry, last week you indicated that you had no apprehension about getting into college, and that if you didn't make it, you would simply join the army for two years. You just said that you were frightened about not being accepted at the state university, and weren't sure what you would do."

> **Ineffective Confrontation:** "Larry, you can really be inconsistent at times. I wish you would make up your mind. One week you say you're not worried about getting into college, and the next week you say you are. Did anyone else in the group pick up Larry's inconsistent thinking?"

• A discrepancy between what a member is saying and what he is doing.

> **Effective Confrontation:** "Bruce, you've said that you are really capable, intelligent and able to handle almost anything that comes your way, and yet you are having so much difficulty in passing three of the four subjects that you are currently taking. What you say you are, and what you do, seem so far apart."

> **Ineffective Confrontation:** "You really are a B.S. artist, Bruce. You say that you are smart, and yet you don't show any of your smarts, especially in the three classes that you're failing. How many here think Bruce is as smart as he thinks he is?"

• A discrepancy between what a member says and what she feels.

> **Effective Confrontation:** "Cindy, you keep telling us how your parents don't bug you, and that you're totally inde-

pendent from their control. Yet you get welled up with emotion whenever you mention how they treat you."

Ineffective Confrontation: "Come on Cindy. I can tell that they get to you by the tears and the dry mouth syndrome whenever their name comes up. They still control you, and you're trying to deny it. You may fool yourself, but you're not fooling me, or the group."

• A discrepancy between what a member is saying, and what you the counselor are feeling in reaction.

Effective Confrontation: "Loretta, you have been saying that you use drugs because of the way it makes you feel, and that you really like being high. Yet you also say that you don't have any friends, and that being liked by the other kids is important. Is there any possible connection between you wanting to be liked, and your taking drugs?

Ineffective Confrontation: "Loretta, I just don't believe you when you say you like to get high, and that's the reason that you take those pills. I think you are trying to be liked by the rest of the eighth-grade kids, and because they think you should do it, you do it, rather than risk their disapproval."

These, then, are typical group counselor confrontations that will arise in most of the groups you lead in your school. Remembering and labeling the discrepant behavior, rather than glossing over it, or just plain "missing it," will give you high ratings on this crucial group counselor leadership skill.

Skill #6. You must also have mastered the skill of *summarizing* in order to be an optimally effective group counselor. You will find yourself being required to provide periodic summaries of group content in order to help the group members focus on essential aspects. Moreover, summarization techniques are also important in preclosure stages, which occur at the end of group sessions, and when shifting focus from one individual to another.

An effective summary brings together much of what the group members have said and points the group toward goal-setting and goal achievement. Solid summarization skills are necessary in order to avoid "tangentialism" within the group. A prudently injected summary of what has taken place can help you to avoid

"dead-horse-beating" behavior and shifting in a thousand different directions dependent only upon the whims of each and every
group member who has a stray thought or a novel idea.

You certainly know the value of effective summarization as a
learning principle. Almost all textbooks provide summaries to re-
capture for the reader what has recently been digested. So, too, are
summaries important and necessary in the learning environment
of a counseling group. Students in school counseling groups tend
to forget what has transpired, or to become repetitive. They soon
forget the purpose of group counseling because they have become
distracted. To learn to summarize well within the group, you will
have to practice this group leadership behavior regularly and help
keep everyone on course. When the focus is about to be shifted,
haul out your summarizing skills. When a session is ending, you
can practice summarizing, and drawing together the salient facts
of the group activity. This means you will have to be storing away
all that transpires within the group in order to make your summaries practical and utilitarian. Each and every summary you state
will have a precise purpose. Either you are facilitating focusing
behavior within the group, or you are helping group members re-
fresh themselves on all that has taken place, or you are facilitating
closure by preceding cut-off activity with a succinct statement
about what has taken place. An example of effective summarization skills on the part of the group counselor:

> "Jerry, everyone has been giving you feedback here in the
> group for the past twenty minutes. Let me attempt to summa-
> rize what has taken place, and help you focus on setting some
> pertinent goals for yourself.
>
> "Mary, Sally, and Mark have been trying to convince you of
> the folly of dropping out of school with only four months left
> until graduation. Mona feels that you have a right to do as you
> choose, even though her own biases crept into her advice-giv-
> ing. Sam and Donna have kept relatively quiet, even though
> they have been intensely participating, and perhaps you would
> like to hear from them before you set your own goals. Almost
> everyone seems adamant that you should give more considera-
> tion to staying in school.
>
> "And you, Jerry, still appear to be as confused as you were
> when you brought it up, even though you have been receiving
> a great deal of friendly support from everyone in the group.
> The group members are almost trying to persuade you to be

like them, and choose school for a short time longer, and some pressure has begun to surface which is making you somewhat anxious."

Ineffective group counselor summaries generally are brought about out of frustration, and consequently are loaded with counselor anxiety about shifting. Generally, when you make a poor summary, it's because you have ignored what has been going on, and chosen instead to bring about closure on the proceedings. For example:

"Well Jerry, I think we've stayed with this topic long enough. It's obvious that everyone has a different opinion about what you should do, and that we are getting nowhere by constantly barraging you with our own personal viewpoints. You can think about what's been said. Let's move on to someone else now."

Your summary has a purpose. The example of ineffective summarization shows only group leader frustration; it is helpful to no one. The well-thought-out summary in the first example shows how the group leader is alert to everything that is taking place. Even if he feels that time is being wasted, he uses the data effectively, rather than chastising the group for not being helpful.

Skill #7. One of the criteria that is used to set you aside from all of the group members is your role as an "expert" in human behavior. You are the leader, and if behavior crops up that is not understood by the others in the group, it is your role to help make that behavior understood. The process of showing the underlying meaning of an experience or statement is called *interpreting,* and as a group counselor you will be called upon to make important interpretations which describe and reformulate group-problem-related material.

One of the things that you will learn very fast is that there is no such thing as a *correct* interpretation when you deal with human behavior. Since interpretations deal with causality or explanations for why a given piece of behavior has occurred, it is only a guess, perhaps an educated guess based upon a pile of data, but nevertheless, a guess. Your explanation may sound plausible and believable to everyone, but that does not necessarily attach *truth* to the interpretation. Perhaps an example of what is meant here is in order.

Delbert and Walter are brothers who were raised in the same environment. They are eleven months apart in age, and both spent their early youth being shipped around together from orphanage to foster home. There is no father in the picture, and the mother is away attempting to earn a living to support herself. Delbert is now a grown man in a counseling group. He is exceedingly quiet, withdrawn, fearful, lacking in self-confidence, easily embarrassed, and prone to look to others for support. Walter is also a member of a counseling group. However, he is outgoing, confident, psychologically independent, able to get along with everyone, and generally the opposite of Delbert in every behavioral and attitudinal aspect. The group counselor makes an interpretation of Delbert's behavior, based upon the available data. He says:

> "Naturally you are fearful and lacking in confidence. When you were little and in need of a loving parent, you were constantly denied. Consequently you failed to develop any ego strength, and the development of your self-concept was thwarted at every turn because you received no models upon which to build strength and positive feelings about yourself. It is expected that you would be shy and always hanging back, because you never had anyone to encourage you when you needed it the most. Naturally you don't like yourself, because in your formative years you had no one to give you love, which in turn would have provided you with self-love. And as an adult, you are suffering from those little-boy influences, and consequently are behaving in those expected ways you learned so well so many years ago."

This sounds like an interpretation based upon sound psychology and certainly one that would help Delbert to see that his childhood was loaded with reinforcement for his poor self-image, that he has carried this image over into his adult life, and that it is the thing he must work on in order to make himself a more fully functioning person. But let's not forget Walter. Another group counselor says to him:

> "Naturally you are self-confident and outgoing, and perhaps even a bit cocky as an adult. When you were growing up you didn't have someone there to take care of you whenever you felt down, and so you had to rely entirely on yourself. Because your parents were not there, you developed a healthy reliance

on yourself. You knew that no one would be there to rescue you and so you had no other alternative but to turn to yourself. This kind of deprivation led you to develop a strong sense of self-confidence, since it was either sink or swim in your childhood days. You looked to yourself for protection, since no one else would provide it. You became a leader because you had no other alternative, and your outgoing personality is a natural result of realizing that you, and only you, were responsible for you being happy. Not having someone around helps you to build a strong self-concept, and you did that as a child, and now you are doing it as an adult. You had an excellent opportunity as a child to work operationally at self-reliance, something that most children have handed to them by overly protective, although well-meaning, parents."

The same background data, the same environment and yet contradictory interpretations. Just as "buyable" and psychologically sound as Delbert's interpretation. Which is correct?

The fallacy of the "truism" that an interpretation is "correct," is that all psychological interpretations are hunches offered by the interpreter. For one piece of group member behavior, you could literally come up with dozens of perfectly sensible interpretations, many of which would be exact opposites.

The purpose of being an effective interpreter as a group leader is not to be correct, or to "wow" your members with dazzling diagnostic coups, but rather to provide some measure of self-understanding which will lead to a change in self-defeating behaviors for your group members. You recognize that only amateurs look for surface and easy interpretations of anything, and that because you are the leader, it is likely that your interpretation will be bought, even if it comes from left field, simply because you carry status as the "expert" in human behavior. Your interpretations should then be based upon some measure of your own understanding about yourself and of how people function in our culture. You are not interested in being *right* when you make an interpretation, nor are you the least bit concerned about razzle-dazzle "wowing" behavior. Your primary interest is in providing self-insight which will lead to behavioral change.

Interpretations are necessary because your counseling group will be composed of group members who have a distorted sense of why they behave the way that they do. (Chapter 5 deals with typical group member behaviors and some hypotheses about the etiology of age-typical self-defeating behavior.) As an interpreter of group member behavior, you are working at the self-understanding portion of group counseling. You are giving your diagnostic opinions (which generally run counter to the group member's opinion, since he is busy defending himself from views that would involve *change* if he accepted them) and attempting to convey unstated meaning for the group member. An example of effective—not necessarily *right*—group leader interpretation, which will convey some meaning for the group members while possibly contradicting their own interpretations, is as follows:

> "Jean, you appear to be intimidated by the other members of this group. You have asserted that it is only natural for you to be afraid of strong people, and that everyone is at one time or another. I would suggest that you have learned to be afraid, and that you use it to keep yourself from becoming anything different. As long as you hang back and act fearful, and tell yourself that it is because others are strong and might hurt you, then you never have to change because it really isn't your fault. Responsibility for your weakness is given by you, to 'them.' So being fearful is something that works for you, and you conveniently use it whenever you are in groups such as this."

This kind of interpretation gives Jean something to think about in terms of assigning responsibility to herself for all that she is, including those things about which she feels she has little or no control. The purpose of the interpretation is not to convince her, but to give her some contrary food for thought that will help her to ultimately change her fearful behavior. The interpretation contradicts her own assertion that it is *natural* to feel embarrassed or afraid, and that she has no control over it because everyone feels that way.

Most ineffective interpretations are those in which the interpreter is either too pedantic or jargonal, or totally off the wall and consequently "turn-offish" as far as the students are concerned. An example:

> "Your fear of losing weight is actually a subconscious manifestation of castration anxiety. Overweight people have repressed their sexuality and denied their own humanness, and you, Freddy, are living with the terrible fear that if you were normal in appearance, you couldn't handle all of the attendant human

responsibilities that go with being normal. And so you, and millions of others like you, wallow around in your own excess baggage, afraid of your own self. When you lose this fear, the fat will come off with little effort."

Obviously this kind of leader interpretation creates a mistrustful mind-set, and does nothing but alienate the group members. Interpretations must lead to self-insight, and if they don't, then they are useless as group leader behaviors.

Skill #8. Another key group leader responsibility is the ability to *restate*, and put what has been said into different words so that the group member(s) may find it more meaningful. You should not confuse this with interpretation, which has been explained as giving the underlying meaning of a group member's statements or behavior. Restating does not mean repeating. You will want to listen carefully to what group members are saying to each other, or about themselves, and then restate it in such a way that it becomes clear and pertinent to the individuals concerned.

This is a specialized group leadership skill that you will have to practice as a way of life, in order to become proficient at it. Restating is not a simple task of looking for synonyms and laying them on the group. It involves putting something into different words when you feel that ambiguous communication is transpiring within the group. When a group member takes a long period of time to explain something about himself that no one has understood, you can restate it in concise language and cut through all of the oatmeal that surrounds so many group counseling utterances. You will be a more effective group counselor when you have mastered this skill of bringing it down to earth, using shorter and nonfuzzy conveyances, and essentially delivering the same meaning, except that now, everyone, including the protagonist, has a clear picture of what is being said. An example of acting as an effective restater is illustrated below:

> Rudy, to the group: "I guess I've always been this way. What I mean is, I'm not sure when it got started, but I know I've been concerned with what others think about me since I was just a little boy. My brother was my idol, and when I was little, I never called the signals when we played neighborhood football. I always waited for someone else to tell me what to do, most of the time I ended up as the center, or 'blocking out' because I

wouldn't speak up, I was sure that they would laugh at me if I said something, so I just said nothing and did what I was told to do. In school, I was always afraid to have the teacher call on me, because I was sure I'd get laughed at by everyone if I gave the wrong answer. And even now, I won't ask a girl to go out with me because I'd be so embarrassed if she said no, and I don't think she would ever say yes. I hate this about myself, but I still keep doing it."

Group counselor: "You've always been fearful and anxious when you are around others who you feel might judge you in some unfavorable way. You'd like to change it, but you're not sure how to go about even starting."

The restating on your part, as a group leader, involves clearly labeling what Rudy has said to the group in succinct terms that are consonant with the message he has delivered, while simultaneously adding a dimension of self-responsibility toward making some kind of change in his life. The restatement conveys the essential meaning of what he said in precise terms that he and the group members can understand. At this point, it is likely that other group members will chime in with helping efforts, and Rudy is on his way toward goal-setting, and becoming a new, less fearful activist in his own life.

Ineffective restatements generally involve repeating what has been said, and offering no new dimension of help within the group. For example, in Rudy's case it might go something like this:

"Rudy, you say you've always been that way, and that you've always been concerned about what others think of you. You told us about three incidents in your life when you waited for someone else to tell you what to do, and now, you're afraid to ask for dates. You feel that no one would want to go out with you anyway."

Here the group leader is a funny-time person, who repeats everything either verbatim, or in brief summaries using precisely the same language. As a group leader, when you take on this kind of posture, you become a phony, engaging in a charade that is deeply resented by everyone in the group, and Rudy receives no help, other than the comfort of knowing that you heard him, and that you can act as a playback whenever you choose. Restatements which simply repeat take on the flavor of a stuttering exercise, and group members become reluctant to participate because they are going to hear Mary Mockingbird giving everything back.

Skill #9. You need to learn how to *establish connections* as a group counselor, which means piecing together for the group fragments of problem-related material whose relatedness is unclear to the group members. In gaining proficiency in this group leadership skill, you will need to acquire fine-tuned listening and remembering acumen. When you, as the group leader, are able to connect bits and pieces of group data from previous sessions and piece them together in a meaningful intervention you are providing persuasive information to the group members, which results in self-insight and ultimate new and effective behavior.

There are several kinds of connections that you can establish as a group leader. The most obvious is the bringing together of data from earlier testimony in previous group sessions so that the members can see how earlier group activities relate to what is being said in the present. Group members may be talking about four or five isolated incidents in their lives which they have never considered as related. Your role as a "connections establisher" will aid them in putting together the puzzle by seeing how the pieces interrelate. For example:

Joshua, at one time or another in the past five weeks, has talked about his grandmother and how he can't get along with her; about Mrs. Carty, his gym teacher whom he can't stand; his mother, whom he's had hundreds of fights with; a neighbor lady who always gets him in trouble; and his older sister, who tries to boss him around and whom he can't stand.

Establishing connections with these five or six group-told incidents over an extended period of time involves a group leader statement such as:

> "Joshua, have you noticed that every time you talk about someone you can't get along with, it involves a woman. You seem to be able to make it in your life, until you are forced to deal with an adult lady, and then everything goes to pieces. From your grandmother and mother, to teachers, neighbors, and your sister, you seem to resent any woman telling you how to behave."

Similar connections can be established by relating together the specific incidents that group members have expressed in such areas as dealing with authority figures, running away from love, approval-seeking, fear of failure, guilt, and on and on through a long list of typical group member behaviors, many of which are reviewed in chapter 5. Bringing the bits together, and connecting them, involves being able to recall what was said earlier, and then searching for some thread that winds through the individual's transmissions. This becomes the avenue of self-awareness for the group member. By seeing that a pattern of some kind is clearly present, he or she can work at setting goals that will involve changing the pattern and hence becoming more in charge of self by being aware of how the pieces correlate.

Ineffective connection establishment by group leaders involves either contriving a connection and working hard to make one exist, or being pushy and demanding with an "Aha, see what I've found" posture on the part of the leader. The foolishly contrived connection goes something like this:

> "Billy, last month in a group session you mentioned that you didn't want to continue in chemistry. Then a couple of weeks later you mentioned how overly organized you are about everything, and that being meticulous was something you didn't like about yourself. Now you are talking about feeling guilty because you didn't attend your grandmother's funeral. You see how they all tell something about you, in that you are afraid of failing in chemistry so you dropped out, then your fear of failing was revealed in how you keep everything so orderly that no one can tell that you are hiding your fear. Your guilt about your grandmother means that you are afraid to appear bad in your parents' eyes and, hence, you are once again afraid of failure."

The "Aha-now-I've-got-ya" connections establisher is exemplified in the following brief leader interaction.

> "Georgina, I think a clear pattern of self-defeating thinking has surfaced here in the group. It's obvious that you have little or no confidence in yourself as a love object. In the first session you talked about rejection by your boyfriend and how that bothered you, then a couple of weeks later you mentioned your mom and how you thought she didn't love you, now it's your sister. In every case you felt that you weren't worth being loved, and even though you may not have realized it, all of these incidents are related. I knew that you felt this way about

yourself, and now that you've seen the evidence, I'm sure that
you can see how you do this all of the time."

In the preceding two examples, the counselor as a group leader
is not moving the individual toward self-understanding by establishing connections. The effective connection is one that provides
insights, and also shows the individual(s) in the group that you as
the leader are ever alert, that you listen to everything that takes
place in the group, and that you will piece together all of the stray
and seemingly disassociated parts to form a meaningful whole for
the individuals in the group.

Skill #10. A leadership skill that is often overlooked is called *lecturing and information-giving.* Perhaps you are surprised that it is
included in this list of specific group leadership behaviors to be
mastered, yet you will be required to engage in some lecturish
kinds of activities as a group counselor; providing information to
the group members is a significant part of your role as a group
counselor. Lecturing is the leadership behavior that requires you
to explain procedural matters to the group and also to talk to the
group as a whole about the process analysis and the operating dynamics of the group. You will need to review the ground rules in
the early sessions, and also you will need to explain about room
changes, time allotments, schedule shifts, and numerous procedural matters that arise in the group. A precise statement about these
matters will be your most effective strategy, rather than making
the mistake of belaboring the information, turning the entire
group meeting into a discussion of mundane procedural concerns.

Your ability to engage in process analysis involves occasional
minilectures to the group which explain what is taking place in
the group. Periodically, group members will ask you questions
about how normal their group is. "Do most groups have these
kinds of problems?" or "Is it unusual for us to be struggling with
silence like this?" These, and many other similar kinds of inquiries, require a minilecture on your part as the group leader. The
important stress here is on the prefix "mini" since you can easily
succumb to the temptation to turn your group into a classroom
wherein you, rather than they, are the focus. It is far better for
you to answer such questions and to periodically talk about group
process than to systematically avoid all such leader behavior. Generally at the end of a session it is fruitful to point out what has

taken place in the group, from a diagnostic and dynamic point of view. A short process analysis might go something like this:

> "As a group we have moved from everybody competing for time to speak to a truly helping unity in which the focus is on single individuals and providing help to each other. If you noticed, I intervened on three occasions to keep us from going into a discussion or a gripe session. There is considerably more confronting and support in the group than there was last week, and many of you are making effective interventions, such as yours, Mary Ann when you interpreted Joe's complaining behavior. Silent periods now seem to bring less discomfort than they did two weeks ago, and the obvious nervousness of being in the spotlight has been almost eliminated. Several individuals who have been nonverbal up until today, have begun to participate, perhaps because they feel a deeper sense of commitment and trust here."

An ineffective group leader lecture which deals with group process is one which focuses on the traditional stuff in textbooks on group dynamics. While it sounds impressive, it has little or no value for the group members, and is "wowing" behavior on the part of the leader. Here is an example:

> "We have now passed the challenging stage and moved into the involvement phase of group counseling. This is attributable to a higher degree of group cohesiveness, and the norms of the group have become firmly established. Several group members are assuming typically occurring group member roles. Joe has become the "isolate" while Mary Anne is a "star" in group dynamics language. We have acquired what theorists call a "syntality" of openness and communication channels are intrinsically rather than extrinsically oriented."

While information-giving may appear to be inconsistent with what you have heard about counselors, you will still be required to engage in this kind of behavior as a regular part of your role as a group leader. Questions about job attainment, going to college, dropping and adding courses, future course planning, how to study more effectively, and on and on through an array of school-related concerns will be brought up. If you avoid the role of information giver by throwing it back in the face of your students you become ingenuine, a phony who speaks in strange evasive ways. If you are lacking in knowledge or awareness, you can give straight information or help students to look in appropriate places to acquire the information. The important notion here is for you to be able to provide information without being thrown by it or being seduced into making the counseling group into an informational session. Providing the information in the counseling group is a big part of what it means to be an effective nonevasive leader, and you will want to assess constantly your skills in this area.

Lecturing and information-giving have been taboo concepts in the lexicons of many practitioners in the field of group counseling. If you avoid these group leadership skills you are likely to become sterile and artificial, and you will be teaching your students that they cannot ask you a normal question without sending you into a funny response such as, "My role does not allow me to lecture or give advice," or "Perhaps someone else can answer Steve's question; I do not give out information, I am here to help you to find it for yourself." These kinds of responses communicate a lack of caring and a weird attachment to evasiveness. Provide the information, describe the group process, state the facts about ground rules, and then get back to the actual counseling work of moving individuals into goal-setting and developing alternatives to self-defeating behaviors.

Skill #11. You will also have to learn the group leadership skill of *initiating.* This means being able to take action to initiate group participation, as well as picking up problem areas after closure has been brought about on a given individual or a number of individuals who share a similar concern. Without the ability to initiate, you will find yourself floundering around at the beginning of your sessions, and also sitting through many painful moments when the group members seem to be saying "Where do we go from here, oh great leader?"

Initiating skills involve having a plan of action at all times, rather than operating willy-nilly and hoping that everything will work itself out. While it may not always be necessary for you to call in your plan, nevertheless, you are always ready to do so. Certainly you do not have to fall in love with your plan and demand that it materialize at all costs. You are flexible enough to allow the group movement to shift into other directions. However, if no shifting has been manifested, or if the direction of the shift is in an inappropriate direction, such as a conversation about the upcoming football game, then you implement your initiating skills and use your plan of action.

You are constantly aware of who needs help. You read the group data regularly, and store away potentially fertile explorations for future times. This squirrelling-away behavior will prove useful in opening up future content areas, but only if you use determination in keeping track of all of the significant group data.

Data collection on your part is the precursor to effective initiating behavior. You notice that Mary Jo was twitchy when Don talked about his father, but of course you didn't take the focus off of Don at that time. When Jody told George that she also was afraid of dating, you received another potential initiation for a later time. Muriel and Sammy were both near tears one time when Mike was talking about how tough it was to lose someone you really love. A potential initiation further down the road. Carole has been turning the group off every time she opens her mouth. Misty still hasn't said a word. Freddy still has those involuntary facial reflexes that are obvious signs of nervousness. Rip is constantly getting disapproving signs about his language. And on and on the list goes. You've been storing it away, and when the moment is ripe, you can initiate meaningful group counseling activity because you have been alert.

You are aware of two special kinds of initiating required by you as the group leader. The first involves getting the group started each week. You will never enter the group without at least Plan A, B, and C to initiate. Plan A involves a report from the previous week. (See chapter 8 for a complete rundown of the *second* counseling session.) Then you will have two individuals in mind whom you would like to see utilize the group for working on their own goals. You will also open up the group with a statement about allowing a time for anyone who would like to take advantage of the group to do so. If no one jumps at the opportunity (they will after they see how many good things come to them when they risk the spotlight), then you can initiate with either individual A or B, both of whom have evidenced some kind of data that you have read, and want to explore. An example of an effective group counselor initiation at the beginning of a group is illustrated below:

> "This is our fourth meeting, and we have six more sessions together. After we hear from John and Sammy about their efforts at achieving their goals, I would like to open the group, and

allow anyone the opportunity to utilize our time here to work on something of concern to themselves. Perhaps some of you have been thinking about taking a personal risk, or you've been wishing that the right moment would come up and you don't want to say at the end of the group that you didn't go to work on your own concern because the time never was just right. This time of silence to contemplate your own concern and ask for group time is important, and I will try to program as many opportunities for anyone to work on themselves, without being asked to do so by another group member, or by me."

If no one picks up this time, then you go on to certain individuals whom you feel have something to work on based upon your data-gathering behavior described earlier. This kind of open-ended initiating allows members to work on themselves voluntarily, and after several such invitations, group members will pick up the ball by themselves. This is in contrast to the ambiguous, ineffective initiation by the leader, which only serves to create more threat and anxiety in the group. For example:

"Here we are in the fourth week and many of you haven't taken any risks at all. I want you to remember that this is your group, and that if you don't take advantage of it, you will be the losers. It's no skin off my nose if you don't want to participate. I am going to leave it up to all of you. Either take the ball and run with it, or sit here and stare at each other."

This kind of approach indicates that the leader feels no sense of responsibility or commitment to making the group a productive experience for everyone. The "It's your group so use it" syndrome abdicates responsibility for you as the leader, and generally will send the group members into greater feelings of discomfort and fuzziness about the purpose of group counseling.

The second kind of initiation by you as the group leader involves picking up on new areas of investigation, after closure has been brought about on a given individual. After a brief summarization which you are practicing in the style of number 6 on your list of group leadership skills, you can shift by opening up the group to anyone who would voluntarily like to use the group (as illustrated above). Or, you can initiate by bringing up some of the data that you have been collecting. This is Plan B, and Plan C involves someone else, should the individual in Plan B decline. An example of this kind of group leader initiating might include a simple statement such as the following:

> "Muriel, you were really reacting to what Mike was saying about losing someone close to you. You didn't say anything out loud, but it was clear that it had some personal meaning for you. Would you like to share it here at this time, and perhaps go to work on it as Mike did?"

Another source of initiating behavior on your part involves going back to the goals that each member has stated for him or herself at the beginning of the group. Reminding given individuals of their goals and asking them directly if they would like to work on them, is a potent initiating behavior. See chapter 7 for a review of beginning the first group strategies, which will give you ample data for conducting the subsequent group sessions, and provide you with an opportunity to call upon your initiating skills throughout the life of the group.

Skill #12. The twelfth group leadership skill that you must master, and which you can constantly rate yourself on, is *reassuring, encouraging, and supporting.* This skill means that you can effectively use psychological support when group member anxieties begin to inhibit rather than foster personal progress within the group. The use of this kind of group leadership skill means being able to recognize when support is important, and when encouragement will amount to nothing more than the reinforcement of a self-defeating need to be coddled and approved.

Whenever a group member begins to examine a self-defeating piece of behavior, he will experience some internal resistance to being completely honest. This resistance is natural, in that you would expect a person to defend and hold onto something that has always been a part of his life-support system. Giving up anything means taking a risk, and just because the behavior itself is not growth-producing for the individual, does not mean that giving it up, or even admitting it's presence, is not threatening. When you ask a person to be honest with himself about the causes of his behavior, he must either defend such an onslaught or admit to alternative ways of thinking and behaving. Admitting to new possibilities for thinking and behaving means having to give up some traditional ways of doing the same, and of course, the giving up of these old manners really means rejecting a part of the self. Herein lies the threat. "If I become something different, then the old me was no good, and I must admit this." As a group leader, you will be constantly asking individuals to reject large chunks of what they have become, things that don't work well for them but nevertheless are part of them. Here is where your reassurance, encouragement, and support are vital if you are to help them change and give up some of this self-forfeiting old behavior.

Your reassurance that they can handle it, that it is tough to admit to many things, about which the person has been misleading himself for a long time, is essential for effective counseling. You understand this as a group leader. You are aware that without your support and encouragement it will be virtually impossible for group members to change, so you must be constantly alert to be a supporting person without being a sympathy distributor. Showing the individual group members that you understand how tough it is, and that you are there to help, is an important activity for you to demonstrate. Without this specific leadership skill, all of your diagnostic and strategic planning will be worth nothing. An example of effective reassuring, encouraging, and supporting on the part of the group leader is illustrated in the examples below. Incidentally, by modeling this kind of behavior, you will be teaching the other members of the group how to behave accordingly.

> Zelda is becoming uncomfortable as she talks about her relationship to her father. She is squirming, and getting choked up. Group leader: "Zelda, it's really tough for you to even talk about your father. You're struggling to get the words out, and you're not even sure if you can do it here. I'd like to help you to be able to handle these feelings better. Perhaps sharing it here in the group will give you the chance to come up with some better ways of dealing with him."

You, as the leader, set a tone of support. Your voice, your posture, your extending yourself by showing her that you are really with it at this time, all help her to deal more effectively with this thing that is possessing her with so much pain. The typically ineffective use of this group leadership skill involves a maudlin attempt to shower the person with sympathy and reinforce the feelings of self-pity, rather than with encouragement to go to work on herself. For example:

> "Zelda, you must feel just awful. Don't cry now honey, everybody has problems, and I'm sure we can help you to feel better.

Can't we, everybody? It's really lonely when you feel unloved, but we all care about you, so don't worry about it dear, things will get better."

This kind of sentimentalism does nothing but make Zelda wonder about your sanity. Certainly it reinforces the notion that this is not a place where I can get any help, but if I want to feel sorrier for myself than I already do, then I just have to bring it up in this group. Maudlin support from the group leader teaches everyone that we don't help people, we just feel sorry for them and show them how much we like them by dispensing heavy doses of "yuk" whenever anyone feels badly

Skill #13. You must become an active interventionist as a group leader. The skill being discussed herein is called *intervening,* or breaking into the group when you feel that inappropriate material is taking up group time. Once again, by demonstrating this skill early in the group, you model how group members can conduct themselves, and thereby later interventions are not necessarily the sole possession of you as the group leader.

Learning the how, when, and why of group leader intervening is one of the most important and most difficult of the group leadership skills you must master. There is so much in this one leadership variable, that we have devoted an entire chapter in a separate text to the subject.[2] You are encouraged to read the entire chapter for a detailed presentation of this crucial skill. A brief synopsis of the contents of that chapter is given here.

Essentially, learning to be an interventionist as a group leader means learning precisely when to intervene in the group activity. You must master a variety of skills, and the ten most common occurrences for intervening are spelled out here, while the rationale and specific examples for each intervention are elaborated in *Counseling Effectively in Groups.*[3] You will want to learn how to intervene when—

1. a group member speaks for everyone,
2. an individual speaks for another individual within the group,

[2] Wayne W. Dyer and John Vriend, *Counseling Techniques That Work* (Washington, D.C.: American Personnel and Guidance Association Press, 1975), chap. 11.

[3] Dyer and Vriend, eds., *Counseling Effectively in Groups* (Englewood Cliffs, N. J.: Educational Technology Publications 1973).

3. a group member focuses on persons, conditions, or events outside the group,
4. someone seeks the approval of the counselor or a group member before and after speaking,
5. someone says, "I don't want to hurt his feelings, so I won't say it,"
6. a group member suggests that his problems are due to someone else,
7. an individual suggests that "I've always been that way,"
8. an individual suggests, "I'll wait, and it will change,"
9. discrepant behavior appears,
10. a member bores the group by rambling.

Each of these occasions calls for an effective intervention on your part. While space limitations prohibit examples of effective interventionism for each, you can see that helping the group members to curtail typically arising group behavior is indeed your responsibility. The most flagrant violation of this specific group leadership skill is the avoidance of making the intervention, or just plain "missing it," and consequently having the group activity continue in an unproductive vein. You will be constantly on guard for signs of the ten occasions for group leader intervention, and you will either encourage another group member to make the intervention at an appropriate time, or assume the role of interventionist yourself.

Skill #14. You will also work at becoming skilled in the area of *dealing with silence.* You will make every effort to avoid being intimidated by silent periods in your group. Begin telling yourself that silence is a far better alternative than having the group engage in talk just for the sake of having noise in the group. Silence is tough for you, because you have been conditioned to find it so. In social settings, the pregnant pause brings everyone's anxiety level upward, and you breathe a sigh of relief when the interminable silence has been broken. Your first few lengthy silent periods will be excrutiatingly painful if you don't remind yourself that silence is a piece of group behavior, that people have a right not to talk, and that the problem is your own. Learning to deal with and explain silence effectively is therefore a crucial part of your inventory of leadership skills to be mastered.

There will be silent periods—of this you can be sure. You can handle these periods of silence if you expect them, wait them out, and interpret them without yourself being flustered and in need of a "noise-fix." The members of your group are not used to talking about themselves. They need time to ponder, to consider if they want to take the risk of self-exposure. Each member of the group has been rubricized as you have, and there will be internal pressure within the group to break the silence. But you, as the leader, need feel none of this pressure. You can feel powerful in that you expected the silence, and that you can behave in all kinds of alternative ways in dealing effectively with the silence. But you are not intimidated. You don't feel like a failure because the noise level is not high. This freeing yourself from the pressures of silence will be your first step in responding effectively to silence, whether it be just a brief respite, or a lengthy contemplative time period for all of the group members. You are not threatened. To be threatened is to render yourself ineffective.

Your first step in effectively handling silence it to refrain from being the perpetual silence breaker yourself. Instead, allow it to happen and check everyone out as the silence progresses. Note who is nervous, looking for someone else to make it end, who seems intimidated, who appears as if they have something they would like to say, but can't muster the courage to let it out. These are your strategies for dealing with the silence. You are by no means inactive at this time. You are gathering data, and also modeling the notion that nothing is necessarily inappropriate about silence, and that you are not the least bit shocked or disappointed by this behavior in the group. A statement to the group, after a silence has been broken by the group members themselves, which demonstrates your unabashed reaction to the silence can go something like this:

> "Silence is something that I expect to occur here in the group. You are not accustomed to talking about yourself, and you will need sometimes to just think about what has taken place and decide if you want to participate at that particular time. I have no expectations for perpetual noise here in the group. In fact, I expect that there will be regularly occurring silent periods. If you are uncomfortable about them, you can talk about that here in the group."

This kind of helpful statement is in contrast to the chewing-the-group-out notion that is exemplified in the leader intervention that follows:

> "If you want to waste your time by not participating, that is
> your business. Silence is really an unproductive way to take up
> group time, but I'm not going to force anyone to talk."

This approach merely lends more significance to the silent periods, and will drive the group members into deeper reluctance than
is already present. Silence is a typically occurring group member
behavior, and to deal with it as anything but that is to let it become your master.

You will also have a repertoire of group leader interventions
that will help you avoid excessive silence within the group. If the
group members are so reluctant that they never initiate and fall
repeatedly into lengthy silences, then you can call upon some of
the data that you have been gathering as the group has progressed.
Here you must be cautious to avoid the "schoolteacher trap," that
is, asking the class a question and then, because of an inability to
suffer more than twenty seconds of silence, providing the answer
or going to the one person who always has the answer. You will
practice giving group members time to think. This is the key to
dealing effectively with silence. Is the time being used to engage
productively in introspection, or is it just plain resistance, manifested in a noncooperative fashion? Generally, the group members
need the time, and you, as the group leader, are impatient with
any display of silence, breaking it with any of a number of little
devices that schoolteachers use in their classrooms.

You can also interpret the silence if it becomes chronic in the
group. A statement to the group, addressed to specific members,
can get them to deal with it and examine it if, in fact, it is a manifestation of resistance and fear in this new setting. An interpretative statement might go something like this:

> "I've noticed that whenever you seem to finish with one per-
> son's concern, the group takes on a silent quality. Almost as if
> everyone is contemplating if they want to take that kind of a
> risk. While the silence is helpful in having you think about it
> in your own heads, sometimes it becomes drawn out, and we
> lose a lot of valuable time. I wonder, Tom, if this is true for
> you? That you see how it helped Marty, but you're not sure if
> you want some of the spotlight, and so you sit quietly, and
> that's the way you deal with your hesitancy?"

This kind of a statement can accompany an opening silence as
well, one in which everyone appears to hang back and avoid get-

ting things started. An interpretation should be loaded with specifics, and not said in a threatening or denouncing fashion.

Skill #15. You are going to work hard at another group leadership behavior, that is, *recognizing and explaining nonverbal behavior.* Once again, you have very little training in this dimension, and so your awareness of the need to be alert in this area is your first priority in gaining skill. Your group members will be communicating in ways that you will never hear. Your eyes will have to be the receiver of the communications, and you must work hard at achieving twenty-twenty vision in this group leadership behavior.

Nonverbal signals are important sources of data from the members of the group. You must first learn to recognize the signals and be alert to pick them up at all times. If you fail to recognize these nonverbal cues, you will be missing a huge hunk of valuable information for use within the counseling group. You can use the nonverbal data to draw someone into the group activity, to give valuable feedback to another member, to provide reactions to someone in the group, to improve communication, to give individuals valuable information about themselves of which they may be totally unaware, to increase self-insight and self-improvement, and to demonstrate to the group members how effective you are personally, and how important it is to be a complete observer of all group activity.

Judy has involuntary facial inflections, Joy raises her eyebrows when Tom mentions his mother's crass behavior, Sam leans forward all the time, Mike moves back whenever he talks, Gary twitches his mustache and sends out nervous signals with his restless behavior, Mary Anne winces, Jimmy never unfolds his arms, Jerry scratches himself at key times, Jill squints her eyes whenever she talks, Marty uses his mouth in a distorted fashion, Harry has a vacuous look about him, Terry looks hurt and vulnerable. The list is potentially endless. Everyone sends out nonverbal data. You will become expert in reading it all. Charting it, storing it away for propitious moments, encouraging other group members to tune into the nonverbal stuff, and teaching everyone in the group that they are not just what they *say*, but what they *do* as well. The nonverbal data are things that each person is doing all the time. Tuning into the data, laying them on the group members at appropriate times, and making yourself literally a receptacle of all the signals your group members are busy sending out, is your mission in improving yourself in this vital group leadership dimension.

Once you have learned to recognize a piece of data, you are going to practice explaining it to the group members. Here, your sense of timing is crucial. You are aware that nonverbal behavior is an omnipresent factor of group counseling. Everyone engages in it all of the time, and so you will not want to be a blurter out of nonverbal signals whenever you read them, since this would occupy all of your time. You will read it from everyone. Who does what with their body? What kinds of messages are being transmitted? Then, when the focus is on a given individual, you will explain your observations, and ask others to give their own observations. Or, you will use the nonverbal signals to verify a discrepancy between what an individual says and what he is doing with his face, hands, and total body. You will not use it to "wow" them. Simply to help them deal with each other in an authentic fashion and to help members on their individual roads to self-actualization. An example of the effective utilization of nonverbal signal reading is provided below:

> "Liz, you seemed to react to Tommy and his difficulty, but you never said anything at the time. You had quizzical looks on your face, and you were wringing your hands furiously as he talked. Perhaps there was something in what he was saying that was particularly troublesome to you."

Or, you could ask others to give Liz feedback about her nonverbal signaling and what it communicated to them. The purpose of your explaining the nonverbal behavior is to put Liz in touch with it, and to help her focus on the aspects of the group activity that her nonverbal behavior symbolized.

Overlooking the nonverbal data represents the most ineffective utilization of this group leadership skill. It means you have not been alert enough to pick up the data, or have assumed that they weren't important enough to bring to the floor of the group counseling activity. If you notice a signal, then it is significant. If you miss it constantly, or are not tuned into the nonverbal behavior, then you will have to develop skills in this area in order to optimize your group leadership proficiency.

You are now getting more alert in this matter of picking up the silent signals of the group members. Another ineffective use of this "silent data" is to play bulldozer with it. For example:

"I saw you smile when Gerald was denying those things about himself. Now tell him what was behind that funny grin."

"Mary, you are a bundle of nerves in this group. You shake when spoken to, you try to hide yourself by folding your arms in front of you, and you stutter as you speak. Now what's behind that nonverbal behavior?"

Another example of the ineffective use of nonverbal behavior is to misuse the data, or to attach significance when there is no cause to do so. For example:

"John, when Suzi mentioned her math teacher, you raised your finger, and then later when the same teacher was mentioned, your foot moved. This time when Mrs. Math Teacher was mentioned you put your elbow in your ear. Now what's going on here, John? Your nonverbal behavior is giving you away."

Obviously, the leader is straining to find something significant in totally meaningless data.

Skill #16. You are going to develop the ability to use *clear, concise, meaningful communications* as a group leader. You are going to eliminate the fuzziness in your communication skills, and work hard at being understood in your group leader activity. This requires much practice on your part. The tendency to be overly intellectual, or interpretative, or jargonish must be suppressed. You will know when you are low on this dimension by the quizzical looks you'll receive from your group members. The whah's and duh's will convey to you that you are not communicating clearly. Group members will constantly ask you to clarify or repeat what you've just said. These are the signals and they work against you in a thousand ways. For every request to clarify, because of your language, there will be ten instances when members have just plain given up and don't have the courage or the inclination to ask you to "run that by me again."

Clear, concise, and meaningful communication involves getting into the language of the group members, saying it so that they can deal with it and understand, rather than trying to impress your nonpresent psychology professor. Thinking to yourself, How can I most effectively get my message across so that they will comprehend and have the benefit of my expertise?—this should be your mind-set while leading the group. Avoid long, windy orations and convoluted interpretations that will lose them. Keep the communication straight, understandable, and significant. Watch for puzzled looks when you are talking and check them out with the group members. Did they comprehend? Can she give it back to me? These are the hallmarks of being high on the communication scale with clear, concise, and meaningful language. Without high grades on this scale, all of your fine intentions and counseling skills will stand you in no stead as a group leader. If you turn them off with your turbid tongue, then the battle has been lost before the forces have been drawn.

Skill #17. You are going to work on your group leadership skills in *facilitating closure*, that is, bringing group focus on an individual or a concern to a close when it has been worked through, and also closing the session at the end of the time. Period. Your closure skills are not to be confused with summarization, for closure means just what it says. You are bringing something to a close and shifting to another area. *Finis!* This is a skill which you have not fully developed, and will have to master as you examine what you need to know to function as a group leader.

You will notice a tendency on the part of the group to get into the beating-a-dead-horse behavior. While you as the leader realize that the group activity has gone beyond helping, there is a lingering-on which is both unproductive and turn-offish. The group will go on and on if you don't implement your closure skills and bring about a shift in the group action. Everyone finds it difficult sometimes to leave a person, to say goodbye. Yet without the goodbye, the thing could drag on forever. It is your responsibility to facilitate closure in these situations. Taking charge when a natural calling for closure is evident is an important task that you must be willing and able to assume.

Closure behavior on your part encompasses two components. In the first, you will have to bring about closure on a given concern or individual in the group, and still have time remaining in that session. You have recognized that continuing the focus on this person is nonproductive, and that you have gone as far as you can go at this time. The key that you look for is, "Have I taken this person through the steps of effective group counseling?" This means making sure you have explored, facilitated self-understanding and all that this means, set goals, developed alternative courses of action, worked at having the individual practice his new behavior in the group, and finally, established psychological homework assignments that clearly meet the SPAMO test (see chapter 6). When you have completed these steps in one fashion or another, then closure is absolutely necessary. If you find yourself wallowing around in the steps, repeating yourself, or having group members asking questions of an individual just for the practice of asking questions, then you are into hanging-on, nonclosure behavior. Closure is demanded. You must make a shift, and you do it by summarizing what has taken place (see Skill #6) and announcing to the individual who is receiving the focus that you feel it is unproductive to continue in this vein. For example:

> "Johnny, I have just summarized all that has taken place up until now. You have a firm understanding of what you have been doing, and you have some goals to work on between now and next week. You can report to us at the beginning of our next session. At this time we can shift the focus of the group, and ask if there is anyone else who would like to use the group to work on a personal difficulty. Unless you feel that continuing would be of some help to you?"

This kind of a no-nonsense approach to closure will facilitate a quick shift of emphasis, and Johnny is spared the ordeal of having to continue as the center of attention when it no longer serves a useful purpose. Your closure statement clearly says that we are going to stop here, and you have checked it out with Johnny to see if he agrees. Of course you have carefully read the signals, and you are sure that the group would get into wheel-spinning behavior if the focus stayed on Johnny any longer. You know that Johnny is ready to go on to other areas, and you have effectively made it happen.

The way in which closure facilitation is most often misused is to not implement it, or to ignore these responsibilities as a group leader. The tendency to stay with a concern until everyone is burned out is characteristic of a group leader who doesn't use his or her closure skills. Conversely, it is possible to attempt to bring about closure too soon, because you as the leader are uncomfortable dealing with a given personal difficulty. Maybe you can't stand talking about death, or homosexuality, or alcoholic parents (because you had one), or any such controversial area. So you effectively shut it off, and make it a taboo topic in the group. The criterion question that you can always use is, "Have we helped this individual proceed through the steps of effective group counseling?" If yes, then closure is called for. If no, then let's get on with the business of group counseling.

Let's assume that you have gone through the steps, and you feel that closure is in order. The most ineffective use of closure facilitation by a group leader involves being overly abrupt and "cutoffish," almost in the authoritarian way a teacher shifts from mathematics time to spelling time in the classroom. For example:

> "We've devoted enough time to Johnny. It's time to move on to someone else. After all we must learn to share the time and plan so that everyone gets a turn."

Here the group leader is a teacher (a lousy one) who is moralizing, and showing no concern for Johnny or anyone else in the group. Closure should be a natural finish to an individual's concern. Not a stultifying experience for everyone in the group.

A second kind of closure involves bringing the session to a close each time. Here, you will want to make it a transitional experience rather than just plain running out of time. After you have summarized very briefly, and psychological homework has been *mutually* agreed upon, you can end the session with a statement about what is going to happen next week.

> "Jeremy, you know what you're going to do. Next week we'll begin with a report from Sally, Mike, and Jeremy. Anyone who would like to get something for themselves can give it some thought for next time. See you all next week, in this room at the same time on Thursday, instead of Wednesday. Any questions? Goodbye."

This kind of an approach brings it neatly to a close without the lingering and prattling that so often characterize floundering counseling groups. It is a clear, concise, and direct closure of the day's activities, and an indication of what you will be focusing on for the next session. No long, windy oration about the process, or anyone's problems. Simply closing.

Skill #18. You must also work at becoming skilled in *focusing* as a group counselor. This involves assisting the group members in staying with pertinent data and focusing on the behavior until it has been worked through by those concerned. Learning to be an effective focuser means arduous practice at avoiding the digressiveness that characterizes most counseling groups. With ten students in a group, there is ten times the potential for digression than in an individual session. You will soon see that any given piece of group data can trigger something in an individual, and that without warning you have been seduced into meanderings that have little or nothing to do with effective group counseling. You must put your focusing skills into practice, and keep the entire group working on meaningful content. Nonfocusing behavior also can be interpreted as avoidance by you as well as by the members of the group.

You will have to work very strenuously at asking yourself if you are indeed pursuing fruitful areas during the meetings of your group. "Should we be here now?" "Is this line of group activity in conjunction with my stated goals for group counseling?" "Are we being sidetracked, and what can I do to bring it back where it belongs?" This type of self-questioning will help you to master your focusing skills, and make a decision about keeping the group focused on group counseling, rather than something of an insignificant nature.

Group members often will take the focus off one individual and bring it to themselves. Here again it is your responsibility to make sure that the focus does not shift entirely to someone else, (it may be propitious to shift temporarily), and particularly to avoid constant shifting and having your group take on the character of a conversation, rather than a helping resource for individuals in the group. Keeping in mind that the business of group counseling is to counsel individuals in groups, you must always ask yourself if someone is being helped at any given, present moment. If not, then it is likely that you will need to practice a focusing intervention. Your group should be kept someplace on your stepladder of group counseling activities; from exploration to trying out new behaviors after goal-setting. You must be counseling. If you are not, then you must work at focusing. Otherwise, you will have a group conversation in which everyone is bouncing off of one another, and no one is being helped.

Effective focusing behavior on your part involves a straight forward presentation of why you are intervening at any given time in the group. You must make focusing interventions which bring the group back without lengthy debates. For example, an effective focusing intervention would be:

> "Merriam, when Gregory started talking about his concern with his alcoholic grandmother, you shifted the focus off of

him and onto yourself. Perhaps we can work with Gregory until he has reached some goals for himself, and then bring it back to you."

Or, in the case of digressing group member(s), an effective focusing intervention would be:

"Karl, you and Freddy are really engaged in a debate with the rest of the group as witnesses. This got started because Sally was talking about her difficulties with Mrs. Fauxpas. Both of you are now trying to win an argument, and Sally has been left in the cold. How about getting back to Sally, and trying to come up with ways for her to deal more effectively with Mrs. F., and you two can catch up on your argument outside of the group."

This kind of focusing intervention identifies how the group got off onto something less than productive, and also brings them quickly back to the central purpose of the counseling group without a lot of reprimanding behavior on the part of the leader.

Most ineffective focusing interventions take on the characteristics of a "chewing out," or they belabor the point to such an extent that the group members end up focusing on why they aren't focusing, which is counterproductive leader behavior. Also, a danger in this focusing area is to allow the digressionary behavior to continue and completely ignore your focusing responsibilities as a group counselor. An example of poor focusing intervention is this:

"Harriet, you've done it again. Every time someone starts to talk about themselves, you conveniently bring it around to something else. And then, everyone in the group starts talking about everything but what we're here for. I want you all to stop changing the subject, and to work on one person at a time, like you're supposed to."

Obviously, you will avoid such reprimanding behavior as a group leader, and exercise your focusing skills in such a way that you bring about new direction in the group, without calling attention to the fact that you are making things happen. The group should shift without having to talk about how they got off on a tangent.

Skill #19. Another skill that you will become proficient at employing as a group leader is *restraining, subduing, and avoiding potentially explosive and divisive group happenings.* While this will not be a frequently called-upon group leadership skill, it will be necessary to know when, how, and why to implement this leadership ability. You will want to avoid being too restraining, and thereby being a group leader who allows little or no controversy to enter your group. On the other hand, you will be cautious about allowing a potentially explosive situation to get out of your grasp and possibly cause a disruption that will divide rather than unite your group in its helping endeavors. You must remember that your goal is to help individuals. This help can come from dealing straight with controversy, but if the group members choose up sides to go to war, then no one will be helped, and your counseling group will disintegrate into a battleground.

Restraining, subduing, and avoiding potentially explosive and divisive group happenings means being able to sense when a given line of group activity is heading in an unproductive direction. Are individuals choosing up sides, and becoming more hostile in their interactions? Is the amount of disagreement reaching an emotional or personal peak, and are some members unable or unwilling to compromise? Is one person sending out cues that he or she wants the focus to shift, and are group members resisting the cues? These are times for calling upon your restraining skills and effectively allowing a cooling-off or refocusing emphasis to materialize in the group. This is important because very little will ever be accomplished in a group that is operating at an explosive emotional level. You will practice picking up the cues. When a potentially divisive occurrence transpires, you will be ready with your effective interventions. You will seldom, if ever, be called upon to exercise this group leadership skill, since counseling groups generally take on a cohesive and helping structure. However, you recognize that it is possible, and you will be ready.

The nature of your restraining behavior will not be to deny or pretend that something is potentially explosive, but rather to deal with it in direct terms. For example:

> "Mary has indicated that she doesn't want to talk about this thing in the group. If you recall, we all agreed that anyone has the right not to have the focus on them if that is their choice. Let's allow Mary to exercise her rights without being pressured here in the group."

"George and Mike, you both seem to be heading on a collision course in which neither of you is listening to the other. Both of you want to win an argument, rather than help each other to listen and change effectively. Suppose you both allow everyone in the group to send you both a one-way message, in which neither of you speaks, and you let in what the others are saying. When that is over, maybe each of you can work at setting a goal for yourself to avoid the getting-worked-up behavior which only gets you more infuriated. Sammy, why don't you send a one-way message to both George and Mike, giving your reactions to what is taking place."

These kinds of strategies for restraining and subduing potentially explosive group situations are indeed leadership skills, and they will help you to avoid what might otherwise become a confrontation that would cause members to doubt your credibility as a group leader. Your role is to help rather than to facilitate divisiveness and ineffectiveness in the group.

Typically ineffective group leadership restraining behaviors involve denying the existence of the potentially dangerous situation, or trying to cool it by sugar-coating the discomfort. For example:

"Now Tony, you really aren't upset just because Jerry called you a dumb ass. It's not nice to get mad at each other, and yelling and carrying on will only make it worse. You're both acting like little children. I know you don't really mean what you said, Jerry."

Or, the group leader admonishes the group for acting badly, and thinks that this will end the potential explosion. Other kinds of ineffective restraining behaviors include: taking on the role of mediator or referee; trying to smooth things over by applying a few niceties to the sore spot; and requiring individuals to apologize to each other. All of these strategies are artificial and simply do not work. While you may cool it for a few seconds, or even eliminate the explosion from the group, you have not taught the group members anything about going to work on themselves, and very likely the explosion will erupt outside of the group. You must be direct, and yet avoid the actual breaking out of violence by helping everyone to see precisely what is happening at a particular present moment. Then use your restraining behavior to cool off the situation while simultaneously working it through in the group.

Also, postponing the working-through until parties have had an opportunity to simmer down can be effective, as long as you are careful to explain to the group that the problem is not being put away but just temporarily tabled.

Skill #20. The final group leadership skill on our list of twenty is *goal-setting.* It appears last on the list deliberately, because it will receive a different treatment from that of all the other nineteen group leadership skills. Without this crucial skill, all of the other nineteen are indeed useless. Goals are such an important part of group counseling, that we have devoted an entire chapter to this specific behavior. Chapter 6 (*Before Your Debut: You Will Learn to Chart Group Member Paths*) discusses the goal-setting process as a group leader. It is filled with suggestions, guidelines, and numerous examples of effective group counselor goal-setting behavior. We refer you to this chapter where you can read, in depth, about effective goal-setting as you work at your group counseling skills.

That concludes the twenty specific group leadership behaviors. While you have much to practice in the way of honing your group leadership behaviors, you also have noted that you are quite capable already of exercising many of these skills. You note that many of these qualities are also necessary for effective individual counseling, and you have been working at being effective in many of them.

Now you have a checklist. You can watch yourself grow and also measure yourself on a scale of highly specific leadership dimensions. You are beginning to see that ad libbing is not an effective strategy for group counseling leaders. The specific components are there. You have a "code of conduct," if you will, and you can consult your code whenever you find yourself floundering around as a practitioner. You will ask yourself, Which skills have I mastered? Where do I need work? and What are my strengths and relative weaknesses? Now you can call yourself on any given dimension, and go to work at being completely effective in every one of the twenty group leadership behaviors that are required for solid leadership. Before, you could always say that there were no firm guidelines for group counselors and how they should behave. Not so now. You have them.

The rating scale is designed to help you assess yourself on the twenty basic group leadership skills elaborated in this chapter.

You can use a one-to-twenty ranking system in which the rank of 1 would indicate the behavior or skill in which you feel most competent to utilize as a group leader, and a rank of 20 for the behavior in which you feel least competent. Also, you may want to use your own personal rating for each of the skills elaborated, or have your co-leader provide a rating for you to compare with your own assessment. The scale is a useful checklist of all of the behaviors discussed in this chapter. They are presented in the order examined in the chapter, and not necessarily in any order of importance.

Group Counselor Leadership Behavior Rating Scale

Rating:

_____ 1. Identifying, labeling, clarifying, and reflecting feeling or emotional data

_____ 2. Identifying, labeling, clarifying, and reflecting behavioral data

_____ 3. Identifying, labeling, clarifying, and reflecting cognitive data

_____ 4. Questioning, drawing out, and evoking problem-related material

_____ 5. Confronting

_____ 6. Summarizing and reviewing important material

_____ 7. Interpreting

_____ 8. Restating

_____ 9. Establishing connections

_____ 10. Lecturing and information giving

_____ 11. Initiating

_____ 12. Reassuring, encouraging, and supporting

_____ 13. Intervening

_____ 14. Dealing with silence

_____ 15. Recognizing and explaining nonverbal behavior

_____ 16. Using clear, concise, meaningful communication

_____ 17. Facilitating closure

_____ 18. Focusing

_____ 19. Restraining, subduing, and avoiding potentially explosive and divisive group happenings

_____ 20. Goal-setting

Now you can go out and use them. Practice them. Measure yourself on each of them. As a group leader you will never act without a rationale. You will teach the group members about what it means to be a client and how good it feels to get counseled. You will be a deliverer of services from a technology of highly specific group leader behaviors. The only way that you will work on yourself is from the point of view of a leader; your own personal stuff will be taboo. And since you have a lot of work to do on your way to group leader mastery, there will be plenty for you to do.

5

Before Your Debut: Anticipating Group Member Behaviors

WELL, YOU'VE come a long way. You have examined your own personal reluctance to make the foray and become an active group counselor. You have identified the causes of your professional inertia, and you have looked very carefully at the reasons for instituting a group counseling effort of your own. You are sure that it is worth doing, you have defined it very exactingly, and you have been thorough about your preliminaries in getting the entire school community ready. Moreover, you have a detailed checklist of group leadership behaviors to follow in evaluating yourself from a technological point of view. Now for the tough stuff. You are going to anticipate group member behaviors. You will work hard at not being taken aback when group members behave in what others might label irregular ways. You are the master of preparation; you will anticipate what might take place, and expect the *expected* rather than being floored by it.

As you work at preparing yourself to anticipate what group members will do and say, you will be able to call upon your group leadership skills in making the transition from typical school discussion groups, to which students have become accustomed, to a counseling group as we have defined it. The group you lead will take on some characteristics that generally typify all beginning counseling groups. You are going to be ready. You will avoid surprises, and painful what-happened feelings, because you are thorough about predicting and planning for typical group member behaviors in counseling groups. You are going to become an interventionist. You will know when, why, and how to intervene in the group counseling activity.

As an interventionist, you will be schooled in knowing when to intervene. Once again, you will not be ill-prepared. You will have a cache of ready interventions as a group leader, and you will be ready to call upon them or have someone in the group do so, whenever a group occurrence calls for some kind of shift toward more effective group counseling practice. In another place we've established the rationale for group intervention, with the leader being ready to intervene as a result of anticipating group member behaviors.

> Significant, on-target "counseling" interventions, whether made by the counselor of the group or by its members, help to keep members working on their goals and give everyone a sense of directionality. Counselees need reinforcement of their progress, and interventions which chip away at impediments to that progress provide support for group counseling as a productively meaningful process. This helps members to feel better about the struggle they are going through on their way to self-enlargement and makes them more willing to work at self-defeating behaviors and less willing to avoid such work. No work, no payoff.[1]

In chapter 4, you read about the group leadership variable which was labeled "intervening." In that section you saw some ten occasions which call for group leader interventions. A thorough reading of chapter 11 in *Counseling Techniques That Work* will give you a detailed analysis of typical occasions for group leader intervention. In anticipating group member behavior, you will be on guard for the following additional kinds of activities which will require you to assume (or help others to assume) the role of group interventionist.

[1] Wayne W. Dyer and John Vriend, *Counseling Techniques That Work* (Washington, D.C.: American Personnel and Guidance Association Press, 1975), p. 201.

The Gripe Session Mentality

Students will make every effort to focus their attention on someone or something about the school that they dislike. Without you as an active, on-guard leader to help shift this trend, the counseling group can easily deteriorate into a meaningless, although interesting, discussion and harangue about the evils of Mrs. Jones, or the multitudinous rules that are anathema to the entire student body. By making the counseling group into a gripe session, you will be teaching your group members to become complainers rather than doers. You will also reinforce the notion that someone else is to blame for their plight. This, of course is, taboo. You are aware that it is always easier to complain, stew, and rue, rather than initiate, shift, and do. Your intervention will take the form of challenging the group members who choose to complain with an intervention that brings the focus back to where it belongs, that is, to the individuals in the group. For example:

> "John, you've talked about Mrs. Jones and her petty regulations, and everyone here seems to agree with you. How is that going to help you, now that you have a unanimous opinion about Mrs. Jones?"

Your sole purpose is to make John, and everyone else, focus on themselves, to see that the world is full of Mrs. Joneses and that learning new and more effective skills in dealing with them is the only solution to the difficulty.

You want them to know that you, as the leader, do not take sides, that you make no moral or legal judgment about Mrs. Jones, or the principal, or the rules; that you feel a commitment to helping them, and that they must begin to examine how they are letting the Mrs. Joneses of the world get to them in a psychologically unhealthy way. By sitting here and talking about her, by getting upset and feeling abused, you point out, the students have given an element of emotional self-control over to someone outside of themselves.

Virtually all counseling groups which have students as group members are susceptible to griping. It is just plain easier to be a complainer, to talk about others, and to get social status by having everyone agree with you, than to actively look at yourself and examine objectively how you are being controlled by others, if that is the case. Look at the conversational groups you participate in, particularly when the common bond is some kind of institutional affiliation. These groups tend to turn into gripe sessions. They are also almost useless, and you have a feeling of impotence after participating in one for a period of time. As a group counseling leader you will anticipate the gripe-session propensity, you will be ready to intervene very early in the initial groups, and you will help the group members see that a counseling group is not just one more place where people congregate for the purpose of social complaining; rather, this place emphasizes self-understanding and self-initiated action to avoid having to be in circumstances where complaining or griping are the only weapons against a seemingly hostile environment. You are armed with anti-griping, other-focused interventions, the kind that make the group a counseling rather than a prattling group. You will set the proper tone early.

FOCUSING ON OTHERS

Besides the griping behavior, you are forewarned that group members will elect to spend a lot of their time talking about others. Parents, peers, teachers, girlfriends, idols, and so on. The students, like everyone else in our culture, have been weaned on conversational groups, thus they will bring the gabby mentality to the counseling group. You, as the well-prepared group leader, have anticipated this inclination to talk about others, and you will make the appropriate intervention to end such wasteful group activity as soon as it appears in the group.

The reason for prohibiting the gab fest is elementary. If the students talk about others, and put their focus on the behavior and attitudes of others, you are reinforcing the notion that others are more important than those present in the group. In addition, you encourage the kind of external thinking that characterizes so many self-forfeiting people in our culture. In the thinking of such persons, the self is not responsible for the emotional condition it finds itself in; by blaming or talking about others they magically assign responsibility to someone external to the self. This kind of warped thinking must be systematically wiped away. Focusing on anyone outside of the group is a waste of precious time. Your interventions will be designed to erase the strong propensity of group members to put responsibility onto others, to talk about those others in blaming ways and then feel comforted because they have once again skirted the real cause of their personal ineffectiveness—which is, of course, themselves and how they react to all the "demented" others that exist in their worlds. You must be ready to intervene when the "others" syndrome surfaces. By pointing to it directly, with interventions that accurately label the other-centered behavior, you will be helping everyone in the group to get past the gossip and onto the real business of group counseling. You are waiting in delightful anticipation for the first "others" stuff to emerge, and you will gently but firmly label, challenge, and eliminate such tendencies later on in the life of the group.

THE AVOIDANCE OF FEELINGS

You will anticipate that the members of your group will find it difficult to talk about and deal directly with feelings in the group. You understand that they have been nurtured on an avoidance-of-feelings teat, and that anyone who talks directly to people about their personal feelings is acting inappropriately in our culture. And so they enter the counseling group with this mentality. You are trying to get people to be straight with each other, and they are busy trying to avoid it at all costs. But you are not surprised by this group activity. You know how tough it is to talk about personal things, and that people will do all that they can to avoid such interaction. In your initial sessions, you are armed with group leader interventions which will ameliorate this group condition. You are an avid anticipator. No surprises here. You expect students to say, "But I don't want to hurt his feelings," and any of a thousand similar avoidance utterances. You are well-armed. You zero in on such a statement and recall the purposes of group counseling, pointing out what a sentence such as that really implies. ("Susie, either you are really afraid that Bruce is so brittle that he would collapse if you told him the truth, or you are fearful that he won't like you if you were to be truthful with him here in the group.") This can be a stimulating introduction to how people are evasive and dishonest with each other, and how to get onto the track of being honest right here in the counseling group.

Your students will try all kinds of tricks to avoid dealing straight with each other. From looking in the other direction, to obvious lies, to nonverbal behaviors which reveal avoidance. The data are unlimited. You are expecting this, and when it surfaces right in the very beginning, you will point to it, label it, talk about it in terms of how it is an impediment to effective group counseling, and most importantly, you will be a model of personal effectiveness in that you will at no time assume the evasive mien yourself. You will always deal honestly with your group members, you will label behavior based upon the available data, and you will discreetly and unpretentiously be the accepting confronter in your role as group leader. That is, no judgment, no ethnocentrism or bias in your counseling interactions. Only straightforward, accepting dealings will emanate from you. This posture will teach others that it doesn't hurt, that no one gets damaged in any way, and that the only way to achieve personal mastery is to be a nonevasive person, first and foremost with yourself, and then with everyone else who crosses your life path.

THE RAMBLING AND BORING STUFF

You can expect members of your counseling group to engage in some tangential discussions if you are not alert to the need for making quick and effective interventions in this area. The propensity to ramble is chronic in beginning counseling groups, largely because it is a leftover response from the ways in which people characteristically behave in conversation groups in our culture. If you've ever tape-recorded a typical conversation you will find almost nothing worth retaining or even remembering. So you will find your group members have a mind-set for rambling and empty digression; you are aware of it, and will be ready with effective interventions.

A student is likely to take off on a tangent from the very outset. A particular concern will surface, and you will soon discover that everyone in the group is asking every conceivable kind of irrelevant question, largely because they want to keep the noise level high, and they equate talking with success in social settings. And so the funny-time questions will fly furiously, and everyone (and certainly the protagonist) will grab at the bait like Charley the Hungry Tuna, and off your group goes, meandering down a path that leads only to boredom and meaningless activity. But you know that the group members just plain want to talk, and they'll talk about anything, just so they can keep on talking.

You are once again armed with an arsenal of ready interventions. You will never hesitate to ask anyone in the group who has just asked a question of someone, "Do you think that that is being *helpful* to Maryanne?" This kind of an orientation will always remind the group members that the purpose of the counseling group is to provide help, rather than to engage in meaningless conversation or to ask questions simply for the purpose of making noise. No, you will disallow such frivolity in your group right from the very beginning, and you will be doing everyone a gigantic service by being professional in this regard from moment one. You need not be harsh or hurtful, simply insistent that this group will focus on helping and nothing else. Also you will guard against the individual who is ready and more than willing to become the group storyteller or the ancient mariner of your group. The tendency to prattle on and bring in every detail of a person's life is very real in many people, and the counseling group can become the ideal forum for such undertakings if you are not alert. You will intervene without hesitation when you feel that any member is rambling on in empty nothingness at the expense of being productive in the group. Your interventions are clear, straight, and not in the least intimidating. You will ask someone else in the group to repeat what the rambler has just conveyed, hopefully someone who has been sending you signals that he or she is really tuned out to Larry Larynx's endless wind. When the task becomes impossible, you can get right into the goal-setting process, firmly yet gently. If everyone in the group is being bored (including you), then you are doing everyone, but most particularly the bore, a favor by demonstrating that this counseling group is not going to be a place that encourages this kind of turn-offish behavior. Hopefully, someone in your group (and every group has one or two) will recognize through the group experience, that they have a communication problem and that they tend to become excessively wordy, and they will work on this as a personal goal. If not, then you have become one more person who reinforces self-defeating behavior, by either ignoring or missing it as a group leader.

You are going to make your counseling group count for everyone, and every piece of self-defeating behavior that surfaces will become a part of the goal-setting orientation that you have committed yourself to in this here group counseling business. You can assuredly count on it, that someone will rise to the surface, who performs either as the irrelevant-question-asker, or as the wordy tangential digressor. You are getting superb at anticipating group member behavior, and you like the sense of expertise that you are beginning to feel.

The Inclination to Intellectualize

You will undoubtedly encounter several intellectualizers and overexplainers in your group. This is one more area in which you are ready to act, rather than being bewildered at the group members' behavior. You know that intellectualizing about something is a way to avoid having to deal with it directly. Explaining something away is always easier than doing something active about the thing that is troublesome. Alas, the intellectualizer must surface. Johnny will very readily explain away Terry's problems with a discourse on a "deprived environmental life space," or Johnny will offer a disquisition on his own self-defeating behavior. Mary will get off on a lengthy description of the need to be approved, and Jerry will writhe in his eloquent prattling about a pet theory of one kind or another. The intellectualizer and the explainer are omnipresent in our culture, and therefore they will permeate every counseling group as well.

Many people have learned the art of intellectualization as a means of keeping the focus off of themselves. It is indeed a useful tool in dealing effectively with many who would choose to pry into scary areas. Simply launch into a theoretical assertion, use some evasive language, and pretty soon the inquisitor will give up, or become too exasperated to pursue it further. So, too, in the counseling group. But you will not be exasperated, because you have anticipated such behavior; nor will you give up in frustration, since you recognize this as an important part of your role as a group counselor. You will label intellectualizing behavior as it becomes evident in the group. You will help the group members to set goals in the direction of becoming more lucid in their communications. Moreover, you will interpret intellectualizing behavior as defensive and essentially avoidance-oriented, and you will help the group members to see that this has become an effective mask upon which they regularly rely, both in the group and in their own personal lives, where it really serves ill purposes on their roads to self-fulfillment and personal mastery.

By labeling the behavior early in the group, by showing the group members who lean toward theorizing that this is one way to turn the group into a dull, nonproductive experience, and by explaining the behavior from the onset, you are indeed actively taking on the role of anticipator and leader in your counseling group. You've been expecting the theoretician, and you are not surprised that many people in your group will try this tack, nor are you in any way scurrilous about the way in which you deal with this behavior. It is an expected manifestation of everyday human behavior in a culture which rewards the theorist for using lofty jargon and evasive language to neatly bypass direct, effective communication. You know that the "As long as I'm not understood, I can't be found out" syndrome is rampant in our culture, and you're not alarmed that the students have begun to latch onto it as a means of putting others off. Like everything else you encounter in the counseling group, you are more effective if you are ready for the behavior than if you let it get the better of you because you are ill-prepared.

THE TENDENCY TOWARD "WE"

So now you are encountering the banding-together syndrome that typifies almost all counseling groups. You're seeing a lot of this *us* and *we* stuff, but once again you are ready, because you've done your psychological homework, and you know that it is easier to deal with a leader who represents being different if everyone is treated alike in the minds of the group members. Your job is to help everyone to begin to think in terms of *I* and *self*, but this is truly a difficult task. The group members are in a category that is different from yours. This is a given. You are the leader, they are the students or clients. And so this arrangement becomes a convenient way of ganging up, if you let it happen.

You recognize why it is occurring. It is simply easier to try to defend what is, and to win arguments and therefore gain status by being in the right camp. You represent a different way of thinking, feeling, and behaving. You are in the business of helping people to change, and the group members are in the business of desperately trying to remain the same. The battle lines are clearly drawn. And the tendency toward we-ness is certainly not baffling to you. If everyone can prove you wrong, or even get the group members to have a unanimous position against you on a purely friendly basis, then the old us-against-you mentality is reinforced, with the "us" taking pleasure in being in the majority. Being on the side of the majority is a goal for many uninformed people, and rightness is associated with the many in our culture, particularly among young people. All of this is something that you are prepared to deal with in the group, on a straight, nonemotional level. You are not interested in winning any battles, or proving anyone right or wrong, only in helping individuals to grow and become more effective human beings. You state this everytime it comes up, you make it clear that this forum is not a debating society, and that no one, least of all you, is concerned about being on the side of right.

But everyone in the group gets a feeling of comfort in identifying with the majority. Hence you will hear a lot of "we feel this way or that way." Whenever it happens, you must be ready with a soft but firm intervention. ("Harry, you just said 'we feel this way.' Are you assuming that everyone in the group is exactly the same, and that you can speak for everyone here?") This is important for many good psychological reasons. Number one being that you are teaching self-determination and responsibility for self, rather than group determination and identification with the collective. You know that you are dealing with individuals, each of whom is unique in a thousand ways, and whenever the *we* notion becomes apparent, you have taken a backward step in the direction of helping individuals via the group counseling approach.

Any time in the counseling group that a member speaks for everyone else, or invokes the *we* as a means of gaining status, you are ready with an appropriate intervention. Moreover, you are ready to interpret this behavior with a simple statement about the counseling group being a place where individuals are given precedence, where people are encouraged to think for themselves, rather than simply letting the collective pronoun do the talking for everyone. You are going to interpret the need for people to initially band together, to protect each other, to use the *we*, as a means of taking on the one person who, as a result of being in a different role, is different from them, and you will in no way be defensive or hyper about your explanation. You expect the collective propensity of the group members, and you are ready to deal effectively with it by always keeping uppermost in your mind the central business of group counseling, that is, counseling *individuals*, who are unique, in *groups*. Without exception, all of your groups will assume this posture initially, and you will always be going up against this barrier as long as you elect to function as a group counselor. But it will never get you down. You are ready.

THE RUSH TOWARD ADVICE AND PREMATURE ACTION

You anticipate that your group members are unsophisticated in counseling and helping activities. They, like almost everyone else, feel that a healthy dose of advice and a ready solution to a problem are sufficient for helping people to change. ("If you have a problem about being shy, all you have to do is start talking to people and you will solve your problem.") Thus, you can anticipate that your group members will also partake of such juicy action-oriented activity in the counseling group. They know nothing of self-understanding, exploration, the development of alternatives and trial-and-error experimentation in new behavioral and thinking modes. Instead, they know about action. "This is what you have to do", "Why not do it this way?" and so on. You know about this. The first time that an individual states a self-defeating behavior and begins to give some background data, you expect someone in the group to give advice and start offering well-intentioned, albeit premature, suggestions for change. You don't chew out the offender, nor are you piqued by this display of nonhelping activity; rather, you are ready with an intervention that will teach the advice giver, along with everyone else in the group, what it is that constitutes help, and how to give it.

> "Is that suggestion helpful to George? Do you think that just telling someone to be different will work? How do you react when someone tells you, or offers you free advice that you aren't ready to take?"

These kinds of interventions demonstrate what tone the counseling group will take, and what gets transacted here in the group. You are also ready to interpret the premature-action mentality in the counseling group, and show the group members that you are not only expecting such behavior, but that you understand it. You point out that it is natural just to offer instant solutions, and far more difficult to help a person help himself by working with that person toward self-understanding, providing him with an opportunity to try out new thinking and behavior, and helping him set achievable goals. You talk about the tendency to tell, to advise, and to assume that because "I can do it" so can everyone else. You explain about how tough it is to genuinely understand another person from their point of view rather than your own. This seldom needs to be explained more than once, and the group members begin to see that rapid-fire questioning and advice are essentially useless in the counseling group.

Thus your anticipatory professionalism in the group counseling has once again averted what might have been a disaster. You might have gotten into a group counseling arrangement in which everyone brought up a concern, and then everyone solved it for the person. Instead, you fostered, right from the beginning, a spirit of patience, tolerance, and empathy for someone else's life concerns, and you helped, through effective straightforward interventions, to maintain a tone of counseling in the group. You knew what constituted effective group counseling, but no one else did, and your modeling behavior paved the way for a smooth transition into the actual counseling process. Without being prepared for the ceaseless interrogation and multifaceted solutions that were to crop up, you might have been befuddled by the group activity, but instead you weathered that storm effectively. By showing a calm understanding of what the group members were doing, and by being ready to label, interpret, and challenge such typical group member behavior, you averted a catastrophic group, which might have rivaled the many school classroom discussion groups, in which ready solutions to complex problems are always offered by untrained observers, solutions that are totally useless and inane, if not insane.

The Tendency Toward Silliness

You are expecting some degree of discomfort in your group members. Virtually all counseling groups with students will exhibit some semblance of characteristic silliness and funny-time behavior. This is something that you are anticipating, and once again you will not be in the least taken aback by such behavior. Particularly at the beginning of your counseling groups, the inclination to avoidance will be manifested in any number of ways, from talking about the upcoming football game to giggling and laughing about Molly's stunt at Friday night's party. The avoidance mechanism is ubiquitous in group counseling.

You recognize that getting down to business right away means getting on with the task of changing behavior, and certainly that potentially painful lure can be at least postponed by some subtle and effective silliness for the purpose of digression in the beginning stages of each counseling group. You are once again alert for this tendency. You are armed with the resolve not to reinforce self-defeating behavior, and therefore you do not participate in any kind of evasive early-session behavior, which can ultimately lead to a conversation group if not checked immediately. You suppress your own inclinations to digress and participate in the avoidance pap that so characterizes the beginning, when everyone is just settling down and saying their hellos. The propensity to giggle, laugh, and generally be unbusinesslike is clear. You don't chew them out or admonish their behavior in the least, rather you are the cool professional, you wait it out, not reinforcing the behavior by participating or laughing yourself. You simply get on with the business of group counseling. And so you will be effective in your efforts to conduct a meaningful counseling experience. If necessary, you interpret the beginning digressive behavior in a calm fashion, noting that it is quite common for people to avoid getting down to work and focusing on self-defeating behavior. You never act hurt or disappointed. You find that just ignoring it, and taking on a serious tone in the beginning, will soon teach everyone that the sooner the group begins to engage in counseling activity, the more time everyone has to use the group productively, and while it is tempting to gab at the beginning, those wasted moments are rued by all when the time for group counseling is ticking away. You, of course, do not assume at all the posture of the totally serious taskmaster. You are more than willing to introduce humor at any time in the life of the group, and in fact have recognized that a group without some laughter and sense of the ridiculous is indeed a lifeless, dull experience. But early on in each session, you are adamant about eliminating the silliness and the gabfesty nature of the group, since you know that the danger is everpresent, and that the entire group experience can turn into a silly but entertaining experience if this behavior is not nipped in the bud. You expect it, it comes, and you gently help it to go away, all because you have anticipated the need for, and the inclination toward, avoidance in behavior change, which of course is the name of the group counseling game.

THE DESIRE FOR THEMES, TOPICS, AND CONVERSATIONS

As you look back at the assumptions included in your extended definition in chapter 2, you recall that there are no themes, topics, or discussions in group counseling. You do not confuse a discussion of drug abuse, homosexuality, pregnancy, and abortion, or any such personal issue, with the business of helping someone (or several people) to deal effectively with these problems as they occur in their everyday lives. Discussion and counseling are not even close in your conceptual framework. Everyone in your group will prefer to have a topic, theme, or discussion to talk endlessly about, and thus avoid getting any personal help in dealing with the concerns of their own lives. A discussion about anything in a counseling group is a genuine cop-out on your part. You are there to help the individuals grow and become more personally productive and effective. Yet everyone will try to get in on the discussion bandwagon. You expect this, and once again you are well prepared. You identify any questions in the group that do not relate specifically to anyone in the group itself. You do not talk *about* problems, rather you talk *to people* about their own difficulties and concerns. You help everyone in the group to see that a centered discussion is appropriate in the social studies, math, science, or English classroom but not in the counseling group. You remind the group members about the purpose of the counseling group, and how this group is different from any of the previous groups in which they found themselves actively participating.

You are deliberately relaxed about this issue, and you are sure that it will crop up, since everyone in the group has had previous school experiences which lead them to believe that conversation is what is expected when students break into small groups in the school. And so your task is difficult. All of the previous experience of your group members leads them toward nice little harmless discussions about the pros and cons of any number of topics, including the rhyme scheme of Petrarchan sonnets and the reproduction patterns of boll weevils in Southern Louisiana, as well as the more common controversies such as democracy versus autocracy, and the inductive versus the deductive method. You remind everyone at every turn, that the work of a counseling group is to help those who are here to become better and happier, and to develop a strong sense of self-confidence in themselves at every stretch of their lives. No hammering out topics here, no conversations on the pros and cons of anything, and no cause-and-effect intellectual discussions in the counseling group.

You intervene every time group members deviate from the counseling focus which you have worked so hard to maintain. When Johnny says something like, "That reminds me of Joe, he had a drug problem ... it seems that this is becoming a social problem", you are quick to bring it back to the group without fanfare, and thus avoid a stereotyped discussion on community drug problems. You help whoever has the concern in the group, and leave the intellectual give and take to the academic atmosphere of the classroom. Here you are dealing with people who have real concerns, and you are studiously tuned into the strong need for keeping to the tone of counseling. (This section might not be as appropriate for very young children, since their ability to deal with each other on a personal level is hampered by developmental exigencies, and often early elementary groups take on a theme-centeredness which can be a provocative group experience. Even here, we would hesitate to call this group counseling, since the goals are more on social interaction and discussion rather than identifying and changing individual behavior and thinking patterns that are in any way self-forfeiting for the youngsters.)

GETTING LOST IN ROLES IN THE GROUP

You anticipate that many of your group members will assume in the group some of the same self-defeating roles they take on regularly in their everyday lives. When these roles emerge in the group, you are prepared to deal with them effectively and to help the individuals set goals for themselves based upon the various roles they assume in the group. You know that someone will want to assume the role of the clown, to make others laugh and thereby draw some attention and status for himself. While you recognize that laughter is indeed the "sunshine of the soul," you also know that if David's only means of getting attention is clowning behavior, then he is exhibiting some self-deprecating behavior that should be pointed out. For example, you might say, "Have you noticed David, that the only way you communicate in the group is by becoming a clown? Is there another side of you that isn't exclusively the funmaker?"

You are not trying to stifle David's creative comedic style, but rather to point out that being the buffoon can indeed be a limiting means of gaining status. You will find many kinds of roles surfacing within the group. When you notice that any individual has limited him or herself by just being in a certain role, you will be ready to help that individual to set new and exciting goals.

You expect role assumption in the group. You know that some people can relate on only one minimal level, and therefore they get into a role, and refuse to get out of it because of the attendant risks involved in trying new behaviors. You expect the clown, the sergeant-at-arms, the provocateur, the intellectualizer, the isolate, the blusher, the rumor-spreader, the tough guy, the brazen one, the bully, the seducer, and the excessive talker to show up in your group. You ready yourself with interventions that make clear what is taking place, and you help individuals set goals that will allow them to be more natural persons, more spontaneous and free of the need to be seen in one certain way, rather than hiding behind the role-mask of approval-getting behavior. You are not trying to stultify creative energies, only to help people see how they come across to you and to the other members of the group. If the roles get in the way, or are assumed for a purpose that is designed to mask the rest of the individual, then perhaps a new goal is in order. In any case, you are not stymied by these roles, you refuse to become annoyed when they crop up, and you go right to work in your leadership role by helping individuals to set attainable, non-role-related goals for themselves right there in the counseling group, which is the safest and most effective environment for working at changing nonproductive behavior.

The Content of Group Counseling
A look at typical concerns that are regularly dealt with in the group counseling setting

You've examined some of the typically occurring group counseling activities for which you need to be adequately prepared, and you have armed yourself with effective anticipatory interventions to cope effectively with these actions. You will not be seduced, alarmed, or intimidated by unexpected actions, simply because you have been very thorough about your preliminaries, and you are expecting what the group members might see as unique behavior, but which you recognize as rather routine group counseling activity. Your expertise is showing and it is sticking out all over the place. You revel in your ability to predict and deal with almost any group counseling action.

Now for the tougher stuff. You want to prepare yourself for the kinds of questions that will be asked of you, particularly about what will be dealt with in the group. You know that the group members will have hundreds of questions about what goes on here. "What do we do, what do you want me to talk about, why can't we talk about the football game, how do we get started?" and on and on they go, questions that are neverending, and which must be dealt with from the very beginning. Moreover, you want to be able to help group members get right down to the business of group counseling; goal-setting and counseling are on your mind, and you want to be ready to get on with it. As you look back at the rationale for group counseling, you begin to recognize why you got into this business in the first place. Remember, the schools don't provide the students with a place to deal with their own personal concerns, to talk about and come up with constructive alternatives to the everyday difficulties they face in their lives, and that is why you wanted to get this counseling group started in the first place. Well, you must be thorough enough in your preliminaries to predict what kinds of things they will want to bring up in the counseling group. You decide to divide them into academic and nonacademic concerns.

Typical Self-Defeating Behaviors (Emotional)

In the nonacademic or personal area, you expect that the students will have self-defeating problems in many areas. Primarily, you are prepared to help the student group members to deal effectively with the whole issue of *approval-seeking*. You know that students have tremendous difficulty about the need for peer-group approval. They are constantly besieged and unnecessarily harassed because they want others in the group to like them, to approve of them, to accept them. You know, while this is certainly nice, and even desirable, that the need for approval should be tackled directly as a self-defeating tendency, and that being depressed because someone (anyone) doesn't like you is essentially a waste of time. So you are prepared to help anyone in the group, who talks in the area of getting others to like them all of the time for almost everything that they do, to set more realistic and less immobilizing goals for themselves. You are going to keep uppermost in your mind that no one can expect others to like them all of the time and maintain any kind of happy equilibrium in their lives. You will be prepared to talk about approval-seeking as a self-deprecating activity, and you will help counsel anyone in the area of becoming more self-confident and self-reliant, rather than focusing their attention on their buddies. Self-determination will be uppermost in your mind, and anyone who begins to talk about others in a way that shows a need for approval will receive your guidance toward self-understanding, in which you provide insight, goals, and suggestions for new self-determining behaviors.

Your students will suffer also from *the not-living-in-the-present-moment trap,* which so engulfs almost everyone in our culture. You recognize that this will crop up over and over again in the course of the group counseling. Planning for the future, living in the past, not knowing how to grab on to the now and live it fully, are characteristic difficulties, and you will be prepared to help your students deal with this problem. Your students will talk about the past as if it is something that exists currently. They will say things like, "That's me, I've always been that way," or "I can't help it." These are the neurotic utterances of someone living in the past and saying to the self that just because I've always been a certain way, I am condemned to a life of living that pattern forever. This is nonsense, and you are ready to counsel in the direction of Aristotle's famous dictum, "Once you lay a brick, and not a moment before, you are indeed a bricklayer." You will help students who are shy, underachieving, boastful, truant, and so forth, to recognize the folly of saying, "I'm that way," or "It's my nature." You are prepared to argue against such illogical self-defeating thinking. You expect much of this kind of behavior, and you are ready to help each student to see that he or she is really a product of their choices and nothing more. That they can, indeed, choose to be something very different from what they have always chosen to be up until now, if only they allow themselves the luxury of believing that they can be different.

Your students will try to *blame,* and you are already prepared to deal with this oh-so-common phenomenon in group counseling. You will not permit the focusing on others that runs so rampant in almost all discussion and rap groups. Instead, you are well equipped to bring the focus right down to those present in the group, and you have a strong rationale for your adamant stance. You are teaching people to focus on themselves, not on others. You are an advocate and spokesman for self-determination and taking responsibility for self, and you are well aware that any extended diatribe that falls into the blaming category is indeed a breach of your philosophical behavior position. Indeed, your group will either deal with each other or remain silent, since to blame others reinforces the neurotic notion that others are in control of us, and this you steadfastly refuse to accept.

You also expect to hear a lot of talk about *worry* in your counseling group, and your students will want to talk about things that concern them in the future. You know that the content of group counseling involves dealing with projections into the future about specific kinds of student-related problems. Therefore, you anticipate hearing the word worry, and you are going to deal with this concept of worry as a waste of time and energy. You are prepared to define worry, as using up the present-moment time to focus on something in the future, and thus being singularly ineffective in the present. If it is going to occur in the future, then any immobilized present-moment time is literally wasted, since nothing can be done about it. Unless, of course something can be done, and then you do it, rather than use up your present moment in worrying behavior. Therefore all human worry is essentially useless, and you will help the members of your counseling group to refocus their energies on present-moment activities that are productive and enjoyable.

You are prepared to diagnose worry for the group members. You are equipped to help each individual set goals that involve using present-moment time in a healthy fashion, and you will demonstrate the folly of worry by illustrating that no amount of worry will ever get anything done. You know that there are only two things to do about worry, and these are to attack the cause of the worry, or to take action about the possible future event that is causing the disaster mentality. In either case, the immobilized mental state can disappear. You know that students worry. They live in anxiety states about hundreds of things, including grades, college, dates, friends, parents, test scores, teachers. They worry. And that worry will surface in the group. You will label it, identify its causes and antecedents, help the students to set goals that involve taking action to eliminate the unnerving worry and learning new behaviors that involve wiping out the worry completely. Thus you are prepared on one more front, and the content of your counseling group is more firmly entrenched in your own think bag.

You know that worry is an immobilizing emotional state that is tied to the future, and that immobilized emotional states tied to the past are called *guilt*. The Big G. Students are full of this and it is an even more destructive and useless emotion than worry. They live in homes which operate exclusively on guilt principles ("If you don't obey me you are a bad girl, and you should feel bad if you are bad"). Schools, too, operate on this touchstone. If the students don't "do it right," as they are told, then guilt results. Teachers spend an awful lot of time in guilt-producing activities.

Guilt is a complete waste of time because it focuses on something that has already occurred. Thus, you will distinguish between the students using their past behavior to learn and grow (which is not guilt at all), and their being immobilized in the present moment over something that is already over, that no amount of pining can change. You will see guilt surfacing all over the group counseling map. From grades, and friends, and past behavior that was disapproved of by parents or academia, the student is overloaded to the point of explosion with various forms of guilt. And you, in your infinite wisdom and effective counseling practices, will help students to identify the guilt, to label it when it occurs, to see the folly of looking backwards and feeling bad now, and to set goals to understand and eliminate guilt in the future.

Essentially, you realize that guilt is someone else's imposition of a value system on the organism. It is the ultimate form of external control, and you will point to this as it arises, and stick it way out in a furrow in a field, for the worms to eat, rather than give it any credence in your counseling group. You are an activist against guilt, and you can predictably assert that the problem of guilt will come up in every session in which students talk of the way in which they feel controlled by others, that is, in every honestly run counseling group. You beat the drums with self-satisfaction, because you are going to make a difference in the lives of these group members, by helping them to rid themselves of the disease germs of worry and guilt. Such a glorious feeling, to know what is going to take place in the group, and to be able to help get rid of such yucky stuff in young people. The business of group counseling is inextricably tied to worry and guilt, two opposite kinds of self-defeating behavior patterns that are united in their zeal to destroy efforts at becoming personally masterful.

You also know that students are going to talk about being afraid of *the unknown*. They will most assuredly bring up concerns about what school will be like when they get into junior high school, high school, or college. How they will function when they are expected to be on their own, what the army will be like, what sex will be like, how tough it will be to make new friends, to be financially independent, to have a job, and on and on through an endless list of fears of the unknown. This, too, is an avoidable thought process that gets cultivated, nurtured, and encouraged in an other-directed culture. "Avoid the mysterious, stay only with the familiar." These are the maxims of a culture that prides itself on keeping the young out of trouble. Thus, young people come to the counseling group with a mind-set about the unknown and an avoidance mechanism for uncertainty. Schools teach certainty. Look for the right answer. Don't dabble in the fuzzy, the gray is an area to avoid and is only for wishy-washy thinkers. You, of course, know that the world's greatest scholars ramble about daily in the gray, and rarely come to rest on either black or white. You are ready to help your clients delve into the mysterious, to understand and avoid the anxiety that goes with checking out the new and adventurous. When Johnny talks about fearing the future, you recognize it as ineffective thinking that helps him to escape his now moments. Living in the present and welcoming the unknown is the mark of the true mental giant. If you stay away from it, you will most assuredly remain just as you are now, *suffering in comfort.*

You see that the fear of the unknown is a cultural problem, and therefore you expect it to come up in virtually all counselor groups. Students will express fears about it, and you will challenge their fears in an uncompromising way. You will point out the folly of reading the same kinds of books, having the same kinds of friends for a lifetime, only seeing one type of movie, or doing just one thing, one way forever. The mysterious is where adventurous and self-actualized living exists. New things bring excitement, the traditional brings routine boredom. Life is about the new, about growing and becoming better in any way. And growth, you will point out, is impossible as long as you avoid the mysterious. The fear is what you will vehemently attack, the disaster-painting, the catastrophizing. This will come up in your group and you, a gentle but firm counselor, are ready with a depot full of ready interventions that will help guide the group member toward growth in the most positive ways.

You must also be ready to deal with a common kind of group counseling phenomenon in school settings, the struggle for *psychological independence.* This, you know, is a giant hurdle for almost every young person alive, particularly those in the high school. You are going to hear much about this in your counseling group. Students wanting freedom from non-freedom-granting parents. Students feeling that they cannot make it on their own. Students not knowing how to deal effectively with parents who won't let go, who insist on keeping them as servants. Psychological independence is a goal for everyone on this planet, yet almost no one achieves it. The ten-month-old child asserts that she can do it herself as her well-meaning daddy holds her coat out to help her; the adolescent insists on getting a driver's license on his birthday of eligibility, thereby gaining a measure of independence. The examples would fill a chonicle ten volumes long. Everyone wants it, but few know how to go after it effectively, without all kinds of hurt feelings on both sides.

As a group counselor, you will be prepared to help students set goals in the area of psychological independence. To help them to talk in doing terms about becoming their own person, this is your own goal. You must work very, very hard at keeping in mind what an important issue this is for the students, and that helping them develop effective strategies for self-understanding and action is of highest priority for you as a group leader. This is the place where they can talk freely about how to achieve psychological independence—not physical or financial, but emotional and personal autonomy. You will work hard in this area, and it will come up often. You are, again, a spokesman for personal autonomy, and you will help each person work hard at setting goals in the area of becoming a complete, psychologically independent individual, one who can interact with everyone, and who doesn't fall apart when someone else lets him or her down.

You also ready yourself to help with *fear of failure*. You are experienced enough to know that virtually all human beings fear failure; and, certainly, young people have learned from a culture which demands excellence and achievement that failure is something assiduously to be avoided. But *you* know that failure is good. That trying something, and then learning from a mistake, is the only way to fly in the skies of self-fulfillment and mental health. You know also, that failure, when it is equated with self-worth, is certainly the bane to self-development. So you expect to hear students talk over and over about not trying certain things, or avoiding risks because they are afraid of messing up. You anticipate a lot of talk about not being good at certain kinds of things, and you are thoroughly prepared to help students to discover that fearing failure is really a fear of not pleasing someone else. Somewhere along the way someone told them that they must do things well—

everything they did. Those things which they did poorly were to be avoided, otherwise they would be admonished for not doing well. Thus a whole behavioral pattern of existence, based upon avoiding the things that might result in failure, was established. On and on through their lives they learned to avoid anything that might smack of mediocrity, and they learned to equate their failures with their self-worth. You will serve as a firm defender of their right to fail, of their being able to be totally self-accepting when they have done something less than perfect. In fact you will be an advocate for possessing a behavioral repertoire of just average things to do, because these things make a person a happier and more experienced individual. Failure will be bandied about frequently in your group, and you—expert counselor—are ready, willing, and desirous of helping students avoid the stereotypical thinking, inherited from a generation weaned on avoiding failure, that the self must be viewed as less than worthy when one doesn't act as a perfect person should. The "Do your best in everything you do" syndrome will be substituted by, "do your best in those things where you choose to excel, and then just 'do' in the rest of the areas of your life." Always having to do your best creates avoidance behavior in almost every area, since absolute perfection is something that humankind has reserved for God but always seems to be trying to lay on itself in neurotic, impossible ways.

You also anticipate that many of the group members will bring to the counseling group the difficulty of having lived a large chunk of their lives in a state of *inertia*, just waiting for things to change. You recognize that many of the students will talk about the future in relationship to jobs, while doing very little preparation in the now. You expect to hear students say, "Oh, that, I'll work on that later, it won't always be that way." You know that students talk in grandiose terms about all of the things they are going to be, and yet large hunks of their present lives are being lived ineffectively. You are prepared to deal with inertia as a strategy for living. You will not be surprised to hear the pronouncements of the students, to be a witness to the great plans with little follow-through. You are doggedly ready to attack the inertia. To label hang-back behavior for what it is, and to interpret, challenge, and counsel in the area of psychological standstillism.

You are aware of the vast numbers of people who operate in this inertia bag, thinking that things will get better with age, and doing little or nothing to make them better. You know that many people have adopted this from a culture that thrives on postponement and procrastination. Students need to feel that the future will be better, but they also need to fully comprehend the notion that nothing will get anywhere without some genuine effort, rather than simply prattling about how things are going to change. You will help to put the group members on the road toward action. Prescribing psychological homework, challenging them to action rather than talk, examining in the group how much of their lives consists of wishing and hoping rather than doing, and, in general, eliminating inertia from their repertoire of ineffective living standards. You are going to be alone in this area, since inertia gets reinforced readily in a group where it is being challenged. There will be a veritable throng of opposition to suggesting that action is a far better strategy than talking. You are ready though. You expect to hear lots of jibberish about how things will change in the future. "When I get away from home, or into the junior high school, when I change teachers, or when I get my license, or when we get married," etc.—futurizing that the future alone, with little or no active behavioral change, will create the "real me." You know it is nonsense, but you also know that students need to think it. Your indefatigable energy will be directed to providing the insight that, for the person who isn't "doing it now," either emotionally or behaviorally, the future will be only a different time slot with another set of excuses for putting things off. You are ready to wipe out inertia.

You are also prepared to fight the ugly demon of *external thinking* in your counseling group. You are too well aware that our culture is an other-directed one, and certainly the students who enter your counseling group will be a product of this culture. You know that families, institutions, television, lyrics of popular songs, advertisers, churches, all preach the message of not thinking for yourself. To trust oneself is to get into trouble. To rely on self is to be an upstart or a troublemaker. Trust the teacher, or mommy or God, or General Motors, or Uncle Sam, anyone but yourself. And here they all are in the group, all external down to their toenails, always assigning responsibility for self to others. Blaming, pleading, demanding the right to be told what, when, why, and how to do it. The external monster will be an omnipresent phenomenon in your group.

You are, nevertheless, ready. You have slain this dragon in yourself, and now you are ready to help others. And so you mount the campaign. When one of them assigns responsibility to another person for something they are feeling emotionally, you help him or her to see what they are doing to themselves. You show how one's emotions are controlled by self, and that emotional upset is not caused by events or people, but by what one tells oneself about those events and people. You are fingering the internal side of the ledger at all times, showing how one is a slave if he must rely on others, illustrating the advantages to having a locus of control in self, rather than in anyone else. It is a struggle, but you are prepared to wage war against it with all artillery ablaze, since the reinforcement for external thinking is so great outside of the group. You are mindful of the obstacles and are always making a strong case for relying on self. Self-reliance is, after all, the curriculum of group counseling, and you never abandon your curriculum, even though the temptation to do so will occur with the resistance to such radical thinking. Imagine being a proponent of taking full responsibility for everything that you do and are. What nonsense. Everyone knows that it is easier to blame, or to assign responsibility to others—parents, teachers, the past, enemies, the government, blacks, whites, Jews, communists, anyone but me. And so you fight the battle alone. But you fight on, and you will make little scratch marks on their personalities by never bending in your efforts to show that the road to self-fulfillment comes to a dead end in other-centeredness, and that the only clear path is one that accepts total responsibility for one's self that avoids at all costs giving control of one's life over to anyone else. You'll hear objections ringing in your ears. "I can't help it, my parents *do* control me, I can't be happy when they run my life." They'll be persuasive all right, but you never swerve. You know that it is they who make themselves unhappy, and that they just plain find it easier and more convenient to shift the causes of their unhappiness to others. You don't get adamant, but you demonstrate down the line that no one, even though they imprison you, can make you unhappy and emotionally distraught unless you choose to tell yourself distraughtful and unhappy things about the conditions of your life. The problems are just about the same for everyone; it is the attitude toward the problems that distinguishes healthy from unhealthy folks, and you are working at making the individuals in your group more internally based. The enemy is external locus of control, and so you spend many group counseling hours in dealing with this strange and trying phenomenon.

Other Typical Student Concerns

ACADEMIC

While working as a group counselor, you are also prepared to deal with many matters that relate to the academic concerns of your students. While many of the personal concerns are rooted in a forest of emotions, and dealing with them is both new and difficult for the group members, there will be many additional school-related and age-typical problem areas that will receive attention in the counseling group. While you are not anxious to wade into solving algebra problems, or learning how to write themes for English classes, you will be expecting to work a great deal of the time on many of the difficulties that young people face daily in the school setting. You also see that the school-related concerns of young people are intertwined with the nonacademic concerns you are expecting and for which you've prepared yourself so diligently. The problem of failing mathematics is not purely an academic question, it is involved with fear of failure, with guilt and worry, and certainly with inertia. Yet there is a sense in which school-related difficulties are separate, the special problems of people who attend school because they are *required* to do so. Schools work hard at eliminating self-determination and independent thinking, and you recognize this and see how important it is for you to be prepared in the whole area of school-specific student concerns.

You know that students are going to have difficulties in their *classrooms*, problems with their *subjects* and problems with their *teachers*. So you take a heavy dose of preparation in initiating and counseling on school-oriented concerns. Certainly classroom behaviors are going to surface. You will help students explore, in safety, strategies for dealing more effectively with academic, self, and school expectations. You will counsel in the direction of self-understanding and goal-setting in academic areas, and you will help students work at establishing their own criteria for self-development in the cognitive realm, focusing exclusively on the self-defeating behaviors that prevent students from reaching their stated objectives. Always, you are the proponent for the group member making his or her own decisions and recognizing how their current behavior is working either productively or counter-productively in their own behalf. At no time do you become an agent for the system, a spy who is trying to change their thinking to suit your own. You know that classrooms of themselves create concerns in students, and you are ready to help students deal with these concerns in an arena of safety and seriousness.

VOCATIONAL AND EDUCATIONAL DECISION MAKING

You will also encourage counseling in the areas of *vocational and educational decision-making.* You are well aware of the crisis that faces all young people about what they will be doing, either in school of for a living, after they leave school. You will help them to explore their own current behavior, and to examine in depth how it is helping them to reach any goals that they might have for themselves down the pike. You know that uncertainty about the future is a source of anxiety, and yet you are mature enough to recognize that nothing is certain, and that being able to deal with uncertainty is one of the component parts of effective living. But you want to guide your group members to plan flexibly, to use their present moments effectively, and most of all, to avoid the ulcer-producing aspects of intense worry about the future. Certainly a hearty look into the group members' vocational and educational concerns will be productive. Also, an overview of their current behaviors and the things they have going for them. Jobs, colleges, training, course planning, requirements, information. All of these are the curriculum of the group, and you will help guide the young people into meaningful group counseling activity that focuses on the acquisition of new thinking and behavior which can lead to the removal of anxiety about their vocational and educational futures. You not only expect to deal with these kinds of concerns, you are prepared to make this happen in the counseling group, since you know how significant these concerns are to everyone.

FINANCIAL MATTERS

Certainly *financial matters* will come up in your counseling group—scholarships, loans, fears about being able to "make it" in the dollars market. These are a few of the crucial uncertainties facing the young person in a school setting. You will help individuals examine their behavior in the whole area of financial aid, whether it be financing college or a hog farm, and you will look at current behavior from the pragmatist's point of view. Most students behave as if they were waiting for someone to drop a fortune into their lap. You will look at new ways of seeking out funding—letters to foundations, interviews, applications, special categories of availability, and personal behavior that works in this dimension. You will talk freely about money, and how significant a role it plays in people's lives. You will counsel to the effect that having personal mastery and fulfillment are not dependent upon the acquisition of wealth, and you will help each person to set goals concerning the avoidance of overdependency on money and living every moment happily and healthily, whether it be with or without money. Most essentially, you will help students to look at their present-moment behavior, in the hopes of some self-awareness and new action in the direction of doing, rather than hoping and wishing that things will eventually work themselves out. Getting a scholarship, a loan, or a good-paying job are skills, and you are prepared to treat these areas as typical counseling concerns, and as problems having to do with learning rather than with socioeconomic status or birthright. You are ready to help them attack their own self-reproaching behavior and to look actively toward being all that they can be in every operational phase of their lives, and this certainly includes the acquisition, the handling, and the absence of MONEY.

LOVE-RELATED CONCERNS

You also expect much counseling focus on *problems related to love.*These include dating, sex, parents, friends, and anyone or anything else that falls into the love category. Dating concerns are real and you know it. "Puppy love" as labeled by unthinking adults, is perhaps the most intense kind of love that anyone ever experiences, and it is loaded with fruit for the counseling group. All kinds of self-defeating thoughts and actions are performed in the name of love. You will help students to put this into a more effective perspective.

Immobilizing behaviors are rampant in the love scene. From dropping out of school, to depression—the gamut of problems is long and wide, and they almost always involve giving others some kind of magic power over oneself, which in turn creates the down moments. You can help students to explore in depth this entire vital area. From sex and birth control, to getting along with those one loves—the possibilities are endless, and always you are going to be counseling rather than having lively discussions. You are determined to help people with problems, rather than to sit around and talk about general topics. All people have difficulties of one kind or another in the love package, and your group will be a place where everyone, or anyone, can deal straight with the present-moment concerns that are messing them up in the receiving and giving of love. Dating will not be treated as an insignificant concern, and "puppy love" will not be the attitude that you bring to these areas. Rather, you are the accomplished professional who recognizes that anyone who is without love in his or her life is an unhappy and potentially troubled individual. Love starts with self-love, and then mushrooms out into giving and receiving love from others all of the time in relationships with the opposite sex, friends, parents and acquaintances. You will help put the students in the group onto the road leading toward complete effectiveness in getting and giving both self-love and other-centered love.

SPECIAL ENVIRONMENTAL CONCERNS

The *problems of living in a specific environment* will also get dealt with in your group. You know that your school is in a special category, and that the students who live or go to school there are having unique problems of their own. Whether it be an inner-city school drowning in poverty, or a school district blessed with affluence; a single ethnic group or a lively integrated mixture; an old school with no facilities, or a modern well-furnished building; a private school or public school; progressive or conservative in its teaching philosophy—whatever it is that stamps it as unique means that you will have unique concerns surfacing in the group. Thus, you are prepared to deal with the special problems of the affluent, the poor, or the in-between, and in each case you make a counseling stand for self-determination and for being emotionally free of control by the environment. You don't accept the notion that just because someone is _____ (you fill in the blank), they are destined to live a life of _____ (fill in again here). You are an agent for self-responsibility, and you don't give up on this stand. Of course, you do not intend to slough off the problems of the _____. You see them as significant, and you deal with them just as you deal with all of the other concerns, from a counseling-for-personal-mastery perspective. But you don't accept the excuse-making that accompanies being a _____, since this is the out that most people are looking for. Your are ready to attack the problems, and to help your students look at their own life circumstances and make decisions about how *they* choose to live their lives, rather than being slaves to an environment they never chose in the first place. Thus, you look at special environmental problems, and you treat them like all the other counseling concerns, as something to understand, develop alternatives to, or change, with the person acting exclusively on the basis of self-directedness rather than other-directedness.

PHYSICAL AND MEDICAL CONCERNS

Finally, you are well prepared to counsel about *physical and medical considerations* if they should appear as a concern of someone in the group. You will not avoid talking about "tough stuff" in this area. Physical handicaps—if they are a concern and if the individual wants to work on accepting and overcoming them —will be a most appropriate area of counseling activity. Similarly, any diseases, infirmities, or physical limitations can be a fruitful area of counseling exploration. Certainly the problem of obesity is not one that can be overlooked in counseling with young people who suffer from this social and physical stigma. You are not going to embarrass anyone, yet you know the folly of ignoring or over-looking something that is vital to self-development. You are going to hear concerns voiced about all kinds of physical and medical labels—clumsiness, short stature, acne, crooked teeth, even bad breath. You'll hear about asthma, and being bowlegged, about hypochondria and lack of energy, about food faddists and drugs, the list is endless. You'll treat them like all counseling group data, as concerns that must be dealt with from the perspective of understanding the self-defeating behavior, and then working hard at becoming a more complete and effective person. The physical nature of the individual is something that he or she carries with them wherever they go, and young people are notoriously abusive toward each other on physical attributes. Small breasts, pimples, overweight, crossed eyes—these are the labels that get attached to others, and they can be hurtful if the individual doesn't know how to sift through these labels and place the kind of insignificance on them that they warrant. The social ostracism which gives rise to neurotic fear is going to be vigorously attacked by you in your counseling activity. The ears are in the self, and if one attaches little or no significance to the labels, and doesn't fear being disliked, then the individual is on the road to self-fulfillment.

But—and you are aware of the importance of the but—students give others great powers, and they don't know (but you do) that no one can hurt anyone with labels, that it is the individual himself who does the hurting by letting others categorize him. Learning to accept oneself without complaint is one of the touchstones of the personally masterful person. Even though the temptation to feel depressed is often overwhelming, and the "need" to be approved is neurotically omnipresent, still one must work at liking self, at being healthily indifferent to the opinions of others. You, in your infinite wisdom, are aware of this and will help your group members to work at being in charge of themselves, at seeing that the judgments of others are just that: the judgments of *others*, not one's own.

That concludes your initial list of concerns that you visualize as being the content of group counseling. You are ready to face your counseling group, in that you are adequately prepared at least to predict what will take place in that mysterious cavern called group counseling. You've done your homework, and you have anticipated group member behaviors all the way from typically arising emotional and personal concerns, to the problems and difficulties inherent in a school setting, problems both academic and school-related but not necessarily curriculum-oriented. You are the masterful anticipator, because you have been thorough in preparing yourself for this venture. You have looked exhaustively into the kinds of behaviors that predictably will surface, you have predisposed yourself to act effectively and successfully in group counseling. For you are well aware that to tread into uncharted waters with little or no knowledge of what to expect, while it may be exciting and adventurous as a strategy for living, is indeed foolhardy as an approach to such an important professional responsibility as counseling and helping to shape people's lives. You do not wish to be constantly consulting your intuition when in the counseling group; rather, you use your awareness and homework on anticipated group member behaviors to weather storms that would otherwise sink the novice sailor who fails to prepare for any contingency. You are now ready to move into the vital area of helping group members to set and achieve personal goals for themselves. Read on for a look at this important goal-setting process in group counseling. It is your *last preparatory* step before plunging into your first counseling session with a group.

6

Before Your Debut:
You Will Learn to
Chart Group Member Paths

GOALS! GOALS! GOALS! You are going to emblazon this term on
your group counseling consciousness. You are going to think of
goals at all times while taking on the role of group counselor. You
will live, breathe, and think in terms of goals. For you know too
well that without goals, counseling is practically impossible. The
name of the game is changing behavior, and you are keenly aware
that behavior has little chance for success if the person is without
objectives or places to land after the trial behavior. You are going
to master the art of goal-setting as a group counselor. You will
never let a moment go by in the group in which you don't consider goals. Helping people work toward being more effective,
that's your mission, and without goals, the mission is aborted
before it even gets off of the launch pad.

You are working hard at the goal-setting process. You have
many unanswered questions about just how to go about setting
goals, even though you know that this word "goal" will become a
kind of watchword in the group. You will never hesitate to bring

it up in the group. Any piece of behavior that is not growth-producing for any individual will be labeled in terms of goals for that person. You aren't afraid to use the term, to get everyone thinking about goals. And you, craftsman that you are, will indeed chart group member paths in the direction of new behaviors or destinations. You are going to be an advocate for thinking about goals in the group. Always, you label behavior this way, because to practice group counseling without goals is like kissing without lips, or sauer without kraut—plainly illogical. Without goals, you are engaging in discussions and rap sessions. You have conversations. When you introduce the notion of goals, you begin to see that you are advocating becoming something *different*, and this is what separates out group counseling from all of the other human social groups. Goals mean that you work toward being better, toward a new destination, and this is indeed the business of group counseling. You are ready to make your counseling group an exclusively goal-oriented experience.

You recognize that goals can take many forms, and that long-range global goals are not even a part of your thinking as a competent professional. Any behavior that is not self-enhancing is ready for the goal-setting process. Johnny gets nervous when he speaks, Mary speaks for Tom, Jerry always says "we feel," Sally is uncertain about challenging anyone, Mercedes is always silent and doesn't like it, and on and on they go. In fact, every kind of behavior that you've read about up until now, in each of the preceding five chapters, is loaded with opportunities for goal-setting. Thus, you must tattoo your brain with the letters G O A L S, and always be thinking about helping individuals to set them as you finalize your preparations for your group counseling professional debut.

You remember, from the extended definition of group counseling and the attendant assumptions related to effective group counseling practices, that goals in group counseling will take on individual rather than a group objectives. You are debunking the silly notion that a group goal is a possibility in a psychological helping group. You remind yourself that everyone is unique, that each person comes to the group with his or her own set of difficulties and areas of concern. Everyone is not the same in your group, so you will guard yourself against coming up with anything so absurd as a goal that fits everyone equally. You remember that *self*-determination is the curriculum here in your counseling group, and that to subjugate each person in favor of a larger goal is a violation of your own stated objectives. If you must have a group goal, try this one, which is mildly acceptable: to help each person set and achieve their own personal goals.

At no time will you make the group more important than the individuals in the group. You are careful to avoid using the *we*, as you recall from your own interventionist strategies detailed in the previous chapter. You help people to think in the *I*. All goals are for people. While you certainly accept the notion that several people might have a similar or even an exact same goal, you do not make it a group goal, since to do so is to accept the folly that the group can be counseled, and grow, and flourish. You are constantly reminding yourself that the "business of group counseling is counseling individuals in groups." You know that virtually all classroom groups are group-goal-centered. The committees, teams, panels, societies, and clubs are social structures which have group objectives as a reason for their very existence. But your counseling group has individuals in it, individuals who function each day in their own existential loneliness, and who must learn that the way to achieve all the things that you have mastered in your case for group counseling in the schools is by working on the "self." Goals, yes, absolutely and regularly, but never do they take on any exotic flavor, other than to be for individuals who can work at carrying them out in their own unique ways.

The group does not exist! It has no life of its own, and at the termination of the counseling process, it will cease to be a helping unit. But the individuals will go on living their lives, and to the extent that each member has set and worked on specific individual goals, the counseling group you are leading will either be effective or be a flop. However, if you have fostered an environment in which everyone likes each other a lot, if you have become a cohesive and friendly unit but no one has grown individually to the extent of functioning more effectively in life, then your group has served no purpose.

Criteria for Effective Goals

Well, you've begun to look at the importance of goal-setting, and you see that the goals are going to be individual rather than collective in nature; now you must look hard at the *criteria* for setting effective goals within the counseling group. You begin by making a checklist for each and every goal that you will help your group members to set.

• *The goal will always be mutually agreed upon.* Here you are keenly aware of the need to avoid imposing your own goals on someone who might not even buy them, let alone have the capacity for carrying a goal to fruition. You are careful to help the individual begin setting his or her own goals. You will avoid taking over and giving a goal, and will substitute for this authoritarian stance one in which you work at helping the group member agree mutually (you and he) to a goal. You will make counseling statements such as:

> "Have you considered any possible alternatives to your present way of acting or reacting? Is it at all possible for you to be different? In what possible ways might you have reacted if you weren't tied to your own characteristic way of behaving?"

These are helpful leads to get the individual thinking about ways of being different and then setting some meaningful goals of his own. Your instinct will be to do it for him, to lay on a goal and then work toward helping him achieve it. But you are going to resist this ploy. You know too well that people strongly resist being told what to do, and so you take a different course of action. If your group member resists thinking in terms of behaving any differently, you will offer suggestions that just might be possible—not for outright purchase, just for speculative consideration. You are interested in helping him grasp at something that might smack of possibility, rather than forcibly laying it on. If you do force it, the group member is likely to accept it readily and then dismiss it just as readily as soon as the session is completed. You will work at making the goals mutal; that is, you will accept them as important and necessary, while your client will see the need for them from his or her own perspective, rather than from yours.

You've seen anxious beginning helpers, who have the "answer" in their own heads and just want the other person to make it a part of his own behavioral self—then all will be cool. But, alas, in the unsophisticated there lies a deep lack of understanding about how people change. They hear it from someone else and it sounds good, but only for the someone else. "Me, I'm different, and that just wouldn't work for me." And so you fight this very thing in yourself at all times. The goal is to be mutual, with the impetus for change most desirably elicited from the thought system of the client. You can help to alter the goal, but you can't productively help at all if you are seeking to impose something that you feel the individual needs.

As an example for all of the criteria in goal setting, let's use the case of *Jack, a group member who asserts that he would like to work at getting over being shy, nonassertive, and nervous in front of other people, particularly in groups.*

You look at your first criterion, and recognize that it would be impossible for Jack to accept what you want for him, that for him just speaking up means taking some risks. If you were to act as a novice (which you won't) you would tell Jack to spend sometime next week in talking to others, to make some phone calls, and to ask some questions in class during the week, then to report back on his success to the group at the next session. But you avoid imposing goals, and work at getting Jack to look at some possible alternatives to his behavior, and if he can't even visualize them, then perhaps you make a suggestion that he might like to work on his shyness right here in the group before trying new things out in his own fearful world. You then suggest one possible goal, which is that Jack talk to someone in the group whom he regards fearfully. If he can't do this, then you can assume the role of a significant other, and help Jack to deal more effectively in his own world by using the principles of role-working. You are working at getting Jack to come up with his own goal, or at least one that he feels is possible for him, by having him perform the new behavior right in the group. In this way, you help him to see that he can be successful in this area, and that the goal is his own. You studiously avoid setting such goals as self-assurance and extraversion, since these are goals that you yourself would like to impose on Jack. You strive to "mutualize" his goals, to have them flow first from Jack's own limited perceptions of how he might indeed be different. Your own goal will be to help Jack to understand his fears and see that they proceed from approval-seeking, fear of failure, other-directedness, and disasterizing of the highest order. But you can't expect him to grasp such crucial understandings and work on them effectively, if you simply give him assignments, while ignoring his need to set his own goals, or at least to play a role in the goal-setting process.

• *All group counseling goals must have a high degree of specificity.* You know about the futility of global goals. "I am going to find myself, I am going to like myself better, I am going to eliminate shyness." Such resolutions are useless as goals, in that they lack specificity; one can never know if, when, how, or why one has "found oneself." The tendency to set global goals is ever present in your group, however, and you must guard doggedly against this temptation. You know that any goal that lacks specificity cannot be carried out, and you are not interested in having your group members set goals just for the hell of it, or to appease some fanciful desire on the part of you or anyone else in the group. Nope, you are a spokesman for getting goals down to specific pieces of sequential behavior; thereby you help assure some degree of success in the achievement of the goals.

A broad goal is an escape, and you know it well. To say that I am going to be "better" is to say nothing at all. Yet, group counselors use these kinds of goals as a cop-out for getting down to specific goals which can then be looked at and carried out in indirect fashion. You will not succumb to this habit. You are going to help each person in the group, not only to set mutually agreed-upon goals, but to put them in terms that are as specific as you and the clients can make them.

In the case of Jack, you are well aware that simply to state as a goal the elimination of fear, anxiety, and shyness is indeed a non-specific approach to the business of goal-setting. Rather, you help Jack set a beginning goal and then refine and expand on his goals in later sessions, as he develops skills and attacks his own personal fears. Thus, you first work on getting Jack to work on his goals in the group, and then you help him set a specific goal for the between-sessions time period. Something like:

> "Next Friday, in math class, at precisely 2:05 PM, you can raise your hand and ask one question of your teacher, regardless of what else is taking place."
>
> Or: "You can go to the shopping center on Saturday afternoon and make an assignment not to leave until you have asked three questions of total strangers, regardless of the absurdity of the inquiries. Also, you can practice the questions right here in the group before you go out there.
>
> Or: "You can make a telephone call to a girl you've wanted to date and just make a point of talking for a total of four minutes before hanging up. Anything beyond four minutes is to be counted as surplus positive anti-shy behavior."

The list is potentially endless; the goal is so specific that Jack fully comprehends what it is that he is going to do, when, how, why, where, under what circumstances, and at precisely what time. These are initial goals, and they can become more general later, but in the beginning of the goal-setting process, careful attention must be paid to the specific nature of each and every goal that group members set and act upon for themselves. You guard religiously against the fuzzy, global goal-setting that characterizes most helping efforts. You are a proponent for goals that work.

• *Group counseling goals must be relevant to the self-defeating behavior of the goal setter.* You are going to be helping many young people in this goal-setting activity, and you must always be on guard against helping students set goals that are completely unrelated to the self-fulfillment and self-enlargement that they are seeking. The goals must be pertinent. They must have utility and practical application in the life of your group member, or else goal-setting will turn out to be an exercise in futility and frustration. Goals without relevance can turn the group members off faster than almost any bungling you might visit on the group as a result of your own inexpertise. You must help the group members to identify the things that are getting in the way of personal mastery, and then specifically set pertinent goals for achievement. Many of the members in your counseling group will want the goal setter to try all kinds of new things, and much of what they ask will be essentially irrelevant to the accomplishment of the individual's stated objectives. Group members will constantly barrage each other for non-helpful data, and then expect the individuals to work at goals in these areas. You are the watchdog against such practices occurring in your group.

Jack wants to work at this shyness in some specific, relevant way. Others in the group, or even Jack himself, might think about their shyness in terms of irrelevant goals (dressing differently, smiling more, or speaking up more at home). You know that Jack must actively work at initiating any self-enhancing behavior on his part. He must speak up in groups and get a feeling for doing it, rather than avoiding group settings. He must talk to strangers and see that he can, in fact, overcome his fears and inertia, and he must take risks with girls and see that he isn't a nerd even if he is refused. These are the areas of Jack's floundering and self-defeating behaviors, and you are going to ensure that any and all goals that Jack sets for himself as targets for the new Jack are going to be pertinent to the stated objectives that Jack has for himself, as well as to that grand objective which you ultimately envision for him, that of being a totally self-reliant, assertive individual.

• *Group counseling goals must be achievable and success-oriented.* Once again you remind yourself that nothing succeeds like success. While you do not equate failure in behavior with failure as a person, you nevertheless recognize the futility of sending a novice out with a goal that he is guaranteed to fail at, and then expect him to want to continue in the process of failure-oriented goals. Your initial goals are loaded in the direction of succeeding. You will not permit anyone to leave your counseling group with a goal in mind that is doomed before it is tried. You load the dice in your favor in this area. The goal is achievable. You not only check it out in the group to help guarantee the success, but you help the individual to make the first goals so small and success-laden, that a spirit of wanting to try more will soon become inculcated in your brave new client. The goal must be attainable. If the individual goes out and fails, he is likely to tell himself something like this: "I knew I couldn't be different, and here I've gone and blown it. I guess I'm just destined to stay the way I am." These are the internal self-sentences of the person who lives with the notion that failure is bad, and that to fail is evidence of being a bad person. You know your students tend to think this way, and so you are instrumental in working with group members to set their goals so small and achievable that any excesses beyond the stated goals can be thought of as bonuses. This is better than setting an initial goal that requires overreaching effort.

In the case of Jack (using role-working), you first have him approach someone in the group who assumes the role of stranger and have him ask a question. Eventually you help him to set an achievable goal outside of the group, such as those illustrated in the previous two sections of this chapter. You have now guaranteed as nearly as possible that Jack will emerge victorious. If, on the other hand, Jack sets a goal for himself which he is unlikely to conquer (and group members are prone to have big eyes and set large, unattainable goals), then you have lost much of your counseling work. If you ask Jack to make sure that he has three dates for the weekend, and that he has a two-hour conversation with someone at his own initiation, and also plan a party for the following week, then you are going to be trapped by your own enthusiasm for Jack to change. And, believe it or not, Jack will likely agree to such a difficult goal, even though he knows he can't handle it yet, simply because he wants to please you and the group, as well as to be able to come back next week and say, "See, I told you I'm shy and I can't change." You know about this, and thus, despite Jack's and the others' protestations that the goal is too easy, you actively work at helping Jack set attainable, success-oriented goals, and you are well aware of why you are behaving in this professional, goal-setting manner.

• *Group counseling goals must be quantifiable and measurable.* You will avoid having group members set goals that are not measurable. You know the folly of having people set out to accomplish something that cannot be measured, and you will apply this learning logic to your group counseling goal-setting activity. The goal has to be measurable. It must have a quality about it in which the client can say to himself, "There, I did it and I know it is done." Thus, a goal of finding out more about colleges is an unmeasurable goal, simply because it lacks precision as well as specificity. But the goal of talking with three admissions counselors before next Friday, and reading Barron's profiles on five colleges of interest, is quantifiable and potentially measurable. Writing down entries in a log when feeling angry, saying how many times and when, is working toward a measurable goal. To the extent you are able, you work at helping students to set goals they can measure.

In Jack's case, it would be foolhardy to have Jack leave the group with a goal of "talking more with girls." On the other hand, a goal whose success he can measure is one in which Jack is enjoined to specify how many times he will initiate conversations, what he will record in his log, what times he will call, even the number of words he will speak if he is chronically and depressingly hangbackish with girls. The measurement of the goal is crucial to Jack's acceptance of the fact that he is indeed changing and growing personally. If he feels that the measured goals are successes for himself, then he can partake of much more in future counseling. If he can't measure his successes, or doesn't know how to measure them, then he will be in a fog about what he is doing—even if he is living more effectively than before he got into that counseling group you are leading so expertly.

• *Group counseling goals must be behavioral and observable.* You are going to work very hard at keeping all goal-setting in the behavioral realm, that is, in observable terms. Someone must be able to look at the goal and then observe that it has been accomplished or that it needs further refinement. The goals that are not behavioral and observable will undoubtedly get passed over in your group member's head. To make a goal that cannot be translated to behavior is to reinforce your client's cop-out behavior. You realize that group counseling is the place where everyone is working on changing their old, self-defeating behaviors and working at becoming different in a more productive vein. And thus you are committed to helping each step upward toward self-actualization by stating and carrying out goal-setting in behavioral observable terminology. A goal that lacks behavioral referents is, as you well know, an exercise in mental masturbation. Without being able to observe their progress, your clients will find it difficult even to assess the progress that they are making or failing to make.

Going back to Jack, a goal in which Jack cannot observe his own progress is worthless. Thus, if you help him set a goal that is designed to make him feel better, or is specified in nonobservable terms, such as getting better or being more effective or taking a risk, then it will be impossible for Jack to look at himself and see if he is growing in this whole shyness area. He needs to observe his behavior, and to have others who can help him to do the same, and you will work diligently at ensuring that all of Jack's goals, whether they be mental or physical, are contracted in specific behavioral terminology, thereby avoiding any and all confusion in his goal-accomplishment world.

• *Group counseling goals are "back-repeatable" and "understandable."* You are a counselor who values the genuine meaning of "understanding." You know enough not to impose your own ideas on others or to assume that just because someone has agreed with you, they in fact understand you in any meaningful way. You are going to translate this maturity of human understanding into your goal-setting work as a group counselor. You see and value the need for each individual in the group to have mutually agreed-upon goals, and to fully comprehend the complex reasons for the goals. You are a proponent of self-understanding in your own counseling philosophy, and you don't let the understanding process stop when you get into goal-setting. Recognizing that it is very easy to get young people to agree to a goal that has been suggested to them, you alertly avoid having others (including yourself) set goals for anyone. You are involved in the process, yet you make it a matter of professional ethics to ensure that any goal, small or large, is fully understood by the client before he or she launches into attempting new and strange behavior for the very first time.

You know that the only way to ensure that self-understanding has taken place, is to help the client articulate the goal in his own terms, along with the rationale for the goal. This is crucial if the goal-setting process is to have any lasting value to the individual. The reason for the goal gets stated by the client, not in your terms, but in her own language and in such a way that it is fully comprehensible to others in the group. You facilitate this kind of group member interaction. You encourage members to ask questions which get at the *why* of the goal, and you also incite the "goalee" to give back the goal in his own terms. Thus you are a supporter of complete self-mastery in the why's and how's of the goal-setting process. You persistently challenge yourself to be the master of effective helping in goal-setting, and without client self-understanding of the goals, then you will be breaking your cardinal principle of being a helper rather than an imposer of your own values and attitudes.

You look back at Jack in your group. He is painfully shy and fearful, and you want to help him set fully effective goals, based upon the solid criteria you are presently reviewing in your mind. But the "understanding" dilemma is most perplexing. "Does he understand what I'm driving at? Does Jack know why he is being moved in the direction of new behavior? Can he give it back to me here in the group in his own words?" These are your self-challenges, and you work hard at helping him to do it. Interventions and goal-setting statements such as:

> "Jack, why do you suppose I am encouraging you to act differently in groups? Or, "Can you state precisely what it is you are going to work at this week, and why?" Or, "Jack, you seem to be resisting trying new behaviors, what do you think you get out of holding on to the old Jack?"

These, and hundreds like them, are intereventions designed to help Jack see for himself, to state in his own language, what the goals are about, why they are being spurred in the group, and what he can get out of the new goal-directed activities. If Jack cannot state them, or explain the why's behind them, then the goals are indeed useless and you need to move back in the group counseling process to further exploration and self-insight before getting into the action-express part of counseling, which involves the setting of, and trying out, of goal-oriented activities. Jack must see in his own head, and be able to give out consciously, the entire rationale for the goal-centered activity. Without it, all of the previous criteria for effective goal-setting are without personal utility for Jack.

You Become an Effective Goal Setter

Well, now you should feel better. You have detailed the criteria upon which you are going to pursue this "charting of group member paths and destinations behavior." You see them in print. You can check yourself off on your goal-setting activity, and measure your own progress in goal-setting (you do have a goal to be effective at facilitating goal-setting) on your own criteria. Here they are in a convenient little checklist. Where are you at each session in this critical area of goal-setting? Are your goals, and those you facilitate in the group—

> high on mutuality?
> specific in nature?
> relevant to the self-defeating behavior?
> achievable and success-oreiented?
> quantifiable and measurable?
> behavioral and observable?
> back-repeatable and understandable?

These are your delectable seven. You will think of them often as the myriad of student concerns surface in your group. Jack will be there in a multitude of forms, and you will always be asking yourself these seven questions as you seek to help others set goals for themselves that ultimately will result in them becoming more self-fulfilled and higher and higher on the ladder of personal mastery. Like any professional, you know that you need to have hard-core criteria to evaluate yourself. And in counseling, without goals there can be no helping. You now have the criteria in your head and in a checklist on your desk, to consult, examine, and evaluate as to how effectively you are delivering the service you are committed to, namely, the fostering of more productive and happier human beings.

You will want to get a lot of practice in goal-setting, since it is going to be your way of life as a professional group counselor. You examined the criteria for setting effective goals, and you have even reviewed some specific examples with your friend, Jack. But you still need some propping-up in this whole area. You will be consciously working on the goal-setting, and as you observe your criteria, you are aware that the goals are specific behaviors that the client or group members must master. But what of your own behaviors in helping the client to be effective in goal mastery? Here you will want to review how you are going to behave in the group as a masterful goal-setting facilitator.

You want to help each individual who has set goals to be able to practice those goals in the group setting. Here your imagination and creative energies are going to be dragged out of the closet, de-rusted, and made ready for application. You will use your role-working strategies. Anyone who is going to work on new behaviors will be given an opportunity to try them out here. Thus, John, who is afraid to talk with admissions counselors, is given practice within the group by having yourself or someone else take on new and exciting roles. Meredith doesn't know how to go about approaching her mother about changing an unreasonable curfew. You arrange a family conference right here in your group. The potentials are limitless. But your own personal goal is to have every goal-setting activity on the part of the group members tested out in the group, evaluated, and demonstrated in an arena where failure is not so threat-laden, and where the individual can learn exactly how to act out his goals in his own life, where it really counts. You are the proponent of making your counseling group into a miniature laboratory, with all the accoutrements necessary for conducting goal-setting experiments. You will be maximizing your success probabilities, and providing each member of the group with invaluable experience in actually participating in their stated hoped-for behavior. You are hereby defied to come up with any conceivable goal that cannot be tested out in the group in some related way. From drugs, to academic difficulties, to the range of emotional concerns, your creative resources will be your most valuable asset as you convert the goal-setting process from the fuzzy and abstract world of verbalizing, to the testable, lived-in world of the doers. You will work hard at providing an atmosphere in the group in which all goals get tried out, critically looked at by the group members, evaluated, refined and retested, before the goal is solidified into a mutual, specific, relevant, achievable, quantifiable, behavioral, and understandable goal for the individual group member's real-world efforts outside of the protective counseling group setting.

So now you have tried out the goal in the group itself, and have reminded yourself once again that *each and every* self-defeating mental or physical behavior is translatable into a *goal.* Your group member has gone out and tried this new behavior, and she is ready to report back on the goal achievement. Once again, you are ready with a repertoire of group leader skills that will facilitate group goal-achievement reporting. (While chapters 7 and 8 deal more in depth with the goal-reporting aspect, nevertheless, a brief overview is relevant here.) The group member leaves the counseling group with a specific set of things to work on before the next session. You will want to begin the next session with a very brief (since you don't want to get seduced into monopoly behavior) report on goal-setting progress. This report will focus exclusively on the group member's (1) new thinking, (2) new feelings, (3) new behavior, and finally (4) his or her continued commitments to upgrade the goals and make them more challenging in light of the longer-range goals.

That does it. You are becoming goal-conscious, and you have some established criteria for helping clients to set goals for practicing the goals in the group, and for evaluating the goal-achievement status of the individual members of the group. You are now getting ready for blast-off. Your preliminaries are thoroughly and meticulously tucked away. You've examined yourself and your fears, and you have laid the groundwork in your school for a schoolwide acceptance of your group counseling efforts. You've assessed your own behavior as a counselor who functions exclusively as a one-to-one helper and have made the decision to get off your duff and become a truly effective counselor via the group approach to the delivery of your services. You've also made some decisions about the group leadership behaviors you are going to have to master in order to become as fully functioning as possible. And you have a complete checklist of specific group counselor behaviors by which you will constantly assess your competency development. You have also fastidiously examined what you are going to expect from your group members as they sample the group counseling goodie bag for the very first time. You are well prepared for their questions, their reservations, their qualms, and the multitudinous roles and self-forfeiting behaviors that they will exhibit. Finally, you have looked hard at the goal-setting process, and once again come up with a checklist of criteria for personal effectiveness in this vital area of group leadership. You are ready. You've done all of your homework, and now you are in the room, meeting your group of anxious students for the very first time. You are about to start, and this is how you are going to do it, while you yourself continue on your unflappable path of effectiveness in group counseling. Let the curtain rise. This is how you begin. . . .

7

Your First Group
Counseling Session

WELL HERE you are. You are walking into the room and your group is awaiting the very first session. You have been complete in your thoroughness about preliminaries; the room is arranged, the students have been given permission to attend, and you are alive with anticipation about inaugurating the project you have so carefully planned. The group members have convened, and you have very cautiously examined what you can expect from the members as they proceed down the path of group counseling. You enter the room and everyone looks to you.

Your first action is to make a well-thought-out opening statement. While you are aware that each individual in the group has some kind of notion about what takes place in the counseling group, you want to be very certain that everyone hears the same opening message from the leader. Thus you are businesslike in your opening statement, and exceedingly clear about what it is that goes on here in this group counseling setting. You also review some of the intake interview information. You will be sure to include a *brief* statement about each of the following eight general areas:

1. The process of group counseling—redefining for clarity
2. What the group leader does
3. Group member expectations
4. Restraining conditions
5. Notes on confidentiality
6. Goal-setting
7. Group counseling payoffs
8. Procedural matters

Your Opening Statement

Your opening statement is directed to the entire group, and this will be one of the few times when you will speak to the group as a whole, other than when explaining procedural matters. You want to begin with a statement that will cool the group members' anxiety about entering the unknown, while simultaneously not reinforcing the tendency for everyone in the very beginning to be conversational, silly, and avoidance-oriented. You notice as you walk in that everyone was talking in small subgroups, and that the activity was almost exlusively conversational in nature. There is no helping activity going on here, you ponder to yourself, and yet you smile inwardly as you reflect on what this group of students will be doing in the near future. You know that they will be helping each other all over the map, and that individuals will be setting goals and exploring ideas that they've never even considered, and yet here now, as you enter the room for the first time, you find them trapped in their typically recurring group behavior, which is "cliquey," inane, and largely superficial. But you don't linger in the anticipation of how much you will teach them in the coming weeks. Now you must attack the reticence, the fear, and the avoidance that is sure to arise. So you look around, sit for a moment, and things get very quiet in anticipation of your first words. You are about to speak for the first time, and you do it with authority, gentleness, and the tone of an expert. You lead off with:

> "Good afternoon" (assuming that you are not meeting before lunch on this day). "We have all had an opportunity to speak briefly before today about the purpose of forming a counseling group. Now that we are all together for the very first time, I would like to review some of the ground rules, and tell you a

little bit about myself, and what my role will be here in our regular meetings. We will be in a counseling group for the next twelve weeks, and that has very special meaning. While all of you have been in lots of groups in your life, you will probably find this group much different than any in your previous experience. We are going to be a *helping* group. Our purpose is not to discuss issues or to have 'rap' sessions about controversial subjects, but rather to help each other. You do not have to be sick or bad to get into a counseling group. Every single person on this planet could benefit from group counseling, if he or she could admit to themselves the possibility that they could 'grow' in some way. Thus, everyone can grow and improve, and to the extent that you would like to become more effective, or 'better' in any way, then you can get something out of this counseling group. No one will be forced to talk about anything they would rather not have mentioned here. Each person has the right to be silent if they so choose, and I will help to make sure that no pressure is put on anyone to speak up against their will. Counseling means helping, not pressuring."

You look around at the group members. They are listening intently, but you still have many more things to say in your opening statement. You are satisfied that you got off to a firm, businesslike beginning. You continue:

"Group counseling is a process in which each person comes to some decisions themselves about how they would like to grow, and then everyone in the group makes every effort to be helpful in having the individuals realize their ambitions. I will be the leader of this group" (and you introduce your co-leader if appropriate) "and in my role as leader, I will be acting somewhat differently than all of you. First, I will never use this group to focus on myself for the purpose of getting help. I am the counselor, and I am here to deliver a service to all of you. Thus, I will be very careful about not getting any counseling help for myself. Not that I couldn't use it in a whole lot of areas, but if I want to be a member of a group, then I will seek out a group in which I am not expected to lead. Secondly, I am a trained counselor." (You now tell a little bit about your professional background.) "Thirdly, as the leader, I will be helping everyone to work on themselves, to be honest with themselves and with each other, and to look toward the possibility of being all that you are capable of becoming. On occasion I will be confronting

and challenging, and I will always be acting in such a way as to
help people in this group to work at becoming as effective as
they choose for themselves at this time in their lives."

Well, you've certainly laid the groundwork. You've mentioned
what goes on here, and you've given a no-nonsense delineation of
your own role, and how it differs from everyone else's in the
group. Now you must make a small statement about expectations.
They are very much with you, and certainly they will be testing
you out on these vaunted pronouncements which you have made.
Of course, you fully intend to deliver on all of your promises. You
continue:

"Each of you has a certain set of expectations about what you
will do here in the counseling group. You are uncertain about
how to behave, and just what it is that you will share. You will
even want to hang back a bit at the beginning, and check *me*
out, and this is quite understandable. You're not even sure if
you want to say anything about yourself here, so you'll be a bit
reluctant in the beginning. I understand this, and I don't expect
you to trust me just because I say that I am trustworthy. I will
work hard at demonstrating that this is a safe, exciting place to
be, and you will become involved not because I tell you to, but
because you will want to gain something for yourself."

Well, that certainly lays it on the line. You have labeled their
feelings, and you have put to rest any notion that you expect everyone to come out of their corners, with their neuroses on their
sleeves, ready to be cleaned up by you. But you must be explicit
about the conditions of the counseling group. So you move on to
your next area of opening statement behavior:

"This group will follow a few very simple rules, and I would
like to lay them out here, and then if anyone feels that they
can't follow them, we can go over the possibilities for amend-
ment here at the beginning, or you may decide that you don't
want to participate, which is, of course, your option to exercise
at any time. We will follow the basic guidelines of all helping
groups, and that is to avoid putting pressure on anyone to
speak. We will not force anyone to say something *that* they
don't wish to say. Also, we will guard against talking to other
people in the school about what goes on here in the counseling
group. I will personally give you my guarantee, that I will not

inform anyone—(including teachers, principals, or parents)—
about what goes on here without first obtaining the consent of
the group members involved. I expect that everyone here will
also conform to this cruicial guideline. In order to establish
trust and openness, it is important for everyone to feel that no
one is going to go squealing to others about what goes on in the
group. This is a hard, fast rule. If anyone feels that he or she
cannot stick by this, then I would ask them to see me personally after the group, and we can work out a way for you to see
me individually, rather than in a group setting. Confidentiality
is very important. Everyone must be able to feel a sense of trust
in this group, and that is why I make such an issue of it here in
the beginning. You will come to trust me, not because I say I
won't talk to others about what goes on here, but because I will
live it each and every day of my professional life. We'll also
have to work hard at not having everyone talk at once, and to
avoid talking about things that don't relate to us personally
here in the group. For example, we will avoid talking about the
football games, national issues, gabby stuff, teachers and other
personalities who are not present here in the group, and generally just plain old conversational stuff that you usually talk
about in other groups. We will deal with each other, and if no
one feels ready to do that, then I will help you to set some goals
for yourselves, and if everyone chooses to be silent, then we
will have silence in preference to conversations and discussions. In fact, we can expect some silence in the group, and
while you will be uncomfortable at first, you will soon come to
welcome it, and see it as a time for personal reflection. Finally,
we will not run away from emotional areas, although we will
not deliberately try to find the touchy parts of each other's
world. There will be no 'attacking' or planned hostility, but we
will be able to talk about things in ourselves that are tough to
talk about, and we will not run from something simply because
it is 'sensitive' or loaded with potential emotions. Everyone is
here simply because they are here. It is no more complicated
than that. And everyone is entitled to what they are, without
being criticized unduly. We will focus on helping, and helping
is done through goal-setting. You will hear the word *goal* regularly here in the counseling group. Every single piece of behavior that is in any one of you, that doesn't get you what you
want, can become a target for goal-setting. So, I'll be labeling
goals all of the time, and helping you to set some personal goals
for achievement, both here in the group, and outside of the
group. All of you will come to see this counseling group as your

own group. I have no set of specific expectations that you must
live up to. You can deal with a myriad of personal concerns,
and you will see this as a safe, exciting place to be, since we will
be doing something that none of your classroom groups do.
That is, focusing on you as individuals with human difficulties.
There will be no grades, no demands, and no rules of conduct
other than those spelled out. You can use this group setting to
get all kinds of goodies for yourself, and I am committed to
helping you get all that you choose for yourself, by being as
straight and honest with you as I know how to be."

Well, that pretty much covers your opening gambit. You've covered all of the bases, and you are ready to field questions. But
before you open it up, you'll quickly review the few procedural
matters.

"We will be meeting once a week here in this room. I've dupli-
cated a copy of the rotating schedule we'll be keeping, and you
can stow it in your notebooks someplace, to remind you of our
meeting place and time each week. The schedule has been
cleared with the principal and all of the teachers, and if you
run into any difficulties, please see me personally after the
group. My office will be open for anyone who would rather talk
to me personally about anything, rather than talking here in
the group. We will go from the beginning of the period, right up
until the end. If you are absent, there will not be group time
available for filling you in on what you missed. However, you
will be able to talk with any group member about what took
place. Remember, we don't talk to others about the content of
the counseling group, but I encourage you to talk among yourselves privately about the group, and even to decide on some
personal strategies for ensuring that you receive time for getting in on the group counseling activity. We will always sit in a
circle, never behind a table, and you may feel free to talk without ever having to ask for my, or anyone else's permission."

That does it. You've said all that you wanted to say for openers.
You now go on to your last statement which is appropriately laconic—"Any questions?"

You anticipate some questions, and you are prepared to answer
them directly. "How will we know what to say? Who goes first?
Can we ask questions whenever we want to?" The questions will
come, and generally you can be assured that they flow from an

anxiety state about being in an "unknown" atmosphere. You will be reassuring in your answers, and you will assure them that almost all answers will come right out of the activity of the next few sessions. You know that you cannot *tell* them what will happen, therefore you will demonstrate it by carrying on with your first-session strategies. Of course, if you are conducting groups with elementary school children, you will gear your opening remarks to their level, and still send essentially the same message.

Phase one of your first session is over. You have introduced yourself and made a clear-headed statement in the way of opening the very first session. You now seek a commitment from each person in the group, to be able to live up to the few ground rules that you have laid down. You ask each member to publicly state that they can live up to the confidentiality requirements that are so necessary for a smooth functioning counseling group. After you receive your commitment, and you assuredly will, you are ready to begin your opening strategies, and here you have once again been the master of careful planning. You have recognized the importance of making the first session a meaningful experience, and therefore you are prepared with a number of strategies for opening the introductory phase of your group.

THE INTRODUCTION PHASE OF YOUR FIRST GROUP SESSION

You are determined not to hang back and wait for something to happen. You assiduously avoid the "It's your group now, you take it from here" syndrome that characterizes floundering "helping" groups. You are ready with a beginning strategy that will have group involvement built into the process, while simultaneously preparing the group members for getting into the self-revelatory behavior that is a necessary precursor to effective later down-the-pike counseling.

You select one of the four beginning strategies that are thoroughly presented in the Appendix. You have an opportunity to try out your own initiating strategy, and you carefully select one of the following (or you add some more to the list) for openers.

Beginning a group:

• Members introduce themselves

• Members introduce themselves with a first-impressions twist

• Group consensus is taken on where to begin

• Leader provides sentence stem for getting started

As you read these strategies from the Group Counseling Strategies Appendix, you see examples of each, along with a rationale for using any of them in the incipient stages of your group. Each of the strategies has a goal-centeredness about it; you will be helping each and every member make a self-introduction, and at the same time you will identify future goals for working on in the counseling group itself. You are a storer away of data, and you record in your head all of the significant things that each member says about him or herself. Whichever strategy you select as appropriate for your particular group, you have a guarantee that your very first session is not going to be a bust, with everyone just sitting around, stupefied by the strange atmosphere that has been created for group counseling. You get right into the openers. You use yourself as a model for demonstrating facets of the beginning strategies, and you carefully help each member over any real or imagined hurdles they may have in this very first effort. The stutterer, the red-faced hang-backer, the potential crier—all are carefully noted internally, and you don't make a big deal out of it when it crops up. You say, "Thank you for telling us about yourself, and perhaps we'll get back to some of your concerns a bit later in the group." Softly, expertly, you show each person that this is not a fearsome exercise at all, and you also demonstrate that talking about oneself is no simple task, but one which requires skill and practice. You are getting into the business of group counseling, that is, of *counseling individuals in groups*, and in these early exercises you are gathering much data that will be helpful in future sessions, just from the way each member goes through the motions of your introductory exercises. As you read through the exercises and make a decision about which one you'll use (see chapter 9), you select a strategy that will be the most effective icebreaker for your particular students. At any rate, you are ready, armed with not just one, but several options for getting everyone into the business of group counseling right from the opening bell.

THE COUNSELING PHASE OF YOUR OPENING SESSION

You remind yourself here, after the introductions are complete, that this is indeed your very first session, and therefore you want everyone to leave with a firm notion in their heads about what takes place in a counseling group. So, you emphatically decide that some counseling must take place in this first session, and thereby you will have answered operationally the question, What is it that we do here? You are anxious to break down resistance and to build trust within the group. You are aware of the fallacious thinking that explains trust in terms of being evasive and easygoing. You decide that in order for the group members to trust you and this whole group counseling bag, they must be introduced to counseling right from the very beginning. Show that there is nothing hurtful about it, demonstrate that counseling is good stuff, that no one one gets damaged or ganged-up on. You cannot let them leave this first session without at least a taste of this luscious pastry called counseling. You think back to your own first experience in a helping group, the leaders who just waited around, or tried to be sugary, or fumbled about in their own anxieties. You know that you didn't trust them then, and certainly no one is going to trust you if you give more of the same here. You know about the components of trust. Nonevasiveness, honest direct dealings, a genuine desire and *ability* to help, all these are crucial elements. And so, you reason, if this is a counseling group, why should I pretend that it is anything different right from the outset, why make it into a gab group, or a discussion group, or even a let's-get-to-know-each-other-group.

You've promised them that they would be participating in a counseling group, and you intend to deliver on that promise. So, you launch into the counseling aspect of your group right away, fully mindful of the need to have everyone leave the group saying, "At least I know what goes on in our group, and I don't have to wonder what in the hell am I doing here, and why did I ever get myself sucked into this." There will be no sour taste in the mouths of your group members, nor will there be a sense of wonderment about returning the following week, because you, in your good judgment, have demonstrated the counseling part of your group counseling adventure, right from day one.

You are now finished with the preliminaries, and the exercise itself was one in which each individual in the group said something about him or herself. In those introductions, you are scrupulously aware of goals for everyone. In fact, you helped the individuals in their introductions by asking them questions about themselves which were designed to help them talk about themselves in future-goal terms. You remember some of the questions you asked to the introductees. Are you a loving person? Are you shy? Would you label yourself as independent? Do you get along with people who are different? Do you need friends? Are you fearful? Can you laugh easily?—an endless list that came from the group members themselves. You hypothesized certain things about group members that were based on hunches, you asked questions based on intuitions you had, and you got the individuals into the goal habit simply by asking, after each negative or potentially self-defeating trait, "Do you like that about yourself?" But you let it drop then. You didn't pursue it. Effective planner that you are, you stored the data away for later use, and kept mental notes on each group member and how they might work at some goals for themselves.

Well, whom do you start with? You want to help someone to get some counseling in this first session, but who? You scan the group and select a person who seems to be ready, an individual who seems unafraid and a bit talkative. But you are looking for more than loquacity, you are looking for a readiness level evidenced by a lack of intimidation. You want to start off by having everyone observe, and participate if possible, in a session that is non-threatening but certainly informative about the process of group counseling. You select the person, the one individual who seems to have some clear goal in mind. Perhaps you noted someone who speaks in a muddled way, meandering all over the map and you'd like to help that person become a clear, concise communicator. You can ask the individual who speaks in such a fashion, if he or she would like to improve in this direction. You can point to someone who showed no hesitancy in bringing up a concern, say, about making it in school. You will not go for the shy person, or the easily embarrassed. You know enough to let them observe for a while, to see the process, and then to ease into the counseling process.

Well, you've selected your individual to begin the group counseling process. You've used the criterion of readiness based upon your intuition and on the behavioral data that have been revealed up until now. You begin by asking the individual (we'll use Yolanda for illustration) to state her concern in goal-setting language, identifying the self-defeating behavior as specifically as possible. Of course, you know that they will find this very difficult to do, so you are prepared to help them. After they try, you say something like, "Perhaps I can show you what I mean. Your immediate goal is to be able to _____," and you lay it out in behavioral terms, somewhat general terms at first, and later in far more specific terms (as in the chapter 6 criteria).

Well, here you are, off and running in your group counseling activity. While you are cognizant of the need to have some counseling take place, you also want to get some group involvement in the beginning. You know that you will be much more active in the first few sessions, simply because no one else in the group knows what to expect or how to behave in a counseling group. You must be a model, and then teach others to act in effective helping ways. So you are not surprised when the predominant activity in the group has you as the focal point. You know this will change very soon, as you demonstrate effective helping interventions and counseling activity. But, nevertheless, you want to avoid a simple individual counseling session as the sole activity for the initial group meeting. But you have been successful up until now, and you remind yourself that the counseling activity is under way, and that everyone present is seeing some effective counseling taking place. You then move your first client into the exploratory phase of counseling, and here you get the others in the group involved. You find out a little bit about your first participant, where the behavior takes place, how long it has been a problem, whom he lives with, how he is managing in his everyday world, how good he is at loving himself, what his self-images are, how his aspirations are lined up, and so forth. You invite group members to ask *meaningful* questions, to test hypotheses, to involve themselves in the exploratory phase. When this is finished, a window on the client's world will have been opened. This will not take the form of an interrogation—of this you are certain. When group members get into firing-line activity, you will quickly and firmly label it "interrogation, gestapo behavior." You will always label any ineffective group member behaviors right away, and then you will be guaranteeing that they will become extinguished early. You ask specific group members (never the *we*) to find out anything they would like to know, and you are consciously mindful of the need to get data onto the floor, in order to help you in later counseling activities with the client or clients who have similar concerns.

You've gotten a window on your client's world, and he or she is not feeling the pressure of having to defend. You know that people like to talk about themselves, and you've capitalized on this in getting out specific data, which can help you to ascertain just how this self-defeating behavior is manifested, when it occurs, with what folks, and how long it has been a part of your client's world. You have scattered answers to these issues, and now you are anxious to move into the gutsy part of the group counseling activity. You march onward to the most difficult element in the counseling process—SELF-UNDERSTANDING.

You want your client (and any others in the group who are experiencing similar, self-defeating behavior) to be able to answer the two questions: What do I get out of this behavior? and, Why has the behavior persisted in me? These are the toughies. You will now take your helper on an excursion toward self-understanding, and you will help the other group members to do the same. You will stay with this until you have some idea that he or she understands this psychological maintenance system for the behavior. Here you will be on guard for the overly anxious group members who will want to give advice and tell the individual what to do. You will label such premature-action behavior as unhelpful, but not by being challenging or direct. A simple turning to the client, and asking, "Do you think that piece of advice is helpful, Yolanda?" will generally suffice. Yolanda has thought of the alternatives before, she just hasn't understood why she behaves the way she does. You are going for a diagnostic insight. You know that every piece of human behavior is caused, and that you want to have your clients see this in themselves. The neurotic rewards that they receive are your goals for understanding.

You work in this self-understanding area, probing with questions such as, "What do you think you get out of this behavior? I wonder why it doesn't go away if it doesn't serve any useful purpose?" These are your probes for getting at self-understanding. You know that many group members will become impatient here, since they are conditioned just to give answers, and to tell someone how to be different. But you will persist, and help to remove any advice-giving attitude in your group. While you may not ever achieve complete client self-understanding, you will at least stay with it until the individual is able to give back some degree of self-understanding about his self-defeating behavior. If the problem is approval-seeking, they should be able to see that pleasing others is easier and less risky than working on themselves and believing in themselves. If it is procrastination, you will help the client to verbalize to the effect that putting it off is a form of self-delusion, and that one will never work at changing so long as one tells the self, "I'll eventually get it done." The diagnostic segment here is crucial, and you will be a firebird of activity in moving group members toward self-insight early on, in the very first group session.

From self-understanding probes and interaction, you will attempt to move into specific goal-setting, and here you have done your preliminary homework, as reviewed in chapter 6. You will attempt to help your client(s) specify, in attainable terms, what some alternatives there might be to their present self-defeating behaviors. You will make every effort to keep goals uppermost in your counseling activities, and certainly the exploration of alternatives is a necessary precursor to actual labeling of goals. You can make leader interventions here, which will help the recipient of the group attention to think in new ways. For example, you will lead into goal-setting by asking, "Yolanda, can you think of any alternatives to the way you react to your father? Not that you are prepared to carry them out, but just imagine 'different' ways that a person might react?" This kind of a probe will get her thinking about a new Yolanda, rather than just being stuck with the old. Here you are going to involve the entire group in your preliminary goal-setting activity. You ask group members to state aloud a possible alternative way of reacting, and perhaps each person can give Yolanda his or her own version of a new tack. You, of course, are not in any way trying to sell Yolanda on a given new strategy, but just to expose her to as many alternatives as possible. You realize, that Yolanda is not ready to buy anything but her old ineffective behavior at this point, but the self-examination that must accompany the consideration of new and unique reaction patterns is what you indirectly strive for in the group. You know that the more Yolanda sees new strategies, the more likely she is to give them some thought later, as she works at being a more effective person in her relationship with here father.

You work at the goal-setting, using your seven criteria in chapter 6. Now you are ready, here in this first session if time allows, to demonstrate trying-out behavior right here in your group. If time is short, you will continue next week, but at least *some* counseling has taken place, and you have met your own goal of having everyone in the group exposed to the what-do-we-do-here of group counseling—which is to *help*, or *counsel*. You are making the group into an experimental laboratory at this point, and you use any of the strategies in the Appendix for giving Yolanda a "doing" experience in becoming different. Your goal is to involve the group in the process of helping, from an experiential point of view. You plan your strategy, and then get your client(s) going in the process. You have a multitude of doing exercises available to you. Perhaps you will become Yolanda, and she can be her obnoxious father; you can role-reverse all over the map, having many other group members take part in the role-working activities. Or, you have Yolanda take a risk, and help her confront all the members of the group who are separately playing the role of Yolanda's father. Perhaps you turn the group into a family discussion, or you get involved in a letter-writing exercise in which Yolanda talks directly to her father about the things she wants him to know, speaking directly to him in the group. See the Appendix for a wide selection of various group leader strategies for getting down to the doing aspect of group counseling.

After you have had some time at working on new behavior in the group, you are ready to help your focusee (Yolanda) to set some behavioral psychological homework for herself, between now and the next group meeting. Once again, you remind yourself of the firm goal-setting criteria that you detailed in chapter 6. You want to ensure some success for Yolanda, and so you gently move her in the direction of firming up some behavioral efforts for her to pursue outside the group. You ask, "Can you think of anything that you can do this week that will help you to work at becoming better in this whole area?" The groundwork is laid and now you will drag out your criteria, and help the goal to get narrowed down to the achievable level that is necessary for effective goal-setting and assigning of psychological homework.

There, you've done it. While it has been hurried, you have at least demonstrated what takes place here in group counseling, and you've had a beautiful introduction for each of the group members present today. You don't chastise yourself if you didn't get completely through the counseling aspect of your first session, but you know that you at least got into the process, and no one will leave your group today and ask, What do we do in group counseling? You have artfully and deliberately provided the answer. You haven't explored in appropriate depth the various stages of group counseling, and how you intend to function within each, but in chapter 9 you will read a more detailed analysis of the ongoing group counseling process. For now, you are satisfied that you have launched your program on a path of effectiveness for all concerned, and you know, but really know, that Yolanda is going to do some heavy thinking about her own world, and that effective change is inevitable, given the behavioral orientation of your group counseling self-understanding, the group try-out, and the out-group assignment that is virtually guaranteed of success.

CLOSING YOUR FIRST GROUP SESSION

But it isn't quite over yet, even though you have had a pinpoint accurate launch. You still must close the first session. Here you are going to follow the same guidelines you employed in opening the session. You will be clear, direct, and very professionally businesslike as you put the wraps on session number one. You have finished with some kind of an assignment (nonimposed) for the focusee(s), and you have a checklist of things you wish to accomplish, just as you did in your opening statement. They include:

1. A brief analysis of the *process* of the group
2. A pointing to resistance as it appears
3. An explanation of your own interventions
4. Reasons why counseling worked and why it didn't
5. A checking-out of who has similar concerns
6. A checking-out of anyone who wants immediate group time
7. A statement about the next meeting time

These are the delightful seven ingredients of your summary of the first session, and you are determined to demonstrate, right down the path, that you are so cooly professional that you are aware of what you are doing at all times, and that in no way are you winging it as leader of this here counseling group.

You begin the closing statement:

"That concludes the first session, but before we adjourn, I'd like to point to the things that were happening in the past hour, and explain why I behaved as a leader in the ways that I did."

Now you are thinking about the process, while you can't give it all back, you have been busy storing away the significant tidbits, and you explain them forthrightly to the group. You continue:

"Perhaps you noticed how quiet it got when I walked into the group in the beginning. All of you were expecting things from me, and your conversations stopped immediately. We started out with my introduction, and then moved immediately into the exercise where each member said something significant about himself. This was tough for many people to do, and the fact that I introduced myself, as an example of how to talk about yourselves, was deliberately planned. I knew that if you saw me talking about myself without pain or embarrassment, and if I demonstrated how to describe yourself without the traditional labels, that you would at least know that it was not an impossible task. The fact that I asked various group members specific personal questions as they were introducing themselves was also planned, since I was trying to get you all thinking in terms of goals for yourselves to use later on in the group. The patterns of silence were uncomfortable for some of you, particularly for you, Sally and Fred, and people found themselves staring at the ceiling and twitching when someone wasn't talking. This is not uncommon, and we will learn to deal with silence here in the group, and rather than being surprised by it, we will expect and often welcome some non-noise behavior. Also, many of you were looking to me to direct the action, and I expected this. Tom, Mary, and Allen, were particularly anxious for me to keep things going. This also will change, as you become experienced in making things happen for yourselves here in *your* group. Finally, when we moved to Yolanda, you George, thought I was picking on her, but actually you were afraid to say anything about it. Many of you tried to get her out of the spotlight by speaking for her, and you assumed that it was a tough place to be and were preparing yourselves for a time later on, when you might be there yourselves. I intervened everytime someone said 'we' or 'us,' and this was also calculated. You remember, George and Tom, you both said it several times. I did this because I am trying to get people to think for themselves, rather than assume that everyone thinks alike just because they are students or in the same age group. Finally, I brought the group into involvement in helping Yolanda work on her concerns, because this is a great trial place where new behavior can be tried out in safety. Then I closed with an assignment for Yolanda, because we are concerned with helping her to be different in her own real world, where it really counts, rather than just here in the group. The group moved from almost asking permission to speak, to a firing-line question-asking phase, and finally into active involvement in trying to help, all in one short hour."

Well, that certainly covers some of the more important process analyses, as well as the interventions that you made while leading this first session, and you even pointed to some of the "protective resistance" that was present in the group. A statement about why things work is also in order. How about:

> "You'll notice that when I shifted the focus from everyone talking about themselves, to focusing on Yolanda, she was able to get some help. When she first started talking about her father, you Mike, said something about your own father, and I immediately asked you if that was helpful to Yolanda. This shifted the focus back to her, and helped her to get some help from the group members. Had I let it continue, perhaps we would have forgotten all about Yolanda, and gotten off to someone else, and then our mission of 'helping' would have been aborted. Of course I remembered what you said about your father, Mike, and some of Yolanda's help will also apply to you, and we will be getting back to your concerns later on."

That certainly explained one intervention, gave the rationale, and showed how you as the skillful leader were thinking all of the time about providing help in the group. Now you want to check out who has similar concerns, and if anyone else received help from the experience that Yolanda just completed. You will not be surprised to learn that staying with one person will be more helpful to everyone than flitting from one to another and getting lots of participation, but little or no growth-producing behavioral insight and change. You ask:

"Is there anyone else in the group who would like to work on something next week?" You are patient enough to wait, and if there are no takers (and later they will be clamoring for group time), then you say: "That's fine, we'll pick up with Yolanda's report next week, and review some of the goals that others have set." No big deal; a simple statement suffices. But you also ask for a show of hands on the question, "Did anyone else receive any help today, as a result of Yolanda's counseling experience?"

You are asking this not for your own gratification, but to demonstrate that people do not have to be constantly talking to get help, and that counseling rather than lots of discussion is the aim of the group counseling activity. The only thing you have to say in your closing is a word or two about logistics. So you finish with, "We will meet in this room, the seventh period, on Wednesday the fifteenth of March. This concludes our first session. Have an effective week."

You've signed off, the students file out, and you sink into a maze of introspection about your blast-off into the exciting adventure of group counseling. You now have your inauguration behind you, and you toss the results about in your swirling head.

Reviewing Your First Session

While the session is over, certainly you have some post-session activity to consider, and you do that as soon after the termination time as possible, even the next hour if you can spare the time. You are ready to review, and to prepare yourself for the second counseling session.

If you taped the first session, an analysis of the tape is definitely in order. You want to take notes on what took place, and (with your co-leader if you have one) listen to the session for the bevy of things you missed the first time around. You know things were flying fast and furiously for a while back there, and having a tape, or at least a "clinic" with your co-leader, will give you an opportunity to put the data into a meaningful form. You are deliberate about your note-taking, and you keep a file on the group, with reminders of the things that individuals said throughout the entire first session. You introspect, think aloud, and put it down on paper. You want to be accurate in your leader interventions in the future, and the only way to establish connections later on is to know what was said early in the group.

Your post-session activity is contingent upon the presence of a tape recorder, a co-leader, or simply a soliloquy with yourself. But whatever the circumstances, you are going to put down potential goals for everyone in the group immediately after the first group. You note key phrases that individuals made, you specify resisting behavior, fears, nervousness, hang-backishness, and the multitude of roles that the group members slipped into during that first hour. You note the cliques, the possible areas of disagreement, the self-concepts, the confidence levels, the speech patterns, the nonverbal behavior, and anything else that you can think of. You get it down on paper, and then store it away for preparation for the next crucial step in your continuing development as a group counselor, that fateful *second* counseling session.

For now you must rest. You've been a busy beaver on this day, and you deserve to take a break. The preparation, the hard work at learning what to do and what to expect, all paid off handsomely. You first session was a gem, you did it all. From opening with verve and confidence, to an ingenious beginning strategy, right down to the programming of some highly effective counseling—which of course has to take place in anything called group counseling—and then to your careful process analysis and professional closing statement.

You did it well, you even reviewed thoroughly afterwards, took copious notes, and coveted feedback from your recorder and co-leader. Now you rest for a minute or two, and get on with the business of making sure that your next session, which is probably the *most important* of all, goes as beautifully as the orchestrated pearl that you just completed. Your second session is on the board. Get ready for a knock-out effort—this is what separates the tots from the giants. An effective second session is most important, and you know that this is the place where so many fall on their faces, the big letdown after the debut. You are brief about your resting, self-applauding behavior. Read on. Work on.

8

Your Second Group Counseling Session

YOU THINK about the books you've read on actors who have
spent months in preparation for their grand opening, who have
worked assiduously for their "opening night" applause. The luster
and excitement of doing it for the first time are primary mo-
tivators, and then comes the big letdown. You've read about plays
that have opened to raves, then folded shortly thereafter. You recognize that the debut, while significant, can also be a downfall if it
isn't put into its proper perspective. You, therefore, are going to
assign more importance to your second session than you did to
your "opening night." There will be no letdown here, you are going to make your second session even more effective than your
first. Your post-debut depression will not immobilize you, because
you are well aware that group counseling is a longitudinal process,
one in which you must be effective over a period of time, and
each session must be one in which counseling services get delivered.

While every session in your group counseling cruise is certainly
crucial, this second session, in which the members of the group

are coming in high from the first experience, takes on a particularly significant flavor. You must herein demonstrate how totally committed you are to the process of helping. Your group leader skills will be on the firing line, and if you make this session work and the group members leave with an air of excitement about this thing called group counseling, then the remaining life of the group will be a delightfully effective experience, in which the participants will anticipate and willingly cooperate for a meaningful group climate. Thus you set about to make session number two a perk-up rather than a letdown following your opening-night success.

You can really prepare yourself for this session, even more so than you did for the initial group meeting. You have a mountain of data from that very first meeting, and you can go to work on compiling and collating that data for effective utilization in many future sessions. First you review all of the names and specifics about each individual, and record them for ready reference. You will be calling everyone by name from now on, and demonstrating at the same time that you think each person is so important that you've quickly emblazoned their names on your consciousness. The facts that you store about each person are contained in the introductory remarks. You keep copious notes on *everything that the group members mentioned about themselves.* You recall (or listen to the tape for complete recall) that Sammy said he was a troublemaker and always late, and Maryann mentioned that she was not happy but she didn't elaborate, and on and on you go. You will be looking over those initial "I am" statements, and have them at your fingertips for ready reference in the group. These data will be useful in later sessions, when contradictory information comes up, and they will be put to excellent use when you are aiding someone in gaining self-insight.

You then shift to the interaction patterns of the first group session. Here again, you have made notes on *how each individual behaved* in that initial meeting. Michael never said a word, Mary interrupted quite regularly, David spoke for Paul on three occasions, Sally was the "rescuer" when things got too hot for Tommy, she picked it up and tried to save him from the hot seat. Each person behaved in characteristic ways that they use in their everyday lives. You are aware that they implement these communication patterns in their own lives, and therefore it is extremely important to note them outside of the sessions, if you are going to assist the counselees in more productive directions. Your data sheet is growing on that first session. So much transpired that you missed many things while you were in there working, but now you are getting at them. You know that you will become more and more immediately perceptive as you continue to lead groups, but for now you are relying on your excellent hindsight to guide you in analyzing your initial group data. You are hearing things on the tape that you weren't even aware of. You are remembering how you reacted at that moment, and now you are undergoing self-analysis to evaluate if it was the most effective response. But you know also that you can't change what took place, so you determine to use the missed opportunities of the first session and to employ your skills in the second. You are beginning to see that you have enough data from this initial session to use for a series of second sessions, so you must be selective about which data you use in the upcoming group. Thus far, you have reviewed the communication patterns of everyone in the group, as well as the personal self-statements, all of which you will want to have at your side in the second group. You look this information over, and then go on to a third category of initial group data.

You want to *identify your resource people*, as well as all of those individuals who fit into other roles in the first session. Who seemed most open to the entire group counseling scheme? Who are the potential "helpers," those individuals who seem to have a deeper sensitivity and willingness to go after self-defeating behaviors? Who are the nongullible ones, the young people with perceptiveness who will be your allies in future sessions. Who are the laughers, and those who can create laughter? Who seems to be admired by all? Certainly this will be an individual that you will want to work with in the months to come. These are your potential supporters, the people who can make your job as group leader more flowing and acceptable to all. On your note pad of data, you place marks next to those would-be allies of the future. You know that as leader of a student counseling group you will often be the only defender of being different, opposed by a collection of mindsets that want to hang on to self-defeating behaviors. You will increase your effectiveness tenfold by getting to the leaders within the group, by helping them to see your pitch about looking honestly at oneself and all the other things you are trying to do through group counseling. Thus you are very careful in identifying the cooperative resource people.

You will also want to *label the resistance in the group.* Who seemed most fearful and "on the spot"? Who wanted to erect roadblocks to your own goals of the first counseling session? Who was vociferous against working with individuals? Who was projecting reluctance by their introductory remarks? You know that some resistance is a given, and that identifying it and devising strategies for dealing with it are very important right from the very beginning. In your second session, you will want to point to some of the first-session resistance, and label it specifically. Also, when it crops up again and again, you will have ready interventions for helping the resisters to see themselves more objectively, as well as to eliminate the troublesome reluctance of individuals to participate, which can become obstructionism if it isn't labeled and dealt with early in the group counseling activity. Once again, you go to your note pad and place appropriate comments next to the resisters in the group, and you make comments about how you will use this data in your upcoming sessions.

You look over your note-taking behavior, and see that you have been thorough in your preparations for your second session. You've examined the behavior of each group member, and made notes about the significant introductory statements that they made about themselves. You have reviewed each individual in terms of his or her interaction behavior in the first session, and you have looked carefully at the various roles assumed by each group member. Finally, you have identified resource people and those who seem to be the more resistant to the process of group counseling. Your notes look something like this (below) as you make plans for the crucial second counseling session—the one in which you are going to pull out all of the plugs so that no feelings of letdown can permeate your group counseling activities.

On and on you go, gathering data that will be helpful to you and the individual group members in making your group counseling strategies for the future. You are a veritable tiger in collecting your information from your tapes, files, and interaction with your co-leader. Your ultimate objective is to create such a huge potential agenda for the group, that you need never again be concerned about what will happen. In addition, you are vitally interested in portraying yourself as the complete expert in what you do. You want them all to see that you have done your homework, that you recall all of the data, that you store away every bit of information about individuals for future reference in helping, and that you treat the contents of the counseling group as exceedingly valuable

Name	Significant Introduction Data	Interaction Patterns	Roles	Reactions
YOLANDA	Sees self as competent, too organized, worries excessively, father problems, excellent student	Challenged Tom, saw me as strong, defended Mary, a real participant, likes to argue	Intellectual, possible devil's advocate	A good ally, resourceful, likes the group, good leadership potential
TOM	Doesn't like self, weak self-image, lacks confidence, sees self as a troublemaker, no girlfriend, thinks he's unattractive	Hangs back, but wants help, asked to be first in the spotlight, a yes-man in many ways, afraid to confront	Potential isolate, will hang back if allowed, an attention-getter with his shy demeanor	Resourceful, will be a big help, likes talking about self, can demonstrate that this isn't a fearsome activity
MARYANN	Sees self as timid, but strong, thinks she's attractive, but poor at giving love, unsure about college, wants to get married and raise babies, identifies strongly with others	Said almost nothing after first remarks, appeared to be with it, but cautious, rescued Tom once, seemed relieved that she was through talking, and not anxious to get on with focus of self	The shy bunny, possibly a rescuer at potentially embarrassing times, not a leader—yet	She may be very resistant to the overall process, may need some adjustment times, seemed to like it when the focus was on Tom, and appeared nervous about having it shift to her
MARK	A laugher, cocky and outspoken, but sees himself as unsure, deliberate and very much concerned with others' opinions	Very confronting but backed down when confronted by another, seemed to be intimidated by Yolanda and George	The sergeant-at-arms type, also the confronter for attention	Somewhat negative, will need to be cautious in approaching him with goals

and therefore not to be treated off-handedly. You are deliriously preparing yourself for the second and later sessions, with diligent post-first-session analysis and data-gathering behavior.

Writing Your Plans

Now you want to write yourself a plan for the second session, one that is so effective that bombing will be truly impossible, but also one that is so flexible that you can shift gears in the middle without causing yourself any anxiety. You are going into session number two with high potential for success. You are prepared either to implement your plan or to forsake it in the event of developments that call for a reshuffling of your projections. You set about to look for your best alternative.

You know that Yolanda had some very important goals to work on during the week, goals that arose out of the first session, so you will get to those goals very early. But first, you must have an opening for the second session. You carefully construct your opening statement. Then you will go to your notes for any number of possibilities for getting into the second session. You decide to build in flexibility, and therefore you will open with an opportunity for anyone to use the group in any way that they might like. Perhaps someone has thought about something during the week, and would like to get right in there and deal with it; or perhaps others saw what Yolanda did and have decided, that IF—and that is a big if—the right opportunity presents itself, they also would like to get some help. So after your opening remarks, which are detailed below, you will first go to Yolanda's report, and then Plan A will specify that anyone can use the group who would like to. You'll spice up your remarks to show that risk-taking is an important part of group counseling, and thereby you open up the group for anyone who has even considered taking the risk. Plan A also involves some silence, and so you decide that you will allow at least four minutes of silence before you go to Plan B. Under no circumstances will you force or otherwise encourage anyone to participate during this time. You will time yourself to allow the silence, and check out those who are giving it some consideration but who seem to lack the present-moment courage (more data for use in later sessions).

Plan A will be adopted IF—and once again you are religious

about this if—someone voluntarily picks up the ball and runs with it. You also decide that you must allow group members to exercise their own judgment about participation and to facilitate self-direction, and you will use this strategy in later sessions as well. You are providing some opportunity for group members to structure the use of their own time. But if no one picks up on Plan A, you are also prepared to go on with Plan B. Of course, since this is only the second session, you anticipate that group members will be somewhat reluctant and still into testing-out behavior. Plan B involves selecting an individual, suggested by your notes, and helping him or her to set some goals, based upon specimen goals that you have constructed out of your copious notes. These specimen goals include:

Yolanda	Dealing with her organized personality, and the extent to which it gets in her way.
	Working on eliminating worry.
	Being more effective in dealing with her father.
Tom	Helping him to establish confidence by seeing how he puts himself down, especially with girls.
	Dealing with his constantly-being-in-trouble syndrome.
	Helping him to see self as attractive.
Maryann	Working on her shyness and helping her to see it for what it is.
	Her mothering role. Will she be an equal in her own eyes in all of her relationships?
Mark	Unsure about future vocation.
	Get him to see that he uses his clown demeanor as an approval-seeking device.

These and many more goals are possibilities for use in your group. You settle on asking Tom if he would like to talk about the concerns he raised in the first session. You are prepared for him to say no, and that will be it; but you are also selecting Tom because you think he has a readiness to get into the counseling activity without being too threatened by the experience.

So Plan B is firm, and then you go to Plan C. Here you will ask Mark to deal with his clowning behavior, and once again, you are prepared for him to say no. If so, that is okay, but it is quite unlikely, given his initial desire to be in the spotlight. You can even go on to Plan D, E, and F if you choose, knowing that there are literally hundreds of potential goals for the group members, based exclusively on your initial-session data.

There you have it, a prescription for success for the second session. First your opening, then to a report by Yolanda, then to Yolanda herself, if she was left in the lurch the previous week when time ran out, then to your flexible silence-producing (maybe) opening, then to Plan A, B, or C. You have thought through your options and gone into the balttleground fully prepared to be effective. No uncertainty here, you are the master, and your second session is built upon your excruciatingly meticulous analysis of your very first session. You are going to wow yourself with this second-session behavior, and while you will never, repeat NEVER, fall so much in love with your plan that you must follow it rigidly, you will at least have a plan that will keep you from those sinking feelings that so often accompany any activity you pursue, in which you suddenly realize that you don't know where you are, or even where you are going. Not so in this activity. You are not the least bit intimidated about consulting your notes at the beginning, showing that you are also concerned about being good at what you do. Of course, you will not read to your group members, but you will have a prescription for success either fully committed to memory, or noted down for consulting as you deliver your second-session masterpiece.

Conducting the Second Session

You're back again, this week has flown by, and you are about to launch into your second counseling session, filled with the notion that this is truly one of the most significant meetings of the entire experience. Your opening statement is well thought out, and you begin.

> "Welcome back for our second meeting together. Last week, you recall, we introduced ourselves in a completely unique fashion"—here you are mindful that someone new might be present, but you don't go into any harangue about it; you note it, and deal with the new member by asking them to give their name, and drop it there, for now—"and after we did so, Yo-

landa had some goals to work on, but before we get to them, I'd like to review some of the ground rules I introduced last week."

There, you've done it again, a businesslike, formal opening, which allays any self-defeating, gossipy, conversational behavior that might have been present when you walked in. The business of group counseling is counseling, and you have just reinforced that notion. You continue:

"We are here to deal with personal and individual concerns that anyone has. No one here is sick or otherwise weird because of participating in this group. We don't talk about what goes on here with others outside the group, and no one is forced to participate or state anything if they choose otherwise. Are there any questions about what we do, and why we meet?"

You, of course, proceed to answer questions that might arise, but you will not be seduced into making the entire session one of questions and answers, since this would be an avoidance mechanism, to shun the sometimes painful but necessary work of change. After the questions, you make one more analysis statement about your reactions from the week before.

"Last week some group members were a bit nervous about self-disclosure, but everyone introduced themselves and said a little bit about themselves. After the introductions, Yolanda received some counseling help from the group, and she dealt with the concerns she has in communicating effectively with her father, who was seen as occasionally unreasonable and overly demanding. During the session, many members tried to rescue Yolanda, and periodically, people even spoke for her, rather than trying to help her become more effective in this area. This was not a surprise, and it was pointed to as it arose. We then left Yolanda with some specific assignments. Before I go on, I'd also like to remind you that we are here exclusively for the purpose of helping each other. I will label anything that comes up that is not helpful, and will attempt to get us back on the helping path."

There goes a brilliant analysis, brief, succinct, and designed to put the group members in the mood for getting down to the business of counseling.

"Before hearing from Yolanda, I would also like to remind everyone that it is not so significant to analyze what goes on here in the group. The most important measure of our effectiveness is what takes place in your own lives out there, where it really counts. Also, we will be following up between sessions, and looking back on the things that happened in earlier sessions in order to treat this experience as one ongoing activity, rather than as something to start anew each week. So we always follow up, and that is what we move into now. Yolanda, why don't you give us a report of your activities this week in relationship to the goals you set for yourself at the end of last week."

You have led off with your first element in the grand scheme for this second session. You are off and running. But you need to be wary here. A report can turn into a lengthy, meandering excursion if you let it, so stay alert, be sure that the report contains the right ingredients (see below). Help Yolanda to be effective in reporting, instead of wandering all over the terrain, as she may want to do since she doesn't have your expertise in delivering an effective report to the group.

The report back to the group will focus exclusively on Yolanda's new self, and the new things she has tried out this past week. You begin by asking her to relate any new "thinking" that went on in her mind since the last group meeting. You are deliberately focusing on the new thinking, because you realize that the mental process must come first, before anything else. All new behaviors originate with an idea, and that new idea we call *thinking*. You are attempting to get Yolanda more in charge of her thinking and consequently more aware of the ways that are possible for her to think. You ask her about her mental world over the last week, and then you lead her carefully into any new feelings that she has had as a result of her newly organized thought processes. Of course, you realize that feelings come from thinking, and you are going to be teaching this vital lesson in every report that comes back to the group. You are attempting to convey the vital message that one can control his self-forfeiting emotions if he learns to think differently and decides to become less emotionally handicapped. It is a mental decision first. Thus you focus exclusively, in the initial stages of the report, on new thinking and the resulting new feeling states that exist.

After Yolanda has briefly described her new mental and emotional reactions, you focus on any new behaviors that she might have tested out during the week. "How did you behave differently? What were you telling yourself? How did you react?" These are the foci of an effective report back to the group. The focus is on the individual (Yolanda) rather than on her father and all of the others who have exercised some control over her in the past. You deliberately concentrate on the new, learned behaviors that Yolanda has attempted, and thus you show her that *she* is your first concern, not the ways in which her environment reacts to her. She is beginning to exercise control over herself, and in your thoroughness about reporting back to the group, you are teaching her a most valuable lesson, namely, that you can be what you choose, if you reprocess your thinking, feeling, and behavior in ways that are designed to be self-enhancing rather than self-debilitating.

The final leg of your reporting back to the group at the beginning involves a recommitment to the process of becoming a more in-charge person. Here you help Yolanda set bigger and better goals, to work at new mastery behaviors in her life, and to commit herself to growth in this one crucial area.

You are very cautious about avoiding the most common pitfall of the report back to the group, which is the tendency to rehash in the second session the same stuff that was worked through the previous week. Here you are determined to be the active professional. You know that many group members would love for the focus to stay on Yolanda forever, thereby eliminating the risk of their ever getting in there and changing themselves. You are conscious of how easy it is to stay with a verbal member who wants to share her new joys, and also how tempting it is to have everyone ask a million extraneous, although interesting, questions about Yolanda and her new self. But you know of this danger. You know the seduction process and how it works in the group. You are conscious of the propensity for staying with old, worked-through counseling stuff. You use counseling probes designed to stay with your four-part technology for reporting. If new goals arise, they can be systematically dealt with in later sessions. For now, you want to keep the involvement at a high peak, and therefore you get the focus to shift from Yolanda to someone else in the group. By no means are you through with Yolanda. She will be coming back into the spotlight, and each week, at the beginning of every session, you will get a brief report from her in order to reinforce the notion that you, and the entire group, are interested in following up on her newly formulated goals for self-sufficiency in her area of concern.

You are now ready to move into your planned post-report strategies elaborated earlier. Your second session has gone effectively, as you predicted. You made your introductory statement, moved right into the reporting behavior after your observations, and now you are anxious to get back into the counseling part of the session. You know that many of the group members will be even better than they were before, since they saw a live model of an effective counselor operating in the group last week. You move into Plan A, like the expert that you are. You begin by saying:

> "At this time I would like to offer an opportunity for anyone who would like to use the group, to do so. You will find that getting into the spotlight, although it is somewhat discomforting, is the most exciting place to be if you are really interested in changing or becoming a more effective person. Many of you will choose to avoid it altogether, and that certainly is your right. But each week, as you see things happening here in the group, you will begin to ask yourself if you would like to get in there. Maybe, on the way to school, you say to yourself, 'I'd really like to get in there and get some help, but I'm just too scared to make a fool of myself.' You might tell yourself any number of things, all of which are designed to protect you from taking a risk. As often as possible, I would like to structure open time, a time for you to give some thought to yourself and seek insight into yourself. You will find that being in there, getting help, is the place to be if you are going to change. But it's risky. And learning to take risks is a part of what you will be learning here in the group. Any change involves risk, and certainly getting in there and asking for help is a change in your behavior, thus it is risky. I encourage you to use this time, but in no way should you feel compelled to do so. I have alternate plans, and if no one picks up on this open time, I will move in another direction. I'd like you to think about this, I'll program in some silence and give you time for looking inward, and I'll ask, 'Is there anyone who would like to use the group today to work on any personal concern, of any kind? If so, please feel free to do so now.'"

Well, you've certainly offered them much to think about, and you've opened it up. The silence is dreadful, and they are squirming about, but you'll give it the full four minutes which you've allotted in your original plan. At last (thirty seconds or so later), someone speaks up and you are off and running in your counseling activity, keeping it within the parameters of what it is that constitutes a group counseling activity. Or perhaps no one picks it up. You calmly move on to Plan B. You begin:

> "Tom, in listening to the tape of the first session, I noticed that you described yourself as someone who has almost no confidence in yourself, and that you are particularly uncomfortable in talking with girls. Do you like this about yourself?"

You notice that Tom is a bit surprised that you picked him, but he is certainly willing to deal with it here in the group. Of course he is. You picked him because you thought he displayed a sense of wanting to talk, particularly by his honest, straight talking about himself in his opening remarks. He was also one of the first to talk in the introductions, and you sensed a lack of fear about speaking honestly. You had criteria, and you used them wisely, and now Tom is in the exploratory part of your counseling. Group members are identifying with him, some key questions are being asked, and you are on your way, helping Tom through the maze toward setting some goals and understanding himself, as well as developing some alternate ways of behaving toward girls right here in the group. You've gotten the counseling ball rolling.

But, you say to yourself, what if Tom hadn't been such a willing subject, what if he had appeared nervous and said that he'd rather not talk about himself today? Then to Plan C you immediately go. You don't make any fuss, or demand that Tom explain himself. A simple "I understand Tom, it's tough to talk about those things now . . . that's okay . . . perhaps we can come back to those concerns at a future time," and Plan C gets put into action. Then Plan D, E, or F (not that you will need any of these in this session, but you are so thorough that you have enough alternatives to go through each person). Then, if everyone says no (which will never happen), you can go back to Yolanda, or you can identify and label the resistance, interpret it, and have a group interaction time on the meaning of change and how tough it is to make it come about.

But you are not worried as you look at this session. It is most likely that someone will pick up the open-time ball, and certainly Tom, whom you selected on the basis of his previous willingness to participate, will pick up the ball and start you running down the field with this counseling activity. You will find that many of your group members have similar concerns, and the group will be a hotbed of counseling activity, with everyone eager to get some help for themselves. If anything, you are becoming aware that the toughest thing you have to do is not to get them to participate, but to keep things orderly and to ask group members to stay with one person long enough to set achievable goals. Students, like everyone else, are experts on themselves, and you are finding that they covet talking about the area of their expertise.

In getting to others in the group, you refer to the Appendix and look at the techniques available for bringing group members into the counseling activity. You finger your beautiful list of possible strategies, eyeing the writing-down of goals for both long-term and short-term periods. Perhaps you go to the technique of having group members assume others' roles; or you ask them to write down goals for one specific day, or to answer key questions such as, "Who in the group is most like you?" You can use any technique that will get individuals onto the goal-setting and involvement program. The strategies are endless. You know that you can use them at any time, then shift the focus to another group member almost at will, because you possess the skills.

You take each group member who sets a goal for himself down the counseling path that is outlined briefly in the previous chapter and examined in more depth in the next chapter. Group counseling is counseling all the way, and you have proven that you can help people to change by implementing effective counseling strategies in your first and second counseling sessions.

Your second group meeting is drawing to a close. You have inaugurated your plan for this session, and demonstrated that the second session, like the first, is one in which a maximum amount of follow-up and counseling is taking place. You close your session with a homework assignment, one that meets the criteria of effective goals which you so carefully outlined in chapter 6. Your closing is businesslike, professional, and one which reexamines the things that have taken place up until now. You know that your third session will begin with a report from both Yolanda and Tom, and that you'll have no difficulty in getting members to go after the help that is so beautifully forthcoming in your counseling group. You are, indeed, off and flying on this exciting group counseling experience and now you can rest momentarily, in preparation for the sessions to come.

Put session two to bed. But no beddie-bye time for you, for now the students genuinely love this new thing called group counseling, and you will have them clamoring for more of the good stuff you are delivering out of that previously exclusive one-to-one counseling office.

9

Your Subsequent
Group Sessions

YOUR FIRST two sessions are now ancient history, and you are concerning yourself with all of the remaining group counseling meetings ahead of you. While you are not able to specify, at this time, a strategy for each future session, you are certainly going to have some very firm guidelines for conducting yourself, and the group, in the weeks to come. One operating variable that permeates your planning for future sessions involves having a delineated but flexible strategy for the *upcoming* sessions. You will never enter your counseling group without a clear plan and several options for running the group on that particular day. Like the skillful navigator that you are, you know where you are headed before you point your craft into the unknown.

Session to Session Follow-Up

Thus armed with your resolve never to enter the group without plans, options, and alternatives, you begin thinking about the life expectancy of your counseling. Ten, twelve, or twenty weeks—no matter; you are going to be the accomplished professional as you work at your own group counseling skills. You recall that session-to-session follow-up was a basic assumption when you defined group counseling way back in chapter 2. Now, in all forthcoming sessions, you are going to heed this resolve, and begin each and every session with a reminder of the previous week's activities and homework assignments. As the weeks go by, you will not forget Yolanda and Tom, who were in the spotlight a long time ago. Each week, no matter how briefly, you are scrupulous to ask Yolanda if she is still working on herself; you ask her for a report, using the same format you elaborated in chapter 8, and you send the message that you are still interested in those who were early focusers. These reports will tend to be mild and very similar from week to week, and certainly you will insist that they be brief. But at all costs, you *do* the follow-up.

Your follow-up efforts then move to those who have unreported assignments and goals to deliver in the counseling group. At the termination of every session, you have been instrumental in helping individuals set behavioral goals, like those you looked at in chapter 6. Psychological homework has been mutually agreed upon, and one or more individuals have spent the between-sessions time trying to engage in some new, growth-producing behaviors. You keep accurate notes on those who have come up with post-group behavioral tasks, and after other group members have given a brief report on their own practical growth over the course of the group, you immediately ask the previous week's focusee to report back. You take on your most skillful posture of reinforcement, helping the group member through the rough spots, never tsk-tsking when an assignment wasn't completed successfully. You remind yourself of the technology of a report, which focuses on new thinking, new feelings, new behaviors, and new commitments. Every group session has this beginning flavor, and you practice starting out your groups in such a way that no one, including yourself, could ever accuse you of not engaging in session-to-session follow-up, or of treating the group counseling process as a series of separate entitites rather than as an ongoing experience with continuity and ground rules. Thus, all of your subsequent group counseling sessions will have this feature of follow-up, both in long-distance terms, that is, going back to session number one, and in the sprints, which means the following-up you do from the session immediately preceding. You are a master at treating group members with dignity, but never, that is NEVER, do you ignore a concern or a goal from a previous group meeting that has not been brought to sufficient closure, so that the individual knows and expects that it has been, at least temporarily, resolved. To forget to ask for a report is to forget what you are doing as a professional, that is, helping people to change their behavior, or counseling. Put more simply: if you forget to ask for a report, you are forgetting a person and saying to the person that their concern was not important enough to go back to and check out for progress in their goal-oriented areas. But you will never forget, because you will be the thorough notetaker and post-group analyzer. And if by chance you forget a given individual from one week to the next (since you will be running many groups as you get proficient in this area), then you will have a standard opening whose effect will be to say, "Let's begin with reports from last week's session and check out the homework assignments that we agreed upon last week. Who would like to begin?" You are covered. You know that you would never even entertain the notion of leaving a group without some assignment, and so in your opening, when your memory fails you (because you didn't have time to listen to your tape, consult your notes, and discuss with your co-leader), you have a built-in mechanism to elicit reports from the previous week. If you have any problem with recall, you might begin with a statement such as, "Johnny, would you summarize everything that happened last week, and precisely where you think we left off?" Here you are getting group member perceptions of the group counseling process and refreshing yourself on all of the events from the previous week's session. You can use any of a variety of techniques to get each session started with the follow-up so necessary for the preservation of continuity, and these will depend entirely on your own ability to recall and record the happenings in the group from session to session.

Keeping Goal-Setting in Mind

You are once again mindful of the goal-setting orientation that you are pledged to maintain throughout the lifetime of your counseling group. Virtually every utterance by a group member is an opportunity to help someone to set goals. You have reread all of your guidelines for effective goal-setting in group counseling, and every single session, nay every single sentence, will be scrutinized by you for possible goal-setting interventions. Mary blushes, Mike stammers, Joe looks to you for approval, Sammy sends out angry tones, George "wishes" a lot, Harry "hopes things will get better," Julie complains, and on and on your observations go. Goals, goals, goals. You think about them, help members to set them continually, and involve yourself in this process from head to toe.

You wind this goal-setting thread throughout your group counseling activities in a way that is nonthreatening, nonimposing, and certainly not sarcastic or put-downish in any way. You want to get everyone talking goals for themselves and others, because once you have it in the form of a goal, then you've got some counseling data to examine. If a group member says it is a goal, even a minigoal, then it can be nurtured, thought through, and worked on in the group. It becomes an acceptable piece of tapestry for weaving in the group. Without a goal orientation, you are likely to be in the realm of discussion, which, of course, does not belong in the counseling group at all. Thus, you have a key question always at the top of your mind: "Do you like that about yourself?" If the answer is no, then it becomes a goal, and consequently pertinent for dealing with in the group. You are ready, at every single moment of the life of your counseling group, to spring into goal-setting action, and thereby ready yourself for the business of group counseling, by which we mean, *counseling individuals in groups*. No goals, no counseling. Onward you plunge, in your subsequent group counseling endeavors. Onward you march as the dedicated doer. The next business at hand is your trek through the counseling process, with the readily established goals you have been nurturing and extrapolating from all group members.

Your Step-By-Step Journey Through the Counseling Process

You think back to your own definition of group counseling. You remind yourself that the process proceeds through naturally progressing steps, and that all of your subsequent group counseling activities will indeed follow this pattern. You, of course, recognize the inclination to stray, to avoid the tedium of the counseling process, but you are going to fight this inclination, until the actual counseling becomes a natural way of behaving. Thus, after a goal has been set, or even hinted at, you are into the counseling process with one or more individuals.

IDENTIFYING SELF-DEFEATING BEHAVIOR

You always begin with the identification of the self-defeating behavior, and label how that behavior gets in the way of the individual's functioning. Here, you are quick to label particular results of the self-defeating behavior, and you encourage the group members to join in hunting down the neurotic payoffs for self-forfeiting thinking and behavior. You have a ready repertoire of neurotic payoffs to suggest. Such suggestions help individuals to explore and identify the reason why they are there in the first place, which is the elimination of all behavior which has no positive reward system built into it.

So you work hard at the beginning, when members are getting into the group counseling activity. You help them always to label the stuff that is hurtful, that has no potential for growth, and you know the behaviors that are typical of school-age clients in the counseling group. You are on guard for such behaviors as: shyness fearfulness, uncomfortable feelings around the opposite sex, communication difficulties, approval-seeking, guilt, worry, a hero worship, avoidance of risk-taking, obesity, poor attendance, poor academic habits, low self-esteem, problems relating to parents, friends, neighbors, et al., talking for others, letting others talk for them, procrastinating, living in the past, having no friends, and on and on the list goes. You have a potentially endless chronicle of possibilities to, first of all, help your group members identify and label. This is your opening gambit in any and all counseling activities that you inaugurate in the counseling group.

EXPLORATION

You then are careful to help your group members who are in the helping process explore areas of their self-defeating behaviors. Here, again, you facilitate self-exploration through skillful hypothesis-testing and intimation, rather than getting into interrogation. You are getting a window on your client's world, and you want the window to be as free of smear marks as possible. And so you explore: when does the self-declining behavior surface, with whom, under what circumstances, how long has it been going on, when did it start, when did it first become noticeable to others, how long have you carried it around, when are you capable of overcoming it, can you ever make it go away, who else in the family knows, or cares? Then you make a brief excursion through the individual's life space to find out a bit more about him or her. Brothers, sisters, parents, friends, background, money, educational attitudes, self-concept—are all fertile areas for exploration, without your having to interrogate or cause the individual to feel that he is completing a questionnaire. You simply talk to him about his background and feelings, before you launch into a frontal attack on the specific behaviors that you are going to help him extinguish. Exploration is a delightful activity, but only if it is done casually, without rapid-fire questioning, and if it has relevance to the area you are pursuing. You are going to avoid wandering right into a problem area, without knowing something about the individual himself, the person who is carrying around the concern. You remind yourself, that you are not in the business of treating problems, but rather in the business of helping individuals who have problems; and while the problem might be labeled exactly the same, no two individuals are the same. Thus, you proceed through the exploration phase with every single person who presents a goal for change in the life of the counseling group. No exceptions here, you say; you must be thinking about people, not problems, so after the concern is on the table, you must suspend it temporarily, until you find out the person(s) this problem is lodged in, and under what conditions and how long it has been surfacing.

SELF-UNDERSTANDING

Onward you go in your group counseling activity. For each and every subsequent session, you are involved in helping people to come to a degree of *self*-understanding. Without this phase, that is, without some work at self-insight, you are simply modifying behavior by shifting from a statement of the concern into a treatment of the concern. The individual, for all intents and purposes, is bypassed in favor of simply eliminating problems. Not you. You always, *always* move toward a measure of self-understanding. You are herein working at helping individuals to answer that crucial question—What do you get out of your behavior? You know that there are payoffs, albeit unhealthy ones, nevertheless payoffs, and you want each and every individual to see them, state them, and understand that they are the reason why the behavior maintains itself and why it persists. You have a storehouse full of possible reasons why a behavior persists in an individual. It reinforces sameness, it eliminates risk-taking, it lets others take care of you, it encourages little girlness (or little boyness), it's easier, it gets the person pity from others or self, it gets approval, it allows the person to continue self-put-down, it facilitates blaming others and thus not working at change, it saves the person having to extend self, it reinforces the idea of worthlessness, it precludes having to be different, and on and on. You know them, and you are going to pursue a line of counseling in which the individual is encouraged to examine every single payoff (both positive and negative) that he or she receives from such behavior.

Under no conditions will you accept "Nothing" as an answer to "What do you get out of this behavior?" You know that all behavior is caused, and even though the individual says "Nothing," what he is really saying is, "I don't get anything good out of it, and I don't want to even consider what the bad things are, since I'd have to work at being different if I knew the negative (turned into positive) rewards for my behavior." So you help each person to examine, in every session, the psychological maintenance system for the behavior, and the answer to the riddle about why it persists in him even though the payoff is self-destructive. Until you get there, you hesitate to move into the next area of counseling with an individual. But once a modicum of evidence appears that self-insight is on the horizon, then you shift into the next stage of your counseling activity, always involving the group members to the extent that they are gaining skills in actually delivering and participating in *counseling* activity.

GOAL-SETTING

Now you pursue goal-setting in depth. You have established some goals right from the outset, and you are ready to get into the development-of-alternatives mode that is characterized by an examination of possible options to the given self-sacrificing behavior. You help the group members chart all kinds of new options; you invite the individual who is receiving the focus to examine as many possible alternatives, even distasteful alternatives, to the way she now conducts her life in this one particular area. The group is a veritable warehouse full of data, and the members will throw them out at will. You want to brainstorm here, to the extent it is possible, rather than simply offer one or two possible different modes of behavior.

TRYING ON NEW BEHAVIORS

When the alternatives are out and visible, you can then turn your group into an actor's delight, trying out all kinds of new behaviors in the safe environment of the counseling group. George can shift from being coy and shy to being aggressive, and if he can't, then someone in the role of George can do so—the possibilities are endless. You want to turn the group into a *doing* activity, using all of the resources to make it a productive experience for all concerned. You are aware of the need to be creative here, and you can readily consult the Appendix for a hodgepodge of creative techniques that work in making use of the trying-it-out-in-the-group phase of your group counseling activity.

You have proceeded with every single concern, down this remarkable ladder of effectiveness. You've tried it out with some degree of success, and the individual is beginning to see some difference in himself as he experiments in heretofore unthought-of behaviors. As in every session, you help the individual to see that the acquisition of new skills involves practice, following insight into the reasons for the new way of doing things. As in learning anything, so you remind your clients, the mind must take over and become an active agent in the beginning stages, constantly reminding the body to do it *this* way, until it becomes *natural*, and the mind then goes back into a passive role. But for now, you are helping individuals bring their consciousness levels up, to make their minds work for them, to practice, practice, and practice some more their new and exciting ways of behaving, ways that will bring about solid payoffs. You are weaning them from their standstillism or, even worse, their regressive back-pedaling to the days when they had to depend on a mommy or a daddy for survival.

PSYCHOLOGICAL HOMEWORK

After you've experimented in the group and worked at new behavior acquisition, you move right into the extra-group activity that the individual will be attempting, that is, into the psychological homework, that heavy stuff of which future reports back to the group will be made. The assignments, you remind yourself, are to fit the criteria that you've previously detailed. Certainly, they must be attainable and be guaranteed of success. The assignments are going to be behavioral, and of course you are going to ensure that the person will be able to succeed completely in carrying out the *mutually*-agreed-upon, new extra-group behaviors for the next week. Without this post-group reinforcement, all of the effective stuff you've accomplished up until now will have been for naught, since the measure of your effectiveness as a group leader is contingent upon what takes place *outside* rather than inside of the group. Your group members live 99 percent of their lives outside the group, and you will constantly remind yourself of this fact as you set about to help group members in all their myriad concerns (you've listed hundreds).

Keeping Counseling Uppermost in Your Mind

You travel this ladder upward everytime you begin with a goal for an individual within the group. Even if several individuals share a similar concern, you help them all to go up this ladder together, moving through the statement of their concerns, past the invaluable exploratory stuff, into the beautiful world of self-understanding. Then past goal-setting and thinking, through a raft of alternatives to the behavior, right into the doing-it-in-the-group scene and, finally, into psychological homework in the form of behavioral goals for the post-session time. Then, of course, you use the next session for reports, follow-up, new commitments, new explorations and refinements of the old "easy" assignments, into applications of the new behaviors in every conceivable area of their lives.

There are multitudinous variations on the theme. You will not just sit around and talk each and every time. But whatever it is you are doing, however varied your activities in the counseling group, you will always be moving through this helping process, a step-by-step progression designed to change behavior—which is what we call *counseling*. You are so intent on sticking to this prescription that you have it uppermost in your cranium at all times. You say to yourself, "Am I counseling now? Is counseling going on at this moment? Is someone getting help? Who is it? Where are we in the helping process?" If you get negative noncounseling responses to your self-inquiries, you then make a mental note to shift, or to identify precisely what is going on and how it got to be that way. Invariably, the answer will revolve around a lapse in your own leadership at a particular time. An allowing of someone to overrun the counseling process, or even being hesitant yourself to get in there because it was easier to digress or to allow a digression. But you are ever mindful of the little "counseling fairy" who pounds away at your occipital lobe and helps you to ask those key questions that will be the agent for bringing you back, each and every time, to bona fide counseling activity. If you can't place the current group counseling activity someplace on the progressive helping ladder, then you just say, "Well, old buddy, somehow I blew it, but we're going back to counseling, and this is what I am going to say to the group member(s) in order to get it back on the helping trail." Simple, no admonishing of yourself, just a correction in midstream to keep you sailing on the current toward your destination of helping individuals to change.

In your subsequent group meetings, you notice that you are not nearly as active as you were in those early group sessions. You are pleased by this development, and recognize it as a factor in effective modeling. In the beginning, you were the only one in the group who had any idea about what it was that constituted the counseling part of this group activity. You were constantly required to model effective interventions, to make the group shift from conversation to helping, to actively demonstrate interpretation, diagnosis, and each of your twenty group leadership skills. Later, as the group progressed, you noticed that other leaders began to emerge. Tom began to say *You* instead of the typical *I* response of the uninformed helper. Others began to see that the business of group counseling was not to have the experiences of others remind them of something similar that happened to them, and then launch into a bouncing-off-each-other group activity, but rather to stay with someone, to hear them out, to work through the counseling process. You are sitting back more these days, seeing the fruits of your early laboring to keep a helping focus omnipresent in the group. You are still as cautiously observant in the group, you still intervene and direct the activity toward meaningful counseling activity, but you see others doing fantastic things that only you could do a few weeks ago.

Thus you begin to foster group leadership activity in the members of the counseling group. You do not feel slighted by their unique capacity to confront, to interpret, to summarize, and so on; rather, you are ever mindful of this being the payoff for all helping action. You remind yourself that you are in the business of putting yourself out of business. You don't want these young people to need you at all. You are not interested in fostering dependence on you, or in creating attitudes which make young people feel that they can't handle something without having you to discuss it with. No. You are breeding effective psychological independence by your own modeling behavior. You are working toward not being needed at all, toward helping these students be able to think for themselves, to solve their own problems, to diagnose their own worlds accurately, and to have their own minds in every single area of their lives. You are still the leader. Make no mistake about that. But your activity is not nearly as frenetic, as deliberate, or as frequent as it was in those early sessions, when you were the only one who knew about counseling. Your thoroughness about preliminaries, and your anticipation of group members' behavior, have led you to this present moment, wherein you see that you have taught others how to help. What more glorious and worthwhile activity is there?

You are going to conduct the future sessions of the group in a variety of ways, using an unlimited array of techniques, and activities that will always fit into the group counseling mold, and simultaneously ensure a dynamic, varied experience for each member of the group. As you thumb forward into the Appendix, and peruse the long list of available techniques, you will be deciding before each session which ones are appropriate for your particular group members. Some you will call upon at the spur of the moment, using a subgrouping design or a role-working strategy because it is called for at that particular time in your group. You will also invent your own strategies, keeping track of them, and reminding yourself of the nuances of a technique that make it effective. Soon you will have a long list of your own, and you will begin to refine them and make them into your own technology for leading a counseling group.

You are so mindful of the need to incorporate variety into your counseling group, and yet maintain the parameters of your definition and assumptions, that the search for new methods will be an unending part of your professional group counseling preparation. You'll be asking yourself, "How can I use role-working to help Mary? How can I get Sammy and Michael involved in this, since I know they have similar concerns? Should I break the group into subgroups now, since many have not contributed at all? What strategy could I use to give Jerry that insight he is lacking now? How can I get Tommy to see that he is not coming across the way he thinks he is? What can I do to make Larue see how stand-offish he appears? What should I do to make Rob see that he really seeks approval from everyone? What could I suggest to help Sandra see how snobby she comes across without turning her off to others? On and on the internal questions flash across the tote board of your mind. You know where you want to go, and what you would like the members to be able to achieve, but what techniques are you going to use? You want to be subtle, yet firm; you want to have them reach their goals, but not prematurely. You are looking for self-insight, without directly telling or preaching. The techniques are the guts of your activity. You look over the Appendix, mull around the ones that sound as if they would work, modify others, completely change others around. But always, you are using technique not for its own sake but to help someone in your group through the seven-step process called *counseling*.

As you design specific how-to's in conducting each subsequent group counseling session, you are conscious of the need to be constantly appraising yourself of your present-moment activity as the group leader. You will ever be the introspective one, looking inward and examining your leadership behavior. You will always be hard on yourself, and demand excellence from yourself, or at least professional, authentic counselor behavior. You will appraise yourself readily and regularly, and you'll be the better for it, as will the students you are serving in the counseling group.

Primarily, you will ever be the diagnostician, attempting to come up with the why's in your counseling group. Trying first to answer the critical diagnostic questions yourself, and then helping the group members to have the same insights themselves, before moving on to the significant task of trying to eliminate the self-crushing thinking and behaviors. Diagnose! You must become expert in this area, with hundreds of possible explanations for why a person would do that to himself. You look for the answers, or at least for plausible hypotheses, that will explain why he or she hangs onto that self-defeating behavior. You remind yourself that all human behavior is caused, and there is a payoff for every kind of behavior, even though the answer to the payoff may be profoundly obscure at the moment. Nevertheless, there is a reason. You are always looking for the reasons that are working for the individual group member. The explanation that will sink in, and help him or her to go about changing. You diagnose internally, not out loud. You are always thinking of new possibilities, new strategies for having the individual see what has become plain to you. Diagnose! You work at it *all* the time. Not just on a part-time basis, but always. You will become so proficient at this skill, that soon things will become evident to you that remain hidden for others. This is because you are working at it, trying to come up with answers that matter, rather than just explaining something away with the classic, "That's just Tom, he's always been that way," or some such absurd evasion. And so, in every group meeting, your mind is occupied with the reasons and with the ways to open up your own diagnostic efforts and abilities to the group members.

Also, in your subsequent sessions, you will work at offering alternatives to the self-defeating behaviors that surface within the group. You are getting to be a masterful alternatives-director, showing by your own model of effectiveness that new and different modes of thinking and behaving are available to those who choose to work on themselves. You will be thinking of new and unique possibilities to the old thinking that hampers group members. The alternatives to being angry, shy, hurt, fearful, shameful, depressed, a poor student, a drug user, a truant, will be examined carefully, after the individuals have gained that crucial diagnostic insight into why a behavior maintains itself in them. You will be ready to be totally nonjudgmental in your helping, ready to examine new alternatives; you will constantly be asking yourself during sessions, "What could he or she do differently that would show them that they don't have to stay locked in that particular way of thinking and behaving?" Always you are trying to help, by directing group activity that will help people to come up with some definitive answers to the question their lives seem to be asking of you—"Why should I be any different?" No imposer of your own morality are you. You will help them to answer that question, in every single group interaction incident, via the helpful, workable group counseling process.

You are going to be reviewing constantly the twenty group leadership behaviors examined and exampled in chapter 4. Your propensity for self-appraisal will help you to conduct your subsequent group counseling sessions in as useful a fashion as possible. You will be the model of effectiveness. Showing by your own living, breathing example, that being "together" is not just some fancy ideal you spout, but a real possibility for their own lives. That they can have the kind of personally masterful life they would choose, at least in the emotional realm, and greater autonomy in the behavioral realm as well.

All of your subsequent group counseling sessions, then, are following the model of group counseling activity that you have dutifully laid down throughout your reading of this book. In a nutshell, all of your activity as a group leader will be in the paradigmatic counseling sample below, or else in one of the ancillary group leadership behaviors. Whenever it is not in this realm, you will initiate quick-shift action to get back on the track leading to bona fide group counseling activity.

Step Ladder of What Constitutes Group Counseling

I Identification of self-defeating behavior
leading to:

II Exploration of:
a. significant historical data
b. demographic factors
c. where the self-defeating behavior occurs
d. historical antecedents of the self-defeating behavior
e. typical day
f. an excursion down this person's life path
Leading to:

III The development of self-understanding:
a. the psychological maintenance system
b. a look at why the behavior persists today
c. all in answer to the question—"What do I get out of my behavior?" and never accepting the answer "Nothing"
Leading to:

IV Goal-setting—the criteria of effective goal-setting:
a. mutually agreed upon
b. specificity
c. relevant to the self-defeating behavior
d. achievable and success-oriented
e. quantifiable and measurable
f. behaviorable and observable
g. back-repeatable and understandable
Leading to:

V   Trying it out in the group:
  a. the development of self-trial strategies
  b. total group involvement in the trial
  c. role-working
  d. the environment remains safe at all times
  e. the evaluation of the new trial behavior
  Leading to:

VI   Psychological homework
  a. new thinking and behavior that meets the goal-setting criteria in IV above
  b. never imposed
  Leading to:

VII   Reporting back to the group:
  a. new thinking
  b. new feelings
  c. new behavior
  d. new commitments
  Leading to:

  e. evaluation of the new efforts
  f. assimilation or recycling for new efforts
  g. incorporation of learned behavior

Thus, you have a map for following your own behavior, and if you are not doing this kind of leadership behavior, and are not engaged in one of the ancillary-to-group-counseling behaviors which include:

Summarizing and reviewing important material,
restating,
lecturing and information-giving,
recognizing and explaining nonverbal behavior,
dealing with silence,
facilitating closure,

then anything else literally does not belong. If you see anything else going on you immediately shift the emphasis. Your subsequent sessions will be taken up with meaningful counseling or counseling-related activities (commensurate counseling behaviors). You have your guidelines, you've traversed the thicket through the first and second sessions, and you have ample bark marks to assist you through the remaining sessions. Now, as you look toward the light in the tunnel, you begin to see that the only hurdle to your total group counseling awareness is facilitating closure on the process itself, that is, bringing the entire group counseling life to an end. Chapter 10 will lead you through the remainder of the tunnel, whereafter you'll emerge as the expert who claims expertise by virtue of having been there, rather than having been told about it.

10

Your Final Group Session: Closing Down

YOU ARE, in contradistinction to Winston Churchill's famous dictum, contemplating the beginning of the end, having dealt very thoroughly with the end of the beginning. You want to keep your word, and end the group counseling meetings on schedule, unless an extension has been agreed upon earlier by all of the group members. But, nevertheless, you must end sometime, and working at having a smooth, efficient terminal procedure is your goal, now that you have churned through the group counseling waters for these many weeks.

You are determined to be as thorough and professional about your wrap-up procedures as you have been in all previous sessions, going way back to that very first session. As in T. S. Eliot's oft quoted line about how the world will end, so too will your counseling group end with a whimper, not with a tumultuous bang! Your closing will be a natural unfolding of events; as in all activities, an end must come, and so there is no big deal made about this being the last session. No party, no tearful farewells, no ritual intended to immortalize the past weeks. Rather, a natural, professional wrap-up of the experience you have all shared called *group counseling*. You think back, as you contemplate your final session, to the rationale for getting into the business of leading a counseling group. You remember that the group is a myth. It doesn't really exist at all as an entity. Rather, you have been working with a collection of individuals, all unique, all separated from each other in multitudinous ways. Throughout the life of your group, you have stressed the importance of the individual over the group. You have discouraged the *we* in favor of the *I* and the *you*. The group hasn't been a paramount consideration all the way, and now, as you begin to think about closing, you will not make the group an entity to be memorialized in status over the individuals who comprised the total unit. No, you think, no big fanfare, no calling attention to the group as something to remember fondly and hold onto. You want everyone to leave the group as stronger individuals, having themselves to cling to, having new and stronger self-assurance models to rely on in times of stress. The individuals here are what count. Each person is better in some way, more effective, and each person has certain areas to ponder, to work on in their own private totebag of goals.

Thus, you are determined to enter the last session with a clear resolve to maintain the same powerful individualizing stance right up to the very end. The focus will be on persons rather than collectives, and your finalizing activities will reinforce the importance of thinking about persons rather than groups, which in fact do not exist at all. Your group is a temporary reality, while individuals are permanent realities, and you are going to avoid the pomp and fanfare that call attention to the significance of the group. You are determined, doggedly so, to make your final session like the rest, one in which you counsel and engage in all of your fully mastered group leadership behaviors. While you will be engaged in more summarizing and closure facilitation in this session than you were in any of the earlier sessions, nevertheless it will indeed be a group counseling session, rather than a party or a postmortem.

You think about these words on the importance of the individual, and you introduce your final session with a statement to the group members that covers the necessary groundwork:

> "We have always stressed the importance of individuals, and as
> you leave, you leave as stronger individuals, more in charge of
> your own world. In that sense there was no group at all, and so

ending our collective counseling sessions just means that you don't have this particular collection of unique individuals to work with you on your own concerns. But there are lots of other collections, and so we end with a whimper, so as not to reinforce the silly notion that somehow this group was more important than any one person in it. We go out as individuals, not as a group.''

Well, you've laid it on them in spades. But you've still got the entire final session to conduct before closing out this exciting learning chapter in your and their lives. Naturally, you begin with the long-range and short-term reports from the previous sessions, here stressing that these are final reports, and that all commitments to future goals and growth must now be internalized, and that group support for goals is not the goal at all, but that it is, rather, having that support system for personal mastery lodged firmly *inside* the constitution of each individual group member.

You think about the post-report activity. You want to be sure that some counseling takes place. Some one, or two, will want to get in on the goodies before the curtain closes. Thus, you've thought about who has been hanging back, and you ask directly if they would like to get in on the counseling. You encourage someone that you've had in mind, the straggler, the one who would like to, but can't muster up the courage. You are determined to have a counseling session, and to go through the steps of effective group counseling, right up to giving an assignment for post-group carry-out by the individual(s) involved. You also check out who, if anyone, has some unresolved business that they would like to take care of in this last session. You provide the open-ended invitation to ensure that anyone who was left out has made that choice by themselves, rather than being forced out by an unconcerned or overlooking group leader. Of course, you remind yourself that you can see any one individual who has been systematically choked off because of the clock. But the bell keeps ringing in your head; you must treat this like any other session. You must be the professional counselor, offering the opportunity, right up until the very end, for anyone to partake of the counseling opportunities offered by this helping unit.

Yet, you know that this session has some special overtones to it. You know there is no tomorrow for this group, and you indeed have some special assignments that you are going to carry out, before the group members leave for the last time. You think about these significant factors before ever entering the last group session. And you come in, prepared to be the master of summarization. You deliver on all of the following components, allowing yourself enough time before the end comes, in order to complete your list of final duties.

• You review the closing structures available to you, and you select the most appropriate technique for winding down (see the Appendix). You launch into this final structure after the counseling phase has been completed, right down to the psychological homework and the ways in which the final session counselees are going to report on their progress—by telephone, to you in your office, to specially assigned group members, and so forth.

• After completing the final structure that you have selected for your terminal group counseling session, you are going to launch into your "special group counselor, final-session summarizing behavior." Here you will want to be cautious about the different kinds of summarizing that are available to you. You recall, as you thumb back through your summarizing skills from chapter 4, that summarization is a highly technical skill, one in which the summarizer must provide useful, translatable-to-action data for the group members. Thus you prepare in advance your group leader summary, and you give some specific thought to each member of the group and what you would like to say to them as you part company.

In putting together your final drawing-together thoughts, you will emphasize telling the group about those members who have grown from the experience, and precisely how this growth is evidenced. Such a leader summary follows:

> "Many of you have changed your behavior as a result of participating in this group. Maynard, you are now able to confront others without being afraid, and this came about as a result of much good practice, both in and outside of the group. Shelly, you have worked at changing your relationship to your mom, and in the past ten weeks, you have had your curfew lifted, you've conducted three intelligent conversations with her, and you have convinced her that you are indeed a person to reckon with, rather than a simple slave to be manipulated at her will.
> "George, you have talked spontaneously throughout this group, and this is something you were unable to do before com-

ing here. In addition, you have initiated much counseling content, and have been helpful in teaching others to work on
themselves by modeling this kind of risk-taking right here in
the group. Mary Jo, you have become adept at eliminating approval-seeking, particularly with your best girlfriend, Gail. You
have taught her how to treat you, by giving her accurate feedback about how you feel when she tries to manipulate you."

On and on you go, in your final summary, providing behavioral
evidence for the group members, so that they leave the counseling
group armed with the new behaviors and well aware of how their
new behavior acquisitions have been observed by at least one
competent assessor of human behavior.

Your summary, which will be complete, will include, in addition to specific behavioral evidence for the growth of the group
members, a precise analysis of *how* and *why* they are each more
effective. In your efforts to be helpful and informative, you are
providing your own diagnostic assessment of the individuals who
have participated in group counseling. A sample of this how-and-
why group leader summarization is given below:

"Mary, in addition to being able to eliminate that shyness that
so characterized you before coming to this group, you have
taken on a more assertive tack, which is indeed an effective
strategy for you. You've become less fearful of approaching
others, by working hard at eliminating the old thinking that
used to fill up your head.

"For example, you used to tell yourself that something bad
might happen if you were to be scorned by a friend, or that
some kind of disaster would overcome you as a result of being
rejected. You have attacked this faulty reasoning, and by fearlessly trying initiating behavior, you've learned that those old
fears were really groundless, and that people actually liked you
better rather than less when you took charge of yourself and
stopped hanging back.

"Also, you have learned that their approval, which you used
to covet, was insignificant, and that you must live your life for
yourself, rather than giving other people power over you. All of
these things you learned by first of all, attacking the self-defeating thinking, and then trying out new and exciting things that
you'd never considered before. You've learned to be a doer,
rather than a fearful worrier. You've learned that the label of
being shy was a shield, and so you've stopped hanging on to

that label, and now you are no longer able to call upon that old self-descriptor."

This kind of fact-filled, diagnosis-loaded, direct summary of the how and why of each individual's new behaviors will reinforce the new thinking and doing that should be characterizing each group member, as well as giving them something firm to leave with—a solid analysis by you, the competent professional. This means a great deal to each member, and you are careful to help each person see how their new behaviors are lodged in new and more effective personal thinking and risk-taking.

Your summary will also point to those who haven't grown, and what they will need to do in the future in order to become as fully functioning as is possible for them. Thus, each individual will leave the group with areas for improvement, since you haven't been in the business of creating gods or symbols of perfection in the past weeks. You leave group members with goals ringing in their ears. Thus, you continue with Mary:

> "While you've been exceedingly successful with your antishy-ness attack, you still have a great deal of work to do on yourself in order to tackle it all the way. You will need to continue with the personal log you are keeping, reminding yourself of all that you must do, and keeping track of your failures, which will ultimately be turned into victories.
>
> "Also, Mary, in dealing with boys, you have still held onto many of those old self-destructive patterns of hanging back. Perhaps making some telephone calls to boys, or even asking for a date would be a positive, down-the-pike advance for you. In addition, you could report to me in the office on a periodic basis, and keep me informed of your progress.
>
> "Should you have any letdowns, or skids, and they are quite predictable, since you've had sixteen years of old-Mary practice and only eight weeks of new-Mary practice, we can work on them together. Also, you might practice getting feedback from two or three group members in the future, and program in regular meeting times to deal with your own progress rate."

And on you go, with Mary and all of the others, detailing the areas for work, showing specifically the need to be conscious at all times of the possibilities for setbacks, and you fearlessly point to those in the group who haven't manifested any (or minimal) growth, at least on a demonstrable level. Never becoming dogmatic or critical, but simply being straight about your observations. Thus you deal with the two or three isolates, or the nonparticipators, not with a cryptic tongue but in the following kind of language:

> "Missy, you've kind of kept clear of the action here in the group over the past twelve weeks, and that certainly is not any indicator of your nonparticipation. One can grow, and be with it, and still choose to maintain an air of silence. But, in your case, I've felt that you wanted to get in on it more, from about the fifth week on. On two or three occasions you made an effort, and then got sidetracked by more verbal group members.
>
> "If one of your goals is to be more initiating and forceful, particularly in group settings, then perhaps you can work on this in the future. If you'd like to talk with me about it privately, I'd be happy to make an appointment with you.
>
> "Also, you haven't been real effective in raising those science grades, and maybe it's related to the same kind of demeanor you've shown in here, just being afraid to tackle it directly and kind of waiting for things to get better. You almost always manage to let others talk for you, and many times you looked relieved when the focus shifted off of you. Also, Missy, you apologize quite often when you speak simultaneously with someone else.
>
> "All of these things are potential goals for you, if you would like to change in these directions. Being in this group has shown you, first-hand, that there are specific areas that you can begin to tackle. You've seen how it works, and you've even helped others to work on themselves. Now, maybe you can transfer what you know to *you.*"

You don't leave Missy hanging, since you are going to point to her growth too, however minimal it was. But you don't hedge here, particularly in this final session, when you want the group members to trek out into their own worlds and become as uniquely effective as they can. With a sugar-coated effort here, you know that you might undo all that you have gained up until now, and thus you are ever direct, honest, gentle, and firm, just like always, as you finalize your summaries to all the group members. Nothing cruel here, simply being the honest counselor, which, you have learned by now, is the only way to help facilitate change and thus growth in the clients you serve.

As you continue summarizing in this final session, you also want to help the group members to see precisely what it was that kept them from being more effective, while pointing directly to the factors which immobilized them, even in the smallest of ways. For example:

> "Tommy, you have grown tremendously here in this counseling group over the past twelve weeks. You are functioning at a higher level in dealing with your friends. You have committed yourself to a vocational choice for the present, and you've taken the necessary steps to ensure that you will have post-high-school training. You've lost some weight here, and you are now dating, which is something you had given little thought to prior to entering this group.
>
> "You also have some areas to work on, and of course you are well aware of them, having dealt with many of your own internal "fears" in the group. You recognize now, that you were the one that kept you from asking for a date, that your own set of fears was something that was lodged in you, rather than in those girls out there. You now see that if you are going to be effective at anything, that blaming is not very worthwhile.
>
> "Previously, you were a first-rate blamer, assigning fault for all of your weaknesses to others. Now you have stopped blaming and thinking those self-hurtful thoughts, and you are on your way to *living* rather than blaming. The immobilizing notions were in *your* head, and to the extent that you are not satisfied, in the future, you will begin by examining your own self, rather than first of all assigning blame to someone else.
>
> "Tommy, you have learned some real valuable stuff here, and taking charge of your own emotional world is probably the most important. Your goals are clear, and many new goals will emerge, but your fundamental pattern of fault-finding has pretty much been erased."

Thus, you point to the new and more productive behaviors, while simultaneously illustrating to each group member how their own thinking is what generally fouled them up in the past. You point to the personal immobilizers wherever they are evident, and you show each person not only what they have learned in group counseling, but what kept them in a frozen state before they learned the many concepts of personal mastery.

As you skate through your summarizing activities, you are always cognizant of the need for providing behavioral data when laying anything on a group member. You are careful to avoid a lapse into theoretical jargon which will confuse and obscure your meaning. Your summarizing activities are always locked dead center on behavior, and as you give each group member their little dose of feedback, both about what they have achieved as well as the areas that need new concerted efforts, your own leadership functions are immersed in the drawing out of behavioral data. You are well prepared for this final session, and the multitudinous notes you have collected will be a boon to your behavioral summarizing activities. You will see the Archimedes look on your group members as you point to the specific behaviors that buttress your summaries and final feedback, and if you fail to cite the behavioral evidence, you will see the puzzled look of Diogenes as he wearily searches for (and never finds) his honest man.

You will also make some summarizing statements to the entire group, wherein you share with everyone your final thoughts about the group experience. You wander into this group summary behavior fully aware of the importance of treating each person as an individual, and yet simultaneously responding to the fact that all have shared in this experience together, and that some wrap-up statements are pertinent for all ears to hear, and for each person to do with as he or she sees fit. Your first group summary revolves around the premise that the data revealed in the group are not nearly as significant as what has been experienced in each member's own private life. Thus you state:

"While each person has used the group in many intensely personal ways, many of which have just been summarized by me here, so too have you grown outside of the group, where it really counts. We have only seen a small chunk of each person's life in the past twelve weeks, yet all of you have had your full measure of time (twenty-four hours in each and every day) to think about, digest, reject or accept, and practice, practice, practice, in your own particular life spaces. That is where it really matters, out there where you live and breathe it each and every day. Thus, you may have tried many new and exciting things which you haven't shared at all here in the group, and you may be miles ahead of yourself and have rightfully chosen to keep it within yourselves. Those of you who have not outwardly shown your growth, may have gained deep insights into yourselves and others, by observing those others take their risks and grow. You may have done things outside in your own lives that the group members are totally unaware of, and this is for each of you to measure and to know. The group is not the important thing here, it is each one of you, as you leave this collection of helpers and begin to work on yourselves to become as fully functioning as you choose to be, in each and every significant area of your lives. Hopefully, you have seen demonstrated here, that complete fulfillment is something that is a product of the choices you make, and that your choices come from having a mind of your own. If we add up each of you, one plus one, plus one, and so on, we will never come up with a collective. Always the sum total is one—you—and your own happiness has been the total stress here."

Thus, you have emphasized the need for each person to think about his choice-making powers as he or she leaves the group for the very last time. Now you must think about a succinct, laconic group process finale, for you recall that you have always had a strong belief that the members of the group were entitled to know where you were coming from as a group leader, and exactly what this process of group counseling has been leading to over the past twelve weeks. You launch your final wrap-up to cover the growth of the group, the relative strengths and weaknesses, particularly focusing on the growth that has taken place in the unit you have labeled a counseling group.

"You have probably all observed many changes that have taken place in this group since we began some twelve weeks ago. While I am not going to go into all of them, I would like to share with you some of the more obvious and relevant facts of our collective life together. First of all, when the group started, people seemed reluctant to make the foray and talk about themselves, and very little helping was being offered in the first few weeks. Gradually, by observing what I was doing, you began to get the idea that we were here to help rather than to have nice neat discussions. This has been a very fast-paced group, with people anxious to get in on the counseling benefits. You all learned fast, and each of you, in your own unique way, was offering help to others. In the early stages, people seemed fearful about self-revelation, but as you began to see that the risk was only in your own minds, you began to clamor for group time, almost to the point of having to assign future group counseling spotlight time for everyone. As a group, you moved quickly through that passive stage, and while you were willing to let me do all of the work, when you observed that I wasn't willing or interested in doing all of the counseling, you began to pick up the ball and run with it.

"You have been a strong group, in that you have not hung back and waited for things to happen, but rather have taken the initiative yourselves. Many of you picked up the leadership cues, and began to become accepting confronters on your own. You moved into the helping phases of counseling, and were anxious to make this a place where useful things would happen. You have all seen how the group developed a sense of unity and support, but this was not any natural thing. We worked hard at this, but not in the way you would traditionally think that unity would be encouraged. We stayed with the counseling ethic all the way, always insisting that people be honest and straight, and directly labeling any attempts to be sugary or dishonest. This is what brought about our feelings of togetherness, and the unity has helped us in working more effectively toward helping everyone who wanted to change some aspects of their lives. You probably noticed that no one was forced to participate, yet some presures did develop for the more silent members to get in on it. This, too, is natural and you should all be aware that I was ever conscious of the need to protect anyone from getting attacked simply because they chose to temporarily hang back. As the group began to really work on the counseling chores, the more silent group members also let down some of their guards, and eventually everyone got in on the action over the entire twelve weeks. Naturally, many group members could have benefited from more participation, but this could be said about any counseling group that ever existed. We can all use more growth, and since counseling means change, and change means growth, certainly we could all use more of this good stuff called counseling.

"The group has been a lesson in communicating effectively. At first, everyone just kind of talked helter-skelter, asking questions of everyone in interrogator fashion. The communicating became much more sophisticated as the group progressed, and the questions tended to be more relevant and purposeful. In addition, the skills of listening became finely honed here in the group, with many superb examples of poor listening in the early sessions, then a sense of having to be particularly attentive if one is going to help someone else. Much of the competing for air time evaporated after a while, and it was replaced with some genuine struggling to come up with some of the why's for a given person's behavior. Finally, as a group, you have matured to the point of being an arena for helping, rather than a simple discussion forum. You have learned about counseling, and what it means to work with a person until they have understood themselves and gone to work attaining skills to change their behavior. This was not accomplished without some very tough wriggling. There were moments of disagreement, frustration, and even anger. You dealt with it in a united fashion, having uppermost in your minds, the need to be a helping unit. As you leave, the group will never exist as an entity, and this is all for the good.

"You leave as you entered, with your individuality intact and most important. But you leave with a new set of principles to guide you in your own personal life struggles. The fundamental knowledge that you are worthwhile and that you truly have a mind of your own. It has been a genuine pleasure, and a learning experience for me as well. As always, I will be available for anyone to talk to, either immediately after the group, or in my office. Goodbye."

That seals it. The group has filed out, and you are left with a few stragglers who want to bend your ear about this or that. But now you are alone, alone with your thoughts and reactions to your first complete group counseling experience. You have been a model of efficiency, and you have MADE A DIFFERENCE. You were professional all the way. From your own self-analysis, to your thorough assessment of the community and school in planning your course of action, right down to each and every session. You analyzed your own behaviors, anticipated the group member reactions, and carefully laid out a technology for conducting the first, second, third, and all sessions right up to the final one. While you would like to keep it going, and your heart tugs, you suppress any inclination to become maudlin about saying goodbye. There are many other groups to lead, and you have work to do. But you have *trail-blazed with conceptual sureness*, and each new group—and you will lead thousands before you retire—will be that much more exciting. As you reflect on your achievements, you see you have reached your own goal. You made a difference in the lives of each and every group member. There is no greater payoff.

have matured to the point of being an arena for helping, rather than a simple discussion forum. You have learned about counseling, and what it means to work with a person until they have understood themselves and gone to work attaining skills to change their behavior. This was not accomplished without some very tough wriggling. There were moments of disagreement, frustration, and even anger. You dealt with it in a united fashion, having uppermost in your minds, the need to be a helping unit. As you leave, the group will never exist as an entity, and this is all for the good.

"You leave as you entered, with your individuality intact and most important. But you leave with a new set of principles to guide you in your own personal life struggles. The fundamental knowledge that you are worthwhile and that you truly have a mind of your own. It has been a genuine pleasure, and a learning experience for me as well. As always, I will be available for anyone to talk to, either immediately after the group, or in my office. Goodbye."

That seals it. The group has filed out, and you are left with a few stragglers who want to bend your ear about this or that. But now you are alone, alone with your thoughts and reactions to your first complete group counseling experience. You have been a model of efficiency, and you have MADE A DIFFERENCE. You were professional all the way. From your own self-analysis, to your thorough assessment of the community and school in planning your course of action, right down to each and every session. You analyzed your own behaviors, anticipated the group member reactions, and carefully laid out a technology for conducting the first, second, third, and all sessions right up to the final one. While you would like to keep it going, and your heart tugs, you suppress any inclination to become maudlin about saying goodbye. There are many other groups to lead, and you have work to do. But you have *trail-blazed with conceptual sureness*, and each new group—and you will lead thousands before you retire—will be that much more exciting. As you reflect on your achievements, you see you have reached your own goal. You made a difference in the lives of each and every group member. There is no greater payoff.

laying anything on a group member. You are careful to avoid a lapse into theoretical jargon which will confuse and obscure your meaning. Your summarizing activities are always locked dead center on behavior, and as you give each group member their little dose of feedback, both about what they have achieved as well as the areas that need new concerted efforts, your own leadership functions are immersed in the drawing out of behavioral data. You are well prepared for this final session, and the multitudinous notes you have collected will be a boon to your behavioral summarizing activities. You will see the Archimedes look on your group members as you point to the specific behaviors that buttress your summaries and final feedback, and if you fail to cite the behavioral evidence, you will see the puzzled look of Diogenes as he wearily searches for (and never finds) his honest man.

You will also make some summarizing statements to the entire group, wherein you share with everyone your final thoughts about the group experience. You wander into this group summary behavior fully aware of the importance of treating each person as an individual, and yet simultaneously responding to the fact that all have shared in this experience together, and that some wrap-up statements are pertinent for all ears to hear, and for each person to do with as he or she sees fit. Your first group summary revolves around the premise that the data revealed in the group are not nearly as significant as what has been experienced in each member's own private life. Thus you state:

> "While each person has used the group in many intensely personal ways, many of which have just been summarized by me here, so too have you grown outside of the group, where it really counts. We have only seen a small chunk of each person's life in the past twelve weeks, yet all of you have had your full measure of time (twenty-four hours in each and every day) to think about, digest, reject or accept, and practice, practice, practice, in your own particular life spaces. That is where it really matters, out there where you live and breathe it each and every day. Thus, you may have tried many new and exciting things which you haven't shared at all here in the group, and you may be miles ahead of yourself and have rightfully chosen to keep it within yourselves. Those of you who have not outwardly shown your growth, may have gained deep insights into yourselves and others, by observing those others take their risks and grow. You may have done things outside in your own lives

that the group members are totally unaware of, and this is for each of you to measure and to know. The group is not the important thing here, it is each one of you, as you leave this collection of helpers and begin to work on yourselves to become as fully functioning as you choose to be, in each and every significant area of your lives. Hopefully, you have seen demonstrated here, that complete fulfillment is something that is a product of the choices you make, and that your choices come from having a mind of your own. If we add up each of you, one plus one, plus one, and so on, we will never come up with a collective. Always the sum total is one—you—and your own happiness has been the total stress here.''

Thus, you have emphasized the need for each person to think about his choice-making powers as he or she leaves the group for the very last time. Now you must think about a succinct, laconic group process finale, for you recall that you have always had a strong belief that the members of the group were entitled to know where you were coming from as a group leader, and exactly what this process of group counseling has been leading to over the past twelve weeks. You launch your final wrap-up to cover the growth of the group, the relative strengths and weaknesses, particularly focusing on the growth that has taken place in the unit you have labeled a counseling group.

"You have probably all observed many changes that have taken place in this group since we began some twelve weeks ago. While I am not going to go into all of them, I would like to share with you some of the more obvious and relevant facts of our collective life together. First of all, when the group started, people seemed reluctant to make the foray and talk about themselves, and very little helping was being offered in the first few weeks. Gradually, by observing what I was doing, you began to get the idea that we were here to help rather than to have nice neat discussions. This has been a very fast-paced group, with people anxious to get in on the counseling benefits. You all learned fast, and each of you, in your own unique way, was offering help to others. In the early stages, people seemed fearful about self-revelation, but as you began to see that the risk was only in your own minds, you began to clamor for group time, almost to the point of having to assign future group counseling spotlight time for everyone. As a group, you moved quickly through that passive stage, and while you were willing

to let me do all of the work, when you observed that I wasn't willing or interested in doing all of the counseling, you began to pick up the ball and run with it.

"You have been a strong group, in that you have not hung back and waited for things to happen, but rather have taken the initiative yourselves. Many of you picked up the leadership cues, and began to become accepting confronters on your own. You moved into the helping phases of counseling, and were anxious to make this a place where useful things would happen. You have all seen how the group developed a sense of unity and support, but this was not any natural thing. We worked hard at this, but not in the way you would traditionally think that unity would be encouraged. We stayed with the counseling ethic all the way, always insisting that people be honest and straight, and directly labeling any attempts to be sugary or dishonest. This is what brought about our feelings of togetherness, and the unity has helped us in working more effectively toward helping everyone who wanted to change some aspects of their lives. You probably noticed that no one was forced to participate, yet some presures did develop for the more silent members to get in on it. This, too, is natural and you should all be aware that I was ever conscious of the need to protect anyone from getting attacked simply because they chose to temporarily hang back. As the group began to really work on the counseling chores, the more silent group members also let down some of their guards, and eventually everyone go in on the action over the entire twelve weeks. Naturally, man group members could have benefited from more participation but this could be said about any counseling group that ever e isted. We can all use more growth, and since counseling mean change, and change means growth, certainly we could all u more of this good stuff called counseling.

"The group has been a lesson in communicating effectivel At first, everyone just kind of talked helter-skelter, asking qu tions of everyone in interrogator fashion. The communicati became much more sophisticated as the group progressed, a the questions tended to be more relevant and purposeful. addition, the skills of listening became finely honed here in group, with many superb examples of poor listening in early sessions, then a sense of having to be particularly att tive if one is going to help someone else. Much of the com ing for air time evaporated after a while, and it was repla with some genuine struggling to come up with some of why's for a given person's behavior. Finally, as a group,

APPENDIX

Group Counseling Techniques, Strategies, and Structures for the Practitioner[1]

BECOMING AN expert in leading counseling groups is a professional development goal of great magnitude. Truly effective group counselors have thousands of hours of practice behind them in this most challenging endeavor. They are lifelong learners committed to becoming more proficient in the delivery of their specialized services and more in charge of their own lives. They constantly seek to refine their skills and knowledge and to increase their professional acumen and repertoire of techniques and

---

[1] The Appendix was published previously as Chapter 10 in *Counseling Techniques That Work*, by Wayne W. Dyer and John Vriend (Washington, D.C.: American Personnel and Guidance Association Press, 1975). Reprinted with the permission of the American Personnel and Guidance Association.

strategies for doing their job in all of the specialized circumstances which crop up regularly in the groups they counsel. In this chapter several specific techniques and strategies are presented for the developing group counseling practitioner. All are consonant with the goal of helping each group member to change and to become self-enhancing and in charge of his or her personal world, and all have been proven useful when applied in group counseling.

Competency in group counseling often means being creative and imaginative, introducing new formats and structures. Restricting group activity to the traditional sitting-around-in-a-circle-and-talking modality can often, like any other overused structure, induce restlessness or boredom in members anticipating the same old tired business they have already experienced. By varying the action and incorporating new strategies, a counselor multiplies his opportunities for effectiveness, just as creative artists and teachers improve their service delivery by varying methods of presentation.

Nowhere is it inscribed that a counseling group must be dull, humorless, or routine. There are times in the practice of any group counselor when he or she feels lost or impotent, when the group seems to be bogged down, when the interest or commitment of some or all group members seems to have waned, or when it appears that the introduction of a new technique, strategy, or structure will revitalize group activity and still promote the goal achievements of individual members. The techniques described in this chapter are basic to a fully functioning group leader. The why's, when's, and how's are detailed. Each technique, strategy, and structure is included because it works. We know they work because we have used them on countless occasions. But what we have elaborated here only constitutes a beginning. Effective group counselors are interested in developing their own strategies and in applying their own new twists to those they pick up from fellow professionals.

The techniques presented here are deliberately brief. First the technique is described, then typical occasions for using it are outlined. Finally, a rationale for including it as a group leader strategy is given along with a brief example of how the technique might actually be employed. The list is obviously not all-inclusive. After examining the various ways we have found a technique to be useful in our own professional practice, we have made the decision to include or exclude it here, eliminating from this collection some which were too esoteric, rarely usable, or of minimal productivity.

Specific Group Counseling Leadership Techniques

BEGINNING A GROUP: MEMBERS INTRODUCE THEMSELVES

After explaining what the business of group counseling is all about, the leader asks each member of the group to introduce him or herself to everyone. But members are enjoined not to use any traditional labels or any role data in identifying themselves. That is, each person is to refrain from mentioning such things as courses of study, job, vocational interests, future plans, family data, hobbies, travels, marital status, age, and so on. Instead, the introduction takes the form of having each person tell what kind of a human being he or she is. The leader asks key questions of each person to help the introductions when necessary, such as, Are you loving? Are you happy? Do you like yourself? When is the last time you cried, and over what? Are you orderly? Are you punctual? Are you frustrated a lot? The leader demonstrates the introduction by modeling his or her own introduction in the preferred style (see example below). Group members do their introductions in whatever order they choose, rather than proceeding in sequence around the group.

The typical occasions for using this technique are limited. It is most appropriate for an initial session, although it could appear in some modified form in a later session if the same kind of personal data had not yet been exchanged among the group members. Participants are often apprehensive about being in a counseling group for the first time, and this introductory technique is an effective icebreaker. Members join in with little hesitancy, particularly after witnessing the leader's own introduction.

The technique is useful for beginning a group because it gives the leader and everyone else in the group a wealth of data about each person. The leader's goal is to help each person to identify some negative as well as positive characteristics in order that counseling goal formulation for all group members can begin to shape up in the counselor's mind. By helping each group member to produce a full self-description, the leader demonstrates an ability to be helpful in the earliest stages of the group, eliciting nonthreatening data in particular from members who find the task difficult because they have not thought of themselves as having worth apart from their roles or associations with others. Essentially the members are answering the question, Who am I? Who am I apart from my social roles, my relationships, my hobbies, my activities, my interests, my plans? Who am I apart from my physical appearance and characteristics? We have even tried this introduction technique in total darkness; then the members have to individuate themselves apart from their physical selves, a way which is more difficult to do. We do not, however, recommend that a group counselor attempt the darkness version until he or she is well practiced in the use of the technique, since initial anxiety might be induced rather than reduced, and eliminating early anxiety about what will happen is part of the rationale behind the use of this technique. The rationale is also lodged in the notion that to have the members searching for meaningful content in an unstructured first session is unproductive and turns off the members to the counseling process. This technique involves each person in the group at the outset, and each member is helped to overcome natural fears about participating; all individuals emerge from the first session having gotten their feet wet.

An example of a leader's own introduction, which could be expanded or altered depending on the age level of the group members, might take the following form:

> My name is William, and I am essentially a happy person. I like myself very much, and I work at being happy every day of my life. I am relatively free of guilt and immobilizing worry, and I like to live by appreciating the present moment rather than thinking about the past or the future. I seldom get frustrated to the point of anger, but several specific things do tend to annoy me. I like humor and fun and create as much of it around me as I can. I am somewhat of a procrastinator, and I am vulnerable at times as well. I am basically an independent person, almost to a fault.

BEGINNING A GROUP: MEMBERS INTRODUCE THEMSELVES, BUT WITH A FIRST IMPRESSIONS TWIST

This technique uses exactly the same group member introduction approach described above. Before beginning the introductions, however, each member is given a card or a piece of paper and asked to write down the names of all group members. Next to the names, members are requested to put down their first impressions of each other, based on whatever data they have, even on intuition. Following the noting of first impressions, the same introduction strategy is employed. As each introduction is completed, the group counselor asks if that person would like to hear what first impressions the others had of him or her. If the response is affirmative, each member reads verbatim what has been written next to the person's name.

This technique is clearly practical only in the initial session. It is an exceedingly useful data-gathering strategy, and it provides instant feedback for every member of the group from the outset. People seldom have the opportunity to discover how they strike others on a first-impression basis. By structuring this kind of an introductory experience, the leader not only gives the members the opportunity to hear and evaluate how they appear to strangers, but desirable group interaction and honest communication are strongly fostered. The data emerging here, often of a mixed nature since different people have different impressions of any given person, will be useful throughout the life of the group. Members will remind each other later of these initial impressions, and they will each remember what others thought about them. The fact that a person appears to be fearful, timid, approval-seeking, or even dull is personal data which that person may find undesirable and choose to change. And a counseling group is a place where changing the impressions we give can most appropriately begin to happen.

Whether the group is composed of strangers or short- and long-term acquaintances, the leader can begin with this first-impressions twist, encouraging members to write whatever comes into their minds about each other, using prior knowledge or data garnered merely from studying each other intensely for a few moments. Members may be encouraged to signify their impressions only with adjectives, as in the following example, or with brief sentences, depending on the size of the group and the time available, including both positive or negative perceived characteristics.

Mike: Strong, likable, apprehensive, curious, attractive, shy, probably moralistic

George: Tired, unconcerned, silent, somewhat fearful, intelligent, guarded

Mary: Wistful, nervous, attractive, queasy, hopeful, studious, reactive

Sammy: Egghead, thinker, bright, insecure, has trouble relating, wants to change

Ramona: Athletic, outdoorsy, wishful, funloving, impulsive, nervous talker

BEGINNING A GROUP: GROUP CONSENSUS ON WHERE TO BEGIN

After defining the group counseling process, confidentiality, and other concerns, the leader asks the group members to write down a self-defeating behavior they would like to change on a piece of paper or an index card. The group leader defines self-defeating behavior and names several that are common among that age group. The leader also cautions that nothing should be written down that a member does not wish to share in the group. The completed cards are collected by the leader, who then redistributes them, instructing members to take any card but their own.

After assigning a number to each card, the leader directs the members to read the cards aloud so that everyone in the group can assign a rating to Card Number 1, Card Number 2, and so on, until every card has been rated by all members. Using a rating scale from 1 to 10, a rating of 5 would indicate absolute indifference to whether or not the group ought to spend time working with the member whose concern has been announced, a 6 or 7 implies a mildly positive attitude toward using group time to help that member, and an 8, 9, or 10 is a very positive rating. Conversely, a rating of 4 or 3 would indicate mildly negative feelings, and 2, 1, or 0 would indicate extremely negative feelings about using group time to work on that behavior. Group members are encouraged to rate each concern as they hear it, based on their own personal attitudes and how relevant the concern is to their own personal interests. When all cards have been rated, the leader asks that they be quickly reread in the same numerical order so that members may recheck the ratings they gave and change them if they wish. Such rechecking is important since the members had not heard all the statements before making their initial ratings.

Next, the members announce the rating they gave to each concern. The leader tallies them, gives the totals for each card, and then collects the cards in the order of the one with the highest collective rating, the next highest, and so on. The card with the highest is then read aloud, the individual who wrote it is identified, and the group counseling begins with the focus on that person's concern. Or the leader can help the group to look at the kinds of concerns which were written and judge their appropriateness (perhaps too impersonal), then give more explicit directions on what constitutes productive group counseling content and repeat the process.

This technique works because it eliminates the excessive feeling-out that typifies so many initial group counseling sessions. The leader comes in with a plan, announces that this is a place where we work on becoming more effective operators in our own life circumstances, and then proceeds to demonstrate his or her seriousness by asking members to go through an exercise that is designed to have each one establish a counseling goal.

With this technique group members can talk about the concerns that received a low rating and why that occurred. Also, if a member did not rate his or her own concern with a 10, this can be pointed out. The opportunities for analyzing the data are unlimited, but the effective leader uses the technique only as a beginning, rather than proceeding through every concern to be on the agenda for subsequent sessions. The effective leader knows that other more important concerns will arise in the group, that the technique is valuable in helping the group to get started productively, and that he or she is using a method to launch the group counseling that assures that everyone in the group will feel comfortable in tackling the concern stated by a given member.

What follows is an example of how the group leader might inaugurate this technique by orally specifying self-defeating behaviors that are typical of many people. (The list is practically endless. By spelling out some of the areas that might productively be worked on in the group, the leader helps members to think about what would be the most significant to them.)

> There are hundreds of things that people have trouble handling in their lives. As I list some of them, see if any of them pertain to you. If you find one that is meaningful for you, state it on your card; or you might have something in mind which I don't mention, so that is what you should write down. At any rate, some people get continually bored, or they worry a lot how others see them, or they are filled with guilt about a number of past deeds, or they are fearful or depressed a great deal. Some individuals don't get along well with key people in their lives or don't know how to get the things they want, or they get hurt a

lot or feel abused, or they are overweight, or smoke excessively, or use drugs and would like to be different. Some folks live in the past, or don't know how to make decisions or plan their futures, or get angry and frustrated, or are afraid of certain things, or are vulnerable, or feel they aren't worth anything.

BEGINNING A GROUP: PROVIDING A SENTENCE STEM FOR GETTING STARTED

After explaining how counseling in a group works and all of the ground rules, the leader asks each member to introduce him or herself by completing a sentence stem such as the following: "What no one has ever understood about me is . . . ," or "I'm different from most people in that I . . . ," or "The thing about myself that I would most like to change is . . . ."

Such sentence completions are effective in giving the group a focused beginning. Although they can be used any time in the life of a group, they work well at the start.

Since most group members are unsure about what they will be doing in the counseling experience, it is beneficial for the leader to know of exercises that will help members to become involved immediately in a businesslike fashion. The sentence completion exercise requires individuals in the group to talk about themselves and to work, even if indirectly at first, at goal setting. By having them state how they are different or what they would like to change, the leader has established an atmosphere from the opening moments in which the focus is on identifying, clarifying, labeling, and going to work on the concerns the members have. The sentence stem can be any from a list designed by the leader; a different stem can be given to each member of the group; or everyone can complete the same stem. At any rate, personal concerns and the unique data about each member receive priority attention at the first session.

As each person is completing the sentence stem, the effective leader helps by asking key questions to draw out additional data and set the stage for the development of behavioral change goals. For modeling purposes, the leader might even complete a sentence stem, such as the following two:

What I would like to change most in myself is the way I always put things off. I am a procrastinator of the worst sort, and I really am going to make an effort to be different.

The thing that no one has ever understood about me is that I genuinely like my privacy. Most of my family members and close friends find this difficult to handle, and they interpret it as rejection on my part. I would like them to know that my seeking out privacy has nothing to do with my attitudes and feelings toward them, but they get upset about my wanting to be alone.

Whenever the leader models a behavior, it is done to demonstrate the technique, not to bring the group focus on him or her. Modeling behavior, therefore, is selected for its potency as an illustration and ought to be clearly identified as such. This same point holds true for every instance of leader modeling presented in the remainder of this list of techniques.

WRITING AN ORAL LETTER

The leader asks a group member to write an oral letter right in the group. The recipient of the letter is an individual who is significant in the member's life, someone to whom the group member is having some difficulty relating or with whom the group member has never resolved a conflict. It is even possible to write a letter to a deceased friend or family member and tell that person what the group member never could say when the person was still living. The letter writer should block out the group and all potential disturbances by closing his or her eyes and actually visualizing the letter recipient. The leader explains that the letter should contain whatever the group member would like to say that has not been previously said, the reasons for any existing bitterness, and how the relationship should change. If the letter writer stumbles or has any difficulty, the leader provides suggestions, whether this is in the opening of the letter or in transitional parts of the body of the letter, being a helpful prompter who is in tune with the kind of message the writer wants to send.

When the letter has been completed, everyone in the group is requested to react and say what thoughts and feelings the letter elecited. Then the group leader rewrites the letter right in the group from the point of view of someone who is totally self-responsible and effective, given the same relational data. Any and all blaming, wishing, other-directedness, complaining, and the like are eliminated in the leader's letter to the same individual. The vital ingredient of the leader's letter is that it contains no reliance on the recipient to be different; it contains total acceptance of the status quo and announces how the writer will think and act in the future with regard to the recipient regardless of what the recipient does. Group members are again encouraged to provide feedback. The letter writer can thus see how an effective person would correspond with someone and how this communication is quite different from his or her own.

This technique is most appropriate when an individual expresses a concern about a significant other that is troublesome, agonizing, bitter, frustrating, and full of upsetting interactional demands and unreasonable behavior. The list of possible recipients is endless; they could include marriage or divorced partners, parents, siblings, current or former employers, friends who act abusively, teachers, any of the former inhabitants in an individual's life who are ghosts in the mind and still exercise some negative psychological impact. The technique is most appropriately invoked after a member has emitted considerable data about relationship difficulties and has expressed obvious frustration about the attitudes and abusive actions of the troublesome other. The leader asks the group member to write a letter with a specific purpose in mind. Talking to someone, rather than about someone, makes the communication patterns clearer and reveals much data about the relationship. From previous hurts to admonitions for past behaviors in past events, the letter-writing format provides a useful way for people to get in touch with core dimensions and feelings, even though it is on a simulated basis.

Frequently, this is an emotional experience for the letter writer. Talking directly to someone with whom one always has had difficulty communicating can be a heavy and trying venture. Opening and closing salutations are trouble spots: some individuals have difficulty saying "Dear" at the start or "Love" at the end; others voice their deepest sentiments for the first time in their lives, perhaps concluding with "May all the damnations of Hell torture you for all eternity," thus releasing the horrible pent-up thoughts they have carried for a long time in their heads; or saying aloud for the first time, "I love you." A typical letter begins with "Dear . . . , I am writing you this letter because I have always found it so difficult to communicate with you in person. You would never listen to what I had to say. Specifically, I want to tell you that. . . ." Then the soliloquy takes on its true pertinence. During the monologue, the effective leader takes notes about what is being said; this is not distracting to the letter writer, who has his or her eyes tightly shut. The notes are taken so that all the information revealed can be accurately treated in the rewriting.

Rewriting the letter is very important. Here the leader is using skills to demonstrate what the group member can say in a more positive and effective manner. The contrast in letters will actively demonstrate differences in effective and self-defeating thinking patterns. Group interaction over the letter is also important because feedback from everyone in the group helps the letter writer to learn how others view and feel about the shared personal data. The group members are each requested to give a brief reaction to what was said in the original letter and to state how they might work at becoming more effective in that particular relationship. Because the letter-writing technique introduces a first-person quality to the relationship between a member and some individual who is not in the group, everyone tends to get involved.

Oral letter writing is indeed a powerful helping tool. It should be used sparingly so that it does not become a gimmick or a game, since it can make a genuine difference in the life of a group member. In our experience, no one who has ever written an oral letter in a counseling group and had it rewritten has ever forgotten the cathartic and reconstructive nature of the technique. More importantly, letter writers later feel that there is no longer any reason to make such communications in their everyday lives.

SUBDIVIDING THE GROUP INTO DYADS OR TRIADS

The group leader brings any two members into the center. They sit facing each other and are given the following directions: "Mary, here's what you are going to do. You are going to say things to Tom based on what you have observed and learned about him in the group that you think will be helpful to him. After this is completed, you will reverse the procedure, and, Tom, you will tell Mary whatever you think will be helpful to her." The leader then assists both partners with this task, prompting them, helping them to recall specifics or to focus on particular behaviors they know about each other from their experience in the group.

The second part of the instructions involves a dialogue between the two members which results in goal-setting. "Both of you have provided each other with some helpful feedback. Now, based on that feedback, try to help each other set a goal which can be attained right here in the group. Mary, tell Tom what you think he could work on in the group that would be of benefit to him and tell him how you think you could help him reach that goal. Don't give up until both of you agree on a worthy goal that is realistically attainable. Tom, you will do the same for Mary." Again the leader assists the partners to complete the task. This dialogue focuses exclusively on what each individual would be able to accomplish in the group sessions themselves, although the specified goals are ones that can be transferred to the lives of both individuals outside the group.

This concludes the demonstration part of the technique. The leader then asks all the group members if it is clearly understood how each is to function in the dyads to which each person will be assigned. The group is then either assigned randomly into pairs or triads or assigned based on a previously determined rationale. The subgroups are given a specific amount of time, thirty minutes or so, to accomplish the task they have seen demonstrated. Specific directions are given to the subgroups, and small talk and conversations are strongly discouraged. The subgroups return at the appointed time. Group members then give feedback about their own behavior in the subgroup and announce their own goal, which at least one other member is privy to and has a commitment to help them achieve. The entire group is now aware of specific new goals for each member.

The most appropriate time for using this technique is about one-third of the way into the total life expectancy of the group, although a leader could induce it at any juncture when it seems fruitful to do so. Many people find it difficult to talk in front of more than a half-dozen others, whereas dealing with one or two individuals is not nearly so anxiety-provoking. In the subgroup demonstration the leader is careful to guarantee effective communication and goal-setting. The small unit task is constructed to give each person something clear, pinpointed, and personally valuable to deal with and to renew each individual's commitment to derive all that is possible from the counseling in the larger group setting. When two people are checking on each other as they work toward their goals in the larger group, their sense of involvement in the process is bolstered. This subgrouping exercise helps members to become more familiar with each other and to gain a sense of trust in working together; it automatically provides witnesses to the processes of feedback and goal-setting. Moreover, the counselor can use the data emanating from the subgroups at any time in the later life of the group. The counselor will find that group members are free and willing to share helpful thoughts and observations and to interact on a dyadic or triadic level provided that a clear and effective demonstration is included in the modeling of this technique.

When the members return to the group, the leader has the option of asking any individual what goals were set for achievement in subsequent group sessions. In addition, the leader can help all members to assess the feedback each received from their partner by checking with the other group members.

When the flame of productive activity in a group is dying, this technique can help to refuel it with a quick revitalizing opportunity for everyone in the group to derive safe feedback and become committed to the goal-setting process in a new way.

A FANTASY

The counselor invites a member who has had some counseling focus in the group to suspend all disbelief for a while and imagine being able to do or have anything he or she desires. The fantasy has no bounds. Anything is possible; the world is at the individual's disposal. The leader helps by telling the person to detail aloud how a few typical days will be used up, particularly eliciting who is present in the fantasy, where the person will go, roles of family members, how time is used, the part money plays, the extent to which love is present. The more involved the member becomes, the richer the fantasy. The member is given free rein—anything goes.

After the fantasizing, the group reacts and helps to analyze it. Follow-up occurs in subsequent group sessions. Are there changes in the routine of the member's life or in the member's thoughts and emotions? Has a new perspective on living taken place?

This technique helps reluctant members to disclose their deepest thoughts and feelings so that the counselor and group members have a real view of their world from the perspective of looking at life goals. When offered the opportunity to engage in a freewheeling expression of personal desires, many individuals find the task difficult because they conceive of themselves as inexorably locked into their social roles and circumstances, which they have accepted as their fate. Their lives seem void of meaning and excite-ment; they feel stuck in their ruts. Their fantasies are frequently unimaginative, crowded with the characteristics of their own rou-tinized living, with little or no flair introduced. The leader who uses this technique will note that most fantasies are about 90 per-cent attainable, given the real-world parameters of the fantasizer's existence. Few people fantasize about strolling on Uranus, being a monarch, sitting on the Supreme Court bench, being the opposite sex, or being lionized for exceptional deeds. The fantasy is usually an extension of a life that is being led in a certain mode with a few minor exceptions added. Seldom is it a radical departure, a look at a new person in wildly different circumstances.

The fantasy technique can be most productive in accelerating goal-setting. When the fantasy is analyzed, it usually becomes evi-dent that everything in it is more than remotely attainable at some level. Group members are helped to learn more about the fantasizer, and their reactions promote relational interactions on a new basis with the given member. The effective leader looks for lack of genuine love in the fantasy, living up to the expectations of others, how significant others in the fantasizer's life are treated, who goes on the trip (almost all fantasies involve travel or getting away), the extent to which power and money get attention, and how many components are currently attainable.

This is an exciting technique for helping members to discover their own most meaningful goals and how their thinking has been affected by the enculturation process, rather than seeing them-selves as free agents with the power to alter their life circum-stances in numerous self-enhancing ways. A miniversion of the fantasy can be employed at any time by having an individual dream aloud about how he or she would like to change a relation-ship, conditions on a job or in a total career or in any life segment; here the leader helps the fantasizer detail all the elements and im-agine all possibilities. But again the purpose is to have the member discover attainable goals.

ROLE-SHIFTING

At the beginning of a group session, slips of paper with mem-bers' names are placed into a receptacle. Group members then draw a name, making certain they have not drawn their own. For the next thirty minutes each person, without revealing the name drawn, assumes the identity and manifests characteristic behaviors of the individual whose name appears on the paper. During this time the leader engages the group in some activity which will involve everyone, perhaps asking the members to examine love in their lives, its meaning and importance, or to focus on how they function as strangers in new social situations. At the end of the thirty minutes, the leader asks each member to guess who he or she thought was impersonating him or her and why. The impersonation identities are not revealed until all the crossfire feedback, the rationale for choices, and the commentary of everyone has been brought out. After the names are revealed, further reactions are elicited.

This technique provides an excellent means for group members to see how they are perceived by others without having to deal with the resistance that so frequently accompanies more direct efforts of feedback stimulation. It is best introduced at the beginning of a session to allow ample time for post-impersonation analysis, and it should not be used until three, four, or more sessions have transpired as the members will not have collected enough behavior data to assume the new temporary roles.

The technique engenders much productive group interaction and provides valuable insight to group members on how they are being seen in the group context. Members are amazed at how they appear to others. The total involvement built into the structure allows members who have been resistant or nonverbal to become engaged in new ways, and their interaction increases. Young people take to this technique quickly, often wanting to repeat it at a later time. The group leader is careful, when giving instructions to the members, to emphasize the importance of emulating both nonverbal and verbal behavior and characteristic thinking and emotional patterns.

THE NICE THING ABOUT BEING ...

The leader asks a member who is receiving counseling focus in the group to give a specific categorical label to a self-defeating personality and behavioral dimension. Such labels as cranky, shy, short-tempered, fearful, fat, lazy, guilty, and approval-seeking are appropriate. The individual is then given the sentence stem: "The nice thing about being [cranky] is. . . ." The member is asked to repeat the stem continually and complete it with as many predicates as possible. Then the other members are asked to state the stem and complete the sentence with their own thoughts. No particular order is imposed on group members to participate in stem completion.

This strategy is best employed when the counseling process with a given individual has been moved to the step of self-understanding. The technique is designed to help a member answer the question, What do I get out of this behavior? By urging that member to answer the question aloud in as many ways as he or she can, the difficult work of acquiring self-understanding is promoted. Similarly, by involving other group members in the exercise, everyone begins to understand how a psychological maintenance system underlies self-defeating behavior and each member acquires some insight into analogous dimensions of his or her own living. The resources of the group are brought to bear on a member's particular concerns in a potent and focused way.

Without the self-understanding which this technique helps to bring about for each member, the counseling seldom effectively proceeds to goal-setting and trying out new behaviors, the more advanced steps in the counseling process. Before members are willing to try changing current behaviors, they must know and judge what is behind them, why the behavioral patterns exist and persist.

Nothing prevents the group leader from contributing to the sentence completion exercise when the group seems to be missing some crucial diagnostic insights or when neurotic or unworthy payoffs for psychologically unhealthy behavior are not being pinpointed.

ONE-WAY MESSAGES

The group member who has received a prolonged period of intense counseling focus is asked to remain silent and not respond while the other members in the group send a one-way message to that person (in no particular order). When all messages are sent, the leader asks the person for reactions. This technique can be used as a closure strategy, when further focus on the individual would reap minimal returns and the time has come to shift the group emphasis to someone else.

This technique is used most effectively when the group appears to be at a standstill, when a group member is argumentative and won't consider what others are saying, or when a member denies and explains away whatever others are offering. Group members frequently are anxious to tell others how they ought to be seen and reject any picture of themselves that is different from what they want to believe is so.

Whenever the technique is employed, it is effective in helping a given member to hear what others have to say and then use his or her personal filtering system to accept or reject such offerings. It is productive in reaching withdrawn members, and it gets all members to interact with the person who is receiving the counseling focus. The person in focus receives many ideas and points of view and learns how others have been reacting to the behavior and self-disclosure data he or she has emitted. The technique serves the additional purpose of eliminating boring interchanges which often lead nowhere, although it should not become a leader device that loses its potency through overuse. The opportunities and rationale for using this strategy are limitless.

REPEAT BACK, THEN RESPOND

The leader joins two members who sit facing each other in the center of the group. Person X makes a statement to person Y which has been difficult to communicate to Y in some earlier group context. Y must repeat back to X's complete satisfaction what was just communicated. Y then reacts to what X said and X repeats back to Y's complete satisfaction. The procedure is repeated throughout the interchange. If the talking member does not agree that his message is correctly received, it is rephrased until it is completely understood. Understanding means that every message is reiterated to the speaker's satisfaction, not by saying "I understand" or nodding the head. When the exchange is over, the other group members give feedback to the principals, concentrating on listening and communication skills.

The leader's hidden agenda for using this technique is to facilitate more effective communication between two people in the group who have shown opposition to each other—two whose values, outlooks on life, personalities, and the like are at such odds that contention continually arises in the group when they have anything to do with each other. If two people in the group will not listen to each other or if alienation or rejection between them is running rampant, this technique is effective in breaking down the barriers. People have differences which often are extreme, sometimes permeating and affecting the entire group. Such individuals can benefit from this listening and communicating technique; it requires positive attention and allows for one's point of view to be completely expressed.

While the two principals are in the center of the large group, the leader helps them get started by reminding them of any contentious intragroup behavior which both have previously manifested. The leader functions as a helper, prompter, and monitor of the exchange, without taking either side, and takes notes about content and behavioral data. The form for the dialogue follows:

> X—Makes opening statement, usually somewhat lengthy.
> Y—Repeats back statement, both its essence and nuances.
> X—Either gives permission for Y to react or restates the part
>   that was missed by Y.
> Y—Restates corrected part to X's satisfaction and then reacts
>   with own statement to X.
> X—Repeats back to Y's satisfaction, and the process continues.

This technique aids in bridging communication gaps in the group; pairs of members are helped to resolve differences. But the most important benefit to all group members comes from learning how tough it is to listen well and communicate effectively without letting one's ego or self-interests intervene. It can be used anytime during the life of the group.

Assistant Leaders

After inquiring if anyone in the group would like to work on leadership skills, the group counselor appoints someone to act as assistant leader for the session. During the session the appointed voluntary assistant does not focus on any personal concerns. All leader behaviors are directed toward serving the other members, and everyone in the group is made aware of this distinction.

Drawing out potential helpers and having them serve in a leadership capacity can be done any time after the group has had two or three opportunities to work together and members have had a chance to see what leaders do in comparison with what members do. Group members serving as assistant leaders practice helping interventions and simultaneously improve their own world in the process. The more one serves in the role of helper, the greater the likelihood for becoming more personally in charge of one's self. The effective counselor must constantly produce active strategies for identifying, labeling, understanding, and changing self-defeating thinking and behaving, and functioning in a leader capacity in the group enables some members to help themselves in safety by helping others.

Any time an assistant leader has been engaged, a period must be set aside for the group members to provide insightful feedback when the leadership experience has terminated. Suggestions and evaluative reactions are crucial to the volunteering leader; both support and criticism are significant for the assistant's self-development and self-confidence. Peers helping peers is certainly one of the most useful and effective strategies which can be implemented in a learning environment such as group counseling.

PROMOTING SPONTANEITY

There are two forms to this technique:
1. The leader asks a group member to act in a spontaneous manner right in the group. The leader's instructions are as follows: "When I point to someone, you are to react with whatever comes into your head, without giving a lot of thought to creating a cautious offering. I will point at random to group members, and you just react with whatever words seem fit." The leader then points to group members and helps the individual to react to them spontaneously.
2. The leader asks a group member to act in a spontaneous manner right in the group. The leader's instructions are as follows: "I am going to give you a word to start with and then you just free-associate with a list of words which come to mind. Without thinking it through, just let the preceding word elicit the next one and state the words aloud." The leader appoints someone to write the words as the individual says them to facilitate a post-free-association analysis.

In using either of these spontaneous behavior-eliciting techniques, the leader is sensitive to the particular circumstances that call for such action. They are most appropriate when a member has talked about being too formal, rigid, organized, careful in dealing with others, planned, dull, lacking in spontaneity, or stereotyped as a totally predictable person in everyday living. After the counselor has helped a member through the steps of exploration, identification of self-defeating behaviors, self-understanding, and goal-setting, he or she can offer the member the opportunity to try out new and different behaviors right in the group which will constitute productive change. At this point one of the two spontaneous behavior techniques or a similarly constructed exercise is appropriate.

By helping a group member to engage in some new and exciting behavior within the safety of the group, the counselor promotes and stimulates the member to initiate self-growth. When the group member sees that it is indeed possible to act extemporaneously without all of the attendant anxiety that has kept him or her from doing this before, the member gains a measure of new learning which enables more effective behavior to emerge outside of the group in his or her private world where it really counts; the member learns to act sometimes on impulse rather than restraining every harmless urge.

These techniques introduce action into the group—actually doing rather than merely talking about different behaviors. Effective counselors have action dimensions of counseling uppermost in their list of interventions, knowing that thinking which is untranslated into doing, however admirable, makes little difference in the lives of the clients they serve.

Taking a Risk in the Group

An individual in the group, who has talked about risk-taking avoidance as a self-defeating mode of operation, is asked to take a risk in the group. The member is requested to choose two or three others and to think of something to say to these members which would involve some risk. The risky communication can be either positive or negative. For some people, saying "I like you" or "I am attracted to you" is more risky than saying "You bore me" or "I've been wanting to tell you how much I tune you out." The greater loading of self-perceived risk, the more likely the individual is to benefit from the exercise. Then the group members provide feedback.

This technique is applicable at almost any time in the life of the group whenever exploration and self-understanding have taken place and an individual has acknowledged that risk-taking avoidance is a part of his or her life pattern. By asking a group member to engage in risk-taking behavior in the safety of the group, the counselor helps that member to test out what it means to take risks, to enlarge his or her behavioral repertoire. The powerful lesson that a disaster does not always happen as a result of taking personal risks, that others have a healthier respect for someone who is unafraid to do so, is programmed right into the counseling activity.

In the post-risking analysis by the entire group, the member is helped to understand what has been accomplished, how the recipients of the member's risk-taking statements viewed the communications, what feelings accompanied the action, and how the activity might be productively transferred to the person's life.

THE THREE MOST IMPORTANT PEOPLE IN YOUR LIFE

In the exploratory stage of counseling an individual, when the leader is attempting to induce self-understanding, this person is asked to go back to a particular age, say five years old, and name in order the three most significant people in his or her life. Then the individual is taken to more advanced ages, say twelve, then sixteen, then twenty-two, at regular intervals, until the present age is reached, in each case responding to the same question. Then projection is introduced. Five, ten, twenty, even thirty years in the future. "Who will the three most important people in your life be?"

This technique helps the counselor to gain valuable insights into an individual's world at various life stages, particularly in the dimension of psychological dependency. The technique can be used at almost any time in the group counseling with a particular individual, or it can be used with the total group, each member going through the exercise. The counselor seeks to determine patterns of dependency in those clients who lack psychological independence, and this technique provides that kind of insight for the client as well as the counselor.

The perceptive counselor recognizes that most people fail to include themselves in the list of the three most important people; even when projecting into the future, the self is conspicuously denied. As the lists of significant others develop, the leader gives no signs of approval or disapproval; relationships are carefully noted, and questions eliciting rationales for the choices are asked.

It is a data-revealing technique which helps every member to see patterns of dependency throughout life and to make new and more self-enhancing judgments for future relationships. In any analysis of the data, the leader seeks to help members include themselves on the list, at the very top, if not now, certainly in the near future.

PROJECT YOURSELF VOCATIONALLY TEN YEARS INTO THE FUTURE, THEN CHANGE SEX

The group leader asks a woman who has been receiving group focus to project what her life will be like in ten years. As she projects herself into her future, the leader asks questions about her work roles, promotions, aspirations, family status, position in the world, number of children and how they are cared for, her relationship to a man or men, and so on. When this is completed, the leader then asks her to restate what her life would be like ten years from now if she were a man. The group leader and members then analyze and note differences.

This technique can be used almost any time within the life of the group to demonstrate the different expectations of women, how many women tend to have lower aspirations than men in almost every way because they live in a sexist culture. It is a particularly appropriate technique for a given group member who seems unaware of the extent to which she is lowering herself when she considers herself and her future.

Essentially the group leader is taking the member on a fantasy trip which helps that person to assess how effectively she is living her current life related to anticipated future moves. The sex shift enables the individual to see how she may be lowering her self-expectations; it is a dynamite method for demonstrating inequities. Lowered self-expectancies can then be challenged and eliminated as a part of the counseling.

KEY QUESTIONS

Who listens the most closely to you in this group? Who is the most like you? The least like you? Who is the most effective? The happiest? Whom would you go to for help? Whom would you like to know better? What would you like to know?

These questions and others like them, which an imaginative counselor might think up, easily occur to a group leader in the course of counseling an individual in the group. Effective group counselors regularly involve other group members to aid in the counseling process. The process here is to have all the group members participate in the exercise of choosing other members on the basis of some criterion. The technique helps to promote productive activity in the group and can be used as a stimulus for group involvement at any time.

But promoting involvement for its own sake is not enough. These questions help to produce insights and aid the goal-setting process. When members assess whom they are most like or unlike in the group, others have different impressions; the discrepancies can be noted, reality reading can be upgraded, and goals can be set for checking impressions outside of the group. The results of informal polls can be used to help people who perceive themselves as different to learn how to deal with each other in ways that promote the acquisition of social skills and reduce fear. Often an individual who is fearful, shy, and weak will choose the strongest person in the group as the one who is most similar when in fact everyone in the group sees that such is not the case and can specify data upon which they base their perceptions. Helping members to know each other better not only provides them with the opportunity to practice important basic social skills but also results in upgrading helping competencies of members in later counseling sessions. Members give reinforcement to each other about themselves in ways they had not thought of previously, and many members are surprised and pleased by the positive statements that other members make about them.

CLOSING THE GROUP: EXCHANGING REACTIONS

In the final session the leader asks each group member to list everyone's name on a piece of paper. Next to each name members are asked to write the single most self-enhancing and the single most self-defeating characteristic of that person. These characteristics are to be as explicitly stated as possible and selected because they are seen as helpful contributions. Then, proceeding around the group in random order, each member declares what he or she has written about himself or herself and then hears what every other group member has written about him or her.

This technique may be used at any time in the life of the group, but it is particularly fitting for a final meeting when evaluation of the counseling and projections for goal achievement for each member beyond the life of the group are appropriate focal areas. The technique structures the final session in such a way as to allow everyone in the group to be in the spotlight and make an assessment of where each person is and might go in the future in self-development. As each member hears from all the other group members and that person's self-data are emphasized, the leader provides a summary of how the counseling experience has been useful, reminding each member of what transpired in the group that had pertinence to the member, reinforcing gains, and helping the member to commit him or herself to realizable goals beyond the life of the group. This provides each person with a sense of closure. Members depart from the group with their own self-assessments and that of their peers fresh in their minds; they know where they are in their lives and have made judgments about where they think they must go.

CLOSING THE GROUP: CONDUCTING A REUNION

In the final group counseling session the leader proposes that the meeting be considered a reunion of the group which is taking place in future time. "Well, here we are, just as we said we would be, on the beach at Acapulco. Exactly one year has passed since we had the last group session, and we have a great deal to tell each other about what we made happen in our lives." Each member understands the fantasy, and the members then begin telling what has happened in their lives, relating everything in the past tense. The leader helps to elicit specifics, particularly progress reports on concerns that were voiced during the life of the counseling group. How much do members weigh; are they still living with their partners; how have the qualities of their significant relationships changed; when did they do this or that; where are they vocationally, educationally, and psychologically; how do they feel about themselves now? The questions are designed to determine specifics and the answers become commitments to create self-change.

The technique of closing the counseling experience with a reunion projected a year or so into the future helps to make the final meeting a commitment session, one in which the participants make social contracts with their peers to accomplish specific goals in their lives in the coming year. The leader helps the group to close on an optimistic note by taking the reunion fantasy seriously. Members like to envision what they will achieve and to be able to state what progress they have made. Group members have grown close to each other during the tenure of their counseling experience together, and a final group meeting which is raggedy or fails to draw each member into the activity in a meaningful way would send some members away with a sense of emptiness and incompletion. Closure is always difficult, and members frequently express sadness at breaking a group, but this is averted with the reunion technique.

This concludes the list of specific group counseling techniques, strategies, and structures. Although each technique described in this appendix has limited application depending on the circumstances of the counseling process itself, they are all useful procedures which enliven the counseling process and make it more effective. Each technique has a rationale for its use, and most can be modified or adapted to many group circumstances. Although many additional fine and useful strategies could be listed, this collection serves as a beginning for the group counselor who is interested in making the group into a more stimulating and productive interpersonal learning environment.

Index